This book has aimed to provide readers with a deeper understanding of sustainability as represented in its diagrams. The intention is to jointly improve our competence in visual thinking and in sustainability literacy. The eponymous Sustainable Lens can be considered as a heads-up display or, even without augmented technology, it presents a model for seeing the world through a sustainability driven perspective.

We started with a visualisation challenge. We finish with a bigger challenge. As you go about your life, stop occasionally, put up a frame (thumbs and fingers work well), and ask yourself how much difference you could make by seeing this scene through a Sustainable Lens?

A Sustainable Lens
by Samuel Mann

Copyright © 2011 Samuel Mann / newSplash studio
All rights reserved
www.newsplash.co.nz

ISBN-13: 978-1468112771
ISBN-10: 1468112775

Enquiries regarding requests to reprint all or part of Sustainable Lens should be addressed to:
the publisher, newSplash studio,
Forth Street, Dunedin. New Zealand

or directly to the author, Samuel Mann,
samuel.mann@op.ac.nz

or order online at www.amazon.com

SUSTAINABLE LENS
A visual guide

for Phoebe, Oliver and Henry

backwords and forewords

all the world's a stage

once upon a planet

sustainable lens

the shape of things

visual thinking

seeing sustainably

green is a verb

caring to act

make it happen

references

acknowledgments

> Please pause! Before reading any further, I invite you to take the *sustainability* visualization challenge. Using only one side of a blank sheet of paper, draw a diagram or picture that captures what you think *sustainability* looks like. Use any combination of points, lines, numbers, symbols, shading, colour and words to communicate what *sustainability* means for you. Your diagram can be as simple or as complex as you wish. And of course, you can use a computer if you prefer.

This book is about the showing and telling of information through figures and diagrams and was largely inspired by Edward Tufte's brilliant book, The Visual Display of Quantitative Information. This image is reproduced on Tufte's cover. It is based on EJ Marey's version of the Paris to Lyon train schedule from his book La Méthod Graphique (Paris, 1878). What do you see?

Did you notice that the cities listed on the y-axis are spaced proportionately according to their distances from one another, or the endpoints of each line that show the departure and arrival times of each train? Or perhaps you were drawn to the slope of each line that encodes the relative speed of each train. Informative, rich in meaning and pattern, wonderfully drawn and a joy to use – what did your visual senses tell you?

In the main body of this book, I invite you to apply what you see and interpret from diagram and picture techniques that are not about train journey information, but rather information whose focus is the visually displayed world of sustainability.

What you do next will depend on the kind of reader you are. You could open the book randomly at any page. You could flip from cover to cover, stopping only when something captures your interest or takes your eye. You could read the book backwards starting from the last full stop. Whatever you decide, you will find some kind of diagram about sustainability on every facing page. On the page opposite, the shaded section at the top presents some brief statements about the diagram. These are for you to use, accept, reject or modify as you see fit. In the text that follows I offer information that I hope will help will both inform and stimulate your thinking.

At any point that seems appropriate, you may wish to compare or redraw the diagram you produced. What does your sustainable picture show? Does it present the same concepts and issues and systems that are depicted in any of the diagrams you have looked at? You can also use the diagrams that are presented to explore and experiment. Simply ask yourself, "What happens if?" What happens if you change the angle of a line and make it steeper? What happens if I add smaller circles? What would happen if that base or column wasn't there? I am sure that like me, you will find the implications of changing a diagram by removing or adding something are far from trivial, and will lead to new and even richer insights.

Please do go on, whether it is backwards or forwards, and join me on a journey that follows the history and development of sustainability through the visual creations of more than one hundred teachers, designers and writers. How accessible are their ideas? What do they want us to understand? Why must the future be conceived as sustainable? What should we do as a consequence? What happens if…?

I offer a language and framework that allows you to explore these questions with me by looking at the world through a *Sustainable Lens*.

My motivation is intrinsically pragmatic; I am deeply committed to a term that is taken for granted by many and seen as much overused by some. Needful to say, I urge you to keep using the word sustainability and to share your involvement with the diagrams with others. I also hope the book will have consequences for both viewers and producers of the images - in order that we can all deepen our understanding of the sustainability conundrum and live out our lives contributing to a better future.

an invitation to pause

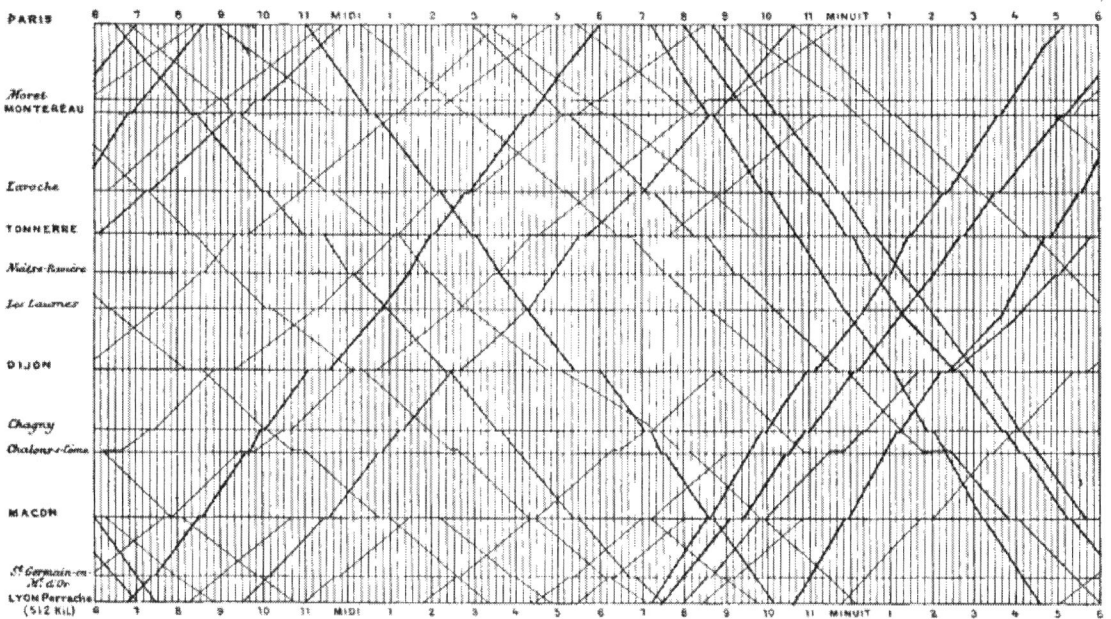

Fig. 5. — Graphique de la marche des trains sur un chemin de fer, d'après la méthode de Ibry.

> My apologies if you picked up this book expecting a handbook on nature photography. I have consciously avoided traditional "green" imagery.

The cover of Schendler's (2009) *Getting Green Done: Hard Truths from the Front Lines of the Sustainability Revolution* shows a dirty and worn workman's glove. It is very different from the usual images associated with sustainability, namely selected charismatic species such as pandas, penguins and polar bears. These charismatic megafauna are not the subjects of *Sustainable Lens*, since the images I present have consequences far beyond conservation awareness.

For many years, this awareness has been animal-centric with its concern for giant pandas, tigers, rhinos, gorillas, elephants and the like (Barash and Webel, 2008). Such focus is intentional and has been used to bring conservation to the forefront of public consciousness (Entwhistle and Dunstone, 2000). The panda, for example, is used to ensure that our attention and emotions are firmly fixed on a single species, rather than endangered species in general. While, this kind of exposure can help to protect the species in question, it down plays or ignores what is going on in the wider habitat.

I have attended many talks about the plight of the polar bear and the erosion of tropical rainforests type, delivered in the name of *sustainability*. However, I wonder if instead of empowering people to take a *sustainable lens* approach, it rather limits their view and constrains what they are able to see and understand about the degradation of natural and human capital. Indeed, idealised imagery of the environment and animals has potentially damaging consequences.

Welling calls this *ecoporn* and suggests that ecoporn-as-porn places the viewer in the same asymmetrical, sexualised relationship to its subjects as standard pornography; even if its primary goal is not sexual arousal. Whether intentional or not, idealised imagery can mask environmental agendas with illusions of beauty and perfection. Hence, instead of educating viewers about ecosystemic degradation and prompting dissent and action, Welling contends that such images can have an anaesthetic effect – they create an illusion of a pure, safe, friendly, ahistorical, depopulated and monolithic world. Nature is located in an indeterminate space far from the viewer's own 'degraded' backyard, which as he points out is paradoxical because it is "…subject to the viewing eye's private, voyeuristic control".

The most urgent need from Welling's perspective is to move beyond apathetic consumer responses by using imagery that helps transform human beings into thoughtful inhabitants of ecosystems. I share his sense of urgency and encourage all of my readers to develop their own *sustainable lens* to assist with that transformation.

The book is laid out in such a way that it can be read from cover-to-cover or opened at a particular page or diagram that draws your interest. While contributing to the overall narrative, each page can be read in isolation. The diagrams are presented clean on the right-hand side so as to celebrate their elegance and to purposefully decontextualise them. While I respect that the original authors' intentions in making such representations may rely upon their original context, a great many of the diagrams included here are more usually seen disassociated from that context. The diagrams take on a life of their own in other situations. If they are to successfully contribute to a *Sustainable Lens*, then they must be able to contribute to new understanding in that new context.

beyond a bit of tail

> Seeing the complexity of information about the world in the form of a single diagram is one thing, understanding its impact as an unsustainable footprint or resource quite another. As you 'pan' in and out of the images, the issue I ask you always to have in mind is how and whether the understandings you generate will change your thinking and actions. Sustainability in this regard is about 'choice' and the moment-by-moment decisions we make as individuals and collectively.

In 1968, astronauts on Apollo 8 took a photograph of the Earth rising above the lunar horizon. The "Earthrise" prompted people to see the world in different light: "Gazing upon our whole planet for the first time, we saw ourselves and our place in the universe with new clarity" (Poole 2008). The whole Earth "Blue Marble" taken in 1972 by the last manned lunar mission Apollo 17 had a similar effect.

The diagram on the left provides a link between the holistic image of earth as a whole and the generative abstraction provided by a diagram. The shrinking Earth here is used to represent the amount of land available per capita - because of population growth, each of us has less than a quarter of the land that our forebears had available a century ago (the numbers are hectares per capita). This sequence of shrinking earths, arranged as in a time lapse allows us to compare land available over the last Century and to predictively explore the future - both through the last two greyed out earths and potentially beyond. Will it, perhaps, stablise at that level? Some of the drivers and implications of this population growth are shown in simplified line graphs. Over the last 20 years trade volumes have tripled, and GDP has increased 50%, but this comes at a cost of increases in carbon emissions. Meanwhile the total land available for agriculture has increased only slightly - despite population growth, there is no more land to feed us.

 "How many planets?" (right) asks the question, "if we all lived like an average <insert your favourite country>, how many planets would we need?". It too, uses the motif of the earth, this time as a direct pictogram, proportional to the number of planets such a lifestyle would require. Note that in a reference to the Earth, those icons representing fractions are drawn with curvatures (more familiar for most of us as we look at the moon). I may not be able to achieve the same impact on you as that stunning photograph clearly had on the crew of Apollo 8, but by sharing our own involvement, responses and experiences about the visual representation of sustainability, I want to help develop and sharpen your *sustainable lens*. This means taking a leaf out of Tufte's book and acknowledging his principles of graphic excellence for displaying quantitative information:

- The well-designed presentation of interesting data – a matter of substance, of statistics and of design
- Complex ideas communicated with clarity, precision and efficiency
- That which gives to the viewer the greatest number of ideas in the shortest time with the least ink in the smallest space
- Multivariate information
- Telling the truth about the data

Tufte (1983) explains: What is to be sought in designs for the display of information is the clear portrayal of complexity. Not the complication of the simple: rather the task of the designer is to give access to the subtle and difficult – that is, the revelation of the complex.

Seeing the complexity of information about the world in the form of a single diagram is one thing, understanding its impact as an unsustainable footprint or resource quite another. As you 'pan' in and out of the images, the issue I ask you always to have in mind is how and whether the understandings you generate will change your thinking and actions. Sustainability in this regard, is akin to Tufte's notion of 'design as choice'. Sustainability is also 'choice' – and the responsibility for that lies with the moment-by-moment decisions we make as individuals and of course collectively!

earth scanning

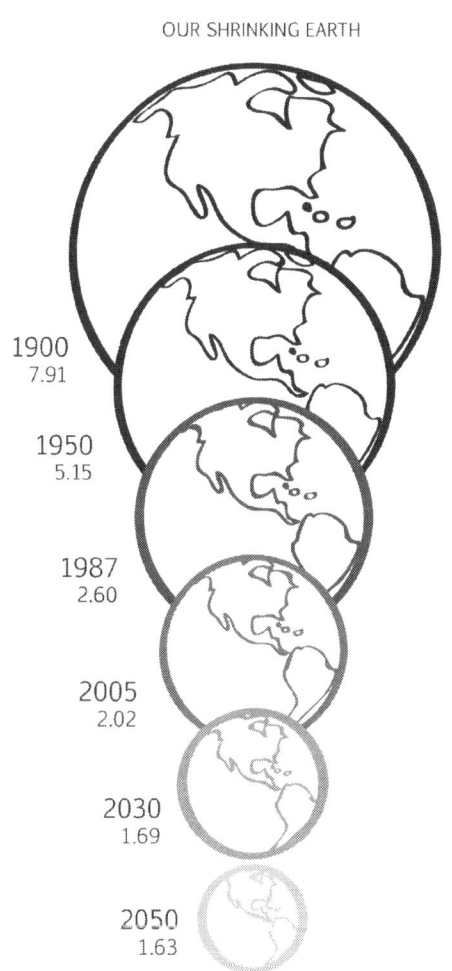

OUR SHRINKING EARTH

1900 — 7.91
1950 — 5.15
1987 — 2.60
2005 — 2.02
2030 — 1.69
2050 — 1.63

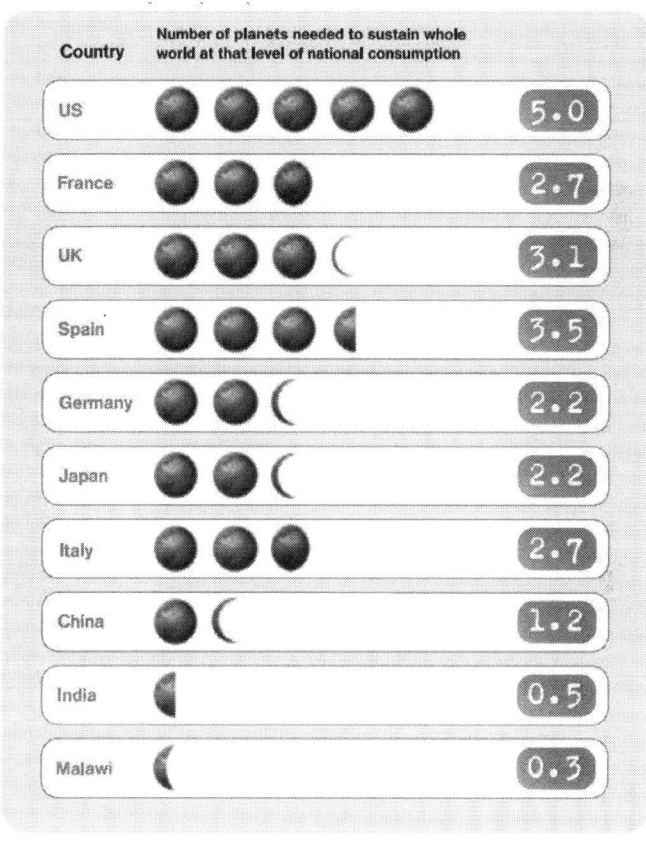

Country	Number of planets needed to sustain whole world at that level of national consumption	
US	●●●●●	5.0
France	●●●	2.7
UK	●●●☾	3.1
Spain	●●●☾	3.5
Germany	●●☾	2.2
Japan	●●☾	2.2
Italy	●●●	2.7
China	●☾	1.2
India	☾	0.5
Malawi	☾	0.3

> Now, a question for you that requires a quick fire response: What does Humpty Dumpty look like?

Did you visualise him as an egg-shaped man with little arms and legs sticking out? Oddly, we are not given any clues about what Humpty looks like in the rhyme, so why do we all think he is egg-shaped?

Erekson (2009) describes how powerful illustrations in picture books can interfere with the visualisation process. Images according to Erekson can be "quirky and unique, yet also familiar and safe". Humpty Dumpty could be imagined or drawn in any number of ways, yet the egg image has become so standard that we rarely seem to think of anything else. Our earliest encounters with nursery rhyme illustration, Erekson argues, define the visualised Humpty Dumpty absolutely.

It is important that the meanings behind this powerful image are clearly understood and do not squeeze out other meanings. To portray an intellectual definition in a visual form, whether artistic, scientific or both, may misrepresent its original meanings. However, such a form also creates the opportunity for a richer understanding of content and intent.

When you drew your sustainability diagram, did it involve three overlapping circles with sustainability (possibly) in the middle? If so, then you drew a picture that is so common in books and articles that it has become virtually synonymous with sustainability. It uses a Venn diagram to represent the key elements of sustainability. These elements have become known as 'the three pillars' - economy, society, and the environment. In the Venn diagram, they represent sustainability as inseparably, infinitely, and indistinguishably intertwined. Or do they?

What the Venn diagram - or 'pillars' - approach does is to pull its three key components together to represent a holistic and philosophical sense of what sustainability is; take these separate elements, now think of them together, but do not expect any guidance as to how they might be integrated.

egg-shaped imagination

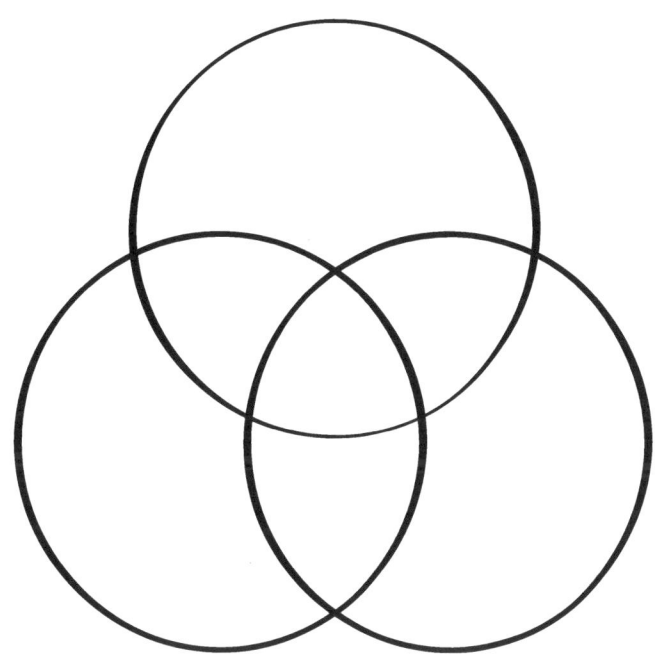

> The concept of *sustainability* has deep roots, and can be traced to Enlightenment thinking. The Age of Discovery, the Wars of Religion, and the mercantile expansions of the 15th and 16th Centuries saw a massive growth in ship building across Europe. This response resulted in increasingly rapid exploitation of domestic natural resources, especially forests and trees. Deforestation led to widespread shortages of wood which soon became an acute political problem that required a sustainable solution. ?

The New Forest (*Nova Foresta* in 1086 Domesday Book) was established as a Royal Park for hunting but with rights for commoners. Over time it was specifically planted (in enclosures, to keep the commoners' stock out) to maintain a resource of timber for the navy. The amount of timber in the New Forest "shew a rapid diminution...owing to the wasteful tendency of the system of government" between 1608 and 1792 (Anon 1853). A 1719 report presented the **"state and produce of timber in this Forest" in a tabular form** (right) and stated "if (removal was) not lessened, must in a short time utterly destroy the forest" (Lewis 1811). Commoners rights included (and still include) collection of fuel wood, cutting peat for fuel, and pannage - turning out pigs to eat fallen acorns. The New Forest can be considered a human ecosystem with human activities playing an active role in maintaining the forest.

Hanns Carl von Carlowitz's 1713 "*Silvicultura Oeconomica*" is considered to be the first text to take a sustainable approach: "continuirliche, beständige und nachhaltende Nutzung" (continuous, permanent and sustainable utilisation) as the rule for forestry. Vehkamäki (2005) argues that the von Carlowitz's aims of saving Europe from running out of wood shows a threefold understanding of sustainability: economic, social and ecological.

In 1804 Hartig described "Forest mensuration and forest management planning… so that the administration looks after interests of future generations so that a fair distribution of interests between the present and future generations will come true" (Vehkamäki 2005).

Heinrich von Cotta's *Anweisung zum Waldbau* (1817: "Instructions for Sylviculture") is considered to be a cornerstone of sustainability. In it he exposes the essential fallacy of forestry (McEvoy 2004), that human intervention improves forests - "we only have a forestry science because we have a dearth of wood". As a result, "…each generation of man has seen a smaller generation of wood".

We seem to accept that we are operating a weakened system:

> *Here and there we admire still the giant oaks and firs, which grew up without any care, while we are perfectly persuaded that we shall never in the same places be able, with any art or care, to reproduce similar trees*

The long period that is necessary for forest development is problematic for Cotta since humans, to use a much quoted phrase, "…cannot see the forest for the trees".

> *Forestry is based on the knowledge of nature, the deeper we penetrate its secrets, the deeper the depths become. The lighter it grows around us, the more unknown things become apparent, and it is a sure sign of shallowness, if anyone believes he knows it all.*

This sentiment is still live. As Kennedy and Koch (2004) argue, forestry science is now in a relationship stage that entails a managing of natural resources for valued people and ecosystem relationships.

Despite these learnings, however, the prevailing attitude through the 16th-19th Centuries was one of overcoming the limitations of nature. The German geographer Carl Ritter, for example, argued that while there was a deterministic relationship between the geography and the people, the measure of progress of civilization was the extent to which that relationship was overcome. Ecological degradation was therefore not a concern for Ritter. Changes in nature were seen as beneficial and in accordance with the hand of the Divine (Clark and Foster *et al*. 2002).

a dearth of wood

State and produce of timber in this Forest, at the under-mentioned periods:

A.D.		Number of Trees	Number of Loads
1608	Timber fit for the Navy	123,927	197,405
	Dotard and decayed trees		118,072
			315,477
1707	Timber fit for the Navy	12,476	19,873
	Dotards not stated		
1764	Timber fit for the Navy	19,836	36,662
	Defective oaks	1,743	3,835
			40,497
1783	Timber fit for the Navy	12,447	19,827
	Defective oaks	596	1,003
			20,830

> The relationship between humanity, resources and caring is starkly illustrated in the diagram showing a stowage system for slaves. Regardless of where people live or the colour of their skin, there is growing recognition that profit comes at a cost.

While the end of the 18th and the 19th Centuries saw the beginnings of the Industrial Revolution and a Victorian obsession with profit, it also saw threads that today make up the fabric of sustainability as people and environment in concert.

First, the slavery abolitionists represented a way of thinking that recognised the importance of all human life. **The Slave Ship Brookes diagram was first used by abolitionists "Plymouth Chapter of the Society for Effecting the Abolition of the Slave Trade" in 1789.** The ship is carrying 454 Africans (above the regulated number but below 609 it had previously carried). While widely regarded as helping bring about British Abolition in 1807, and widely recognised even today, the diagram is criticised as dehumanising individuals at the very moment when the need to proclaim their humanity is paramount (Wood 2000).

Second, people began to reconnect the dots joining people and their environment. In 1864, George Marsh wrote *Man and nature; or, Physical geography as modified by human action*. While his treatise is theologically based, Marsh reminds human beings that while they have the right to use and benefit from natural resources, that does not include the right to damage or alienate them. He writes:

> *Man has too long forgotten that the earth was given to him for usufruct alone, not for consumption, still less for profligate waste*

The legal term usufruct is appropriate since it refers to the right to use and benefit from a resource, but in the process not to damage or alienate it. Marsh was well aware that humans modify the natural world by cutting forests, draining swamps, and depleting wildlife, for instance. These actions were and are often seen as progress, but Marsh sought to highlight the negative side of such behaviour (Lee 2005).

> *The earth is fast becoming an unfit home for its noblest inhabitant, and another era of equal human crime and human improvidence, and of like duration with that through which traces of that crime and that improvidence extend, would reduce it to such a condition of impoverished productiveness, of shattered surface, of climatic excess, as to threaten the depravation, barbarism, and perhaps even extinction of the species.*

In arguing that "man in fact made the world", Marsh was inverting contemporary thought. Marsh argued that environmental degradation was indeed a problem and were caused by "ignorant disregard of the laws of nature" (he gave examples such as water flow in the Aidironack being affected by deforestation).

Apart from highlighting mankind's role as the cause of environmental degradation, Marsh (1864) also offered advice about the "restoration of disturbed harmonies". He promoted the need for a different sort of relationship "on lands laid waste by human improvidence or malice", and urged the pioneer settler "…to become a co-worker with nature in the reconstruction of the damaged fabric which the negligence or the wantonness of the formers lodgers has rendered untenantable" (1864).

Third, John Ruskin began to question the very basis of Victorian society. He observed that the same economic system that creates glittering wealth also spawns what he called *illth* — poverty, pollution, despair, illness. It makes life comfortable for some, but it does so at considerable discomfort to others (Hunt and Holland 1982).

the cost of profit

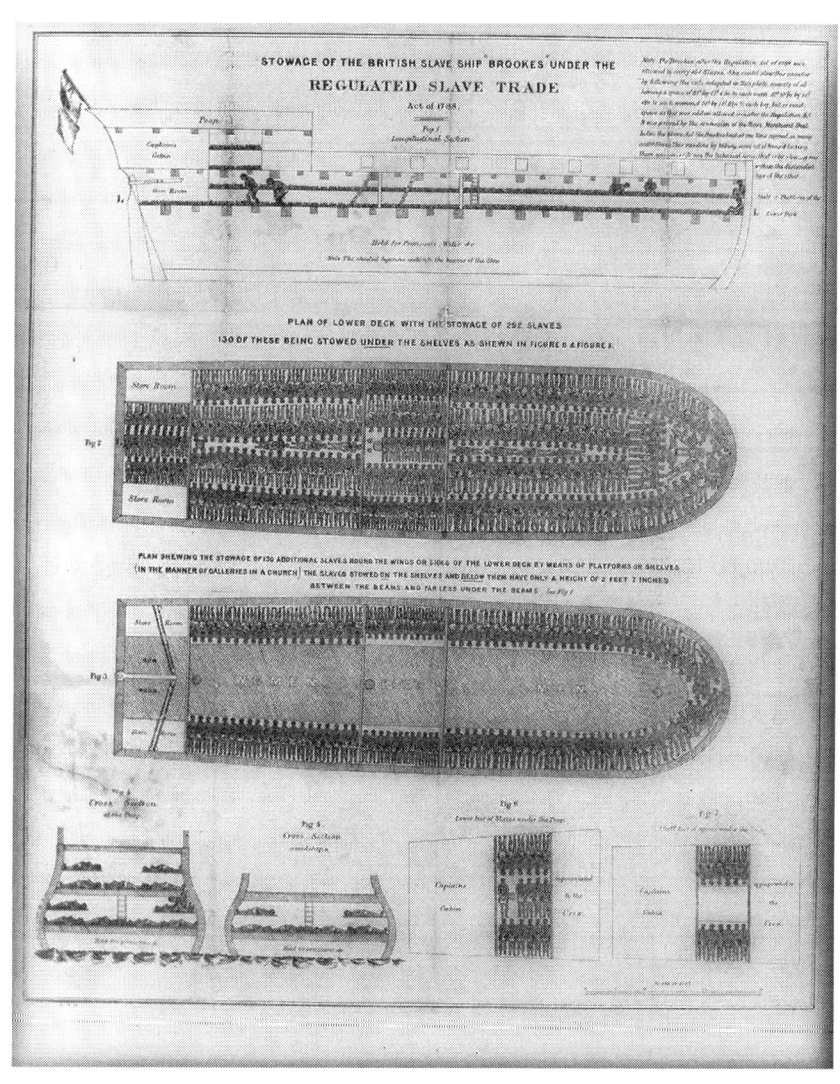

> With the growth of environmentalism in the early 1900's, sustainability involves two streams of thinking that are seen to be inextricably linked – the challenge of a growing world population and the need to develop an ethical framework for the use of resources.

There has been an increasing awareness that human use of the Earth is approaching a range of environmental and resource limits and that this trend is escalating at an alarming rate. In 1949 M. King Hubbert argued that United States oil production would peak in the early 1970s (while dismissed at the time, US production peaked in 1970 - Deffeyes 2008).

The consumption of energy from fossil fuels is thus seen to be but a "pip," rising sharply from zero to a maximum, and almost as sharply declining, and thus representing but a moment in the total of human history.

With time stretched in thousands of years into the past and future, **Hubbert's series of graphs (left) show the impact of this exhaustion of energy supplies.** The top diagram on the left shows energy from fossil fuels; the next renewable energy under different scenarios; the third shows energy per capita; and the bottom image on the left shows human population. This last figure shows a catastrophic collapse unless we overcome the "cultural lag" and see the evolution of a "culture more nearly in conformity with the limitations imposed upon us by the basic properties of matter and energy"

It is clear, therefore, that our present position on the nearly vertical front slopes of these curves is a precarious one, and that the events which we are witnessing and experiencing, far from being "normal," are among the most abnormal and anomalous in the history of the world.

A growing number of writers began to add their voices to the dangers of a world population boom that was projected as unsupportable by finite resources. The seminal books and articles of brothers H.T. and E.P. Odum on ecosystem ecology from the early 1950's onwards; Rachel Carson's (1962) Silent Spring, widely credited with launching the environmental movement; and the foundation of the global think tank (the Club of Rome) in 1963 by Aurelion Peccei and Alexander King all made huge impact in helping to raise public consciousness of a world under pressure.

The Club of Rome's (Meadows *et al.* 1972, 2004) *Limits to Growth*, for example, sold over 12 million copies in more than 30 translations and became the bestselling environmental book in world history (it is still in print today with a 30 year update in 2004). It was also the first real attempt to make the science of what was to become sustainability available to the public.

The **two diagrams on the right are taken from Limits to Growth and model a view of the world as a comprehensive system.** In the model on the top right, the plotted variables follow historical values from 1900 to 1970. Food, industrial output and population grow exponentially until a rapidly diminishing resource base forces a slowdown in industrial growth. Because of natural delays in the system, population and pollution increase after industrialisation peaks. Population growth is halted by a rising death rate due to decreased food and medical services.

The model on the lower right is an attempt to stabilise sustainability far into the future by introducing regulating and technological polices, such as resource recycling, methods to restore soil, and longer capital lifetimes. Notice that the resources still decline, but the rate slows, allowing time for technology and industry to adapt. The value of industrial production is replaced by the value of food and services. There is some hope for human kind.

ups and downs

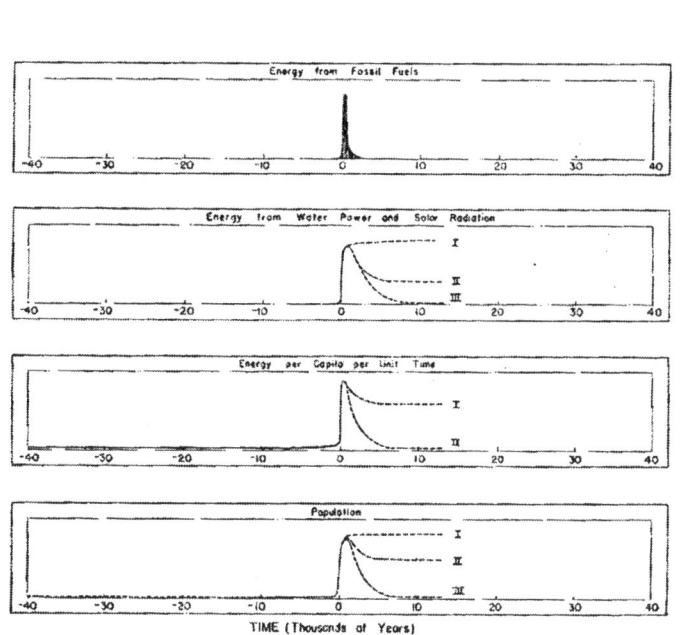
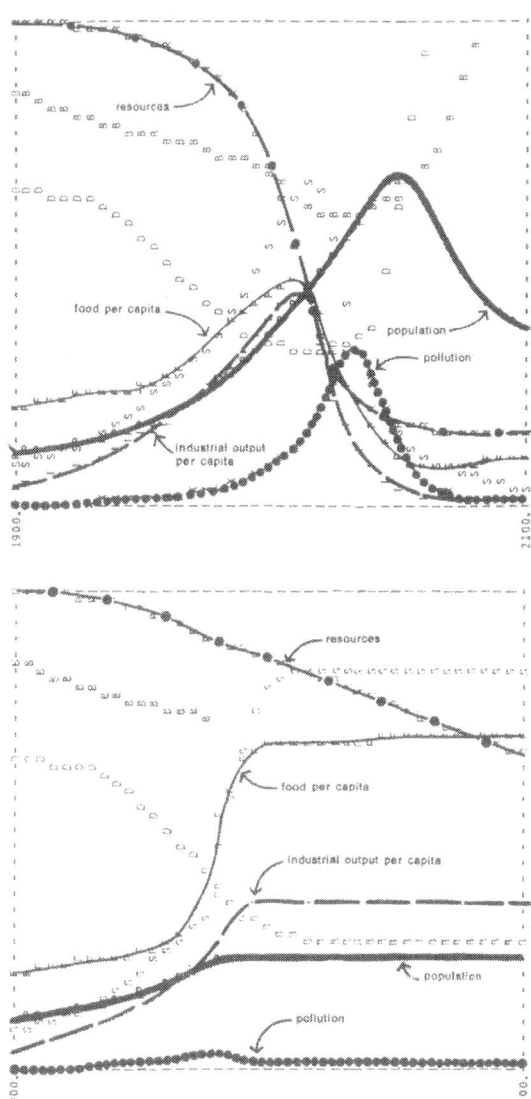

once upon a planet

> Man has the fundamental right to freedom, equality and adequate conditions of life, in an environment of a quality that permits a life of dignity and well being (United Nations Conference on the Human Environment, 1972).

During his term in office as the 32nd President of the United States, Theodore Roosevelt supported conservation strategies aimed at maximising the long term economic benefits of natural resources. In 1949, Aldo Leopold published his "land ethic".

> *The land ethic simply enlarges the boundaries of the community to include soils, waters, plants, and animals, or collectively: the land…[A] land ethic changes the role of Homo sapiens from conqueror of the land-community to plain member and citizen of it. It implies respect for his fellow-members, and also respect for the community as such.*

The United Nations Conference on the Human Environment (also known as the Stockholm Conference) was held in Stockholm Sweden in June 1972. It was the UN's first major conference on international environmental issues, and marked a turning point in the development of international environmental politics. The Stockholm Conference established the solemn responsibility of governments to protect and improve the environment for both present and future generations.

Instead of treating the biosphere and human development as "separate topics of personal concern – tableaux disjointed in time and space" (Caldwell 1984), we begin to see acceptance of the notion of "ecologically sustainable development." The *World Conservation Strategy* was formulated by the International Union for the Conservation of Nature and Natural Resources (IUCN) in cooperation with the U.N. Environmental Program (UNEP) and World Wildlife Fund (WWF), FAO and UNESCO. The World Conservation Strategy was launched in 1980 in 30 countries, and now many countries are adopting conservation strategies formulated within the guidelines suggested.

Subtitled Living Resource Conservation for Sustainable Development, the strategy begins with a foreword:

> *Human beings, in their quest for economic development and enjoyment of the riches of nature, must come to terms with the reality of resource limitation and the carrying capacities of ecosystems', and must take account of the needs of future generations. This is the message of conservation. For if the object of development is to provide for social and economic welfare, the object of conservation is to ensure Earth's capacity to sustain development and to support all life.*

The strategy combined three objectives:

- maintaining essential ecological processes and life support systems,

- preserving genetic diversity, and

- ensuring the sustainable utilization of species and ecosystems.

The strategy then – saw conservation as a means to achieve social and economic objectives, and social and economic constraints as barriers to achieving conservation objectives. In diagrammatic terms, **The World Conservation Strategy places these objectives on the same page and indicates that they should be considered as equals.** Economic, social and environmental issues are seen as part of the same agenda.

all was equal

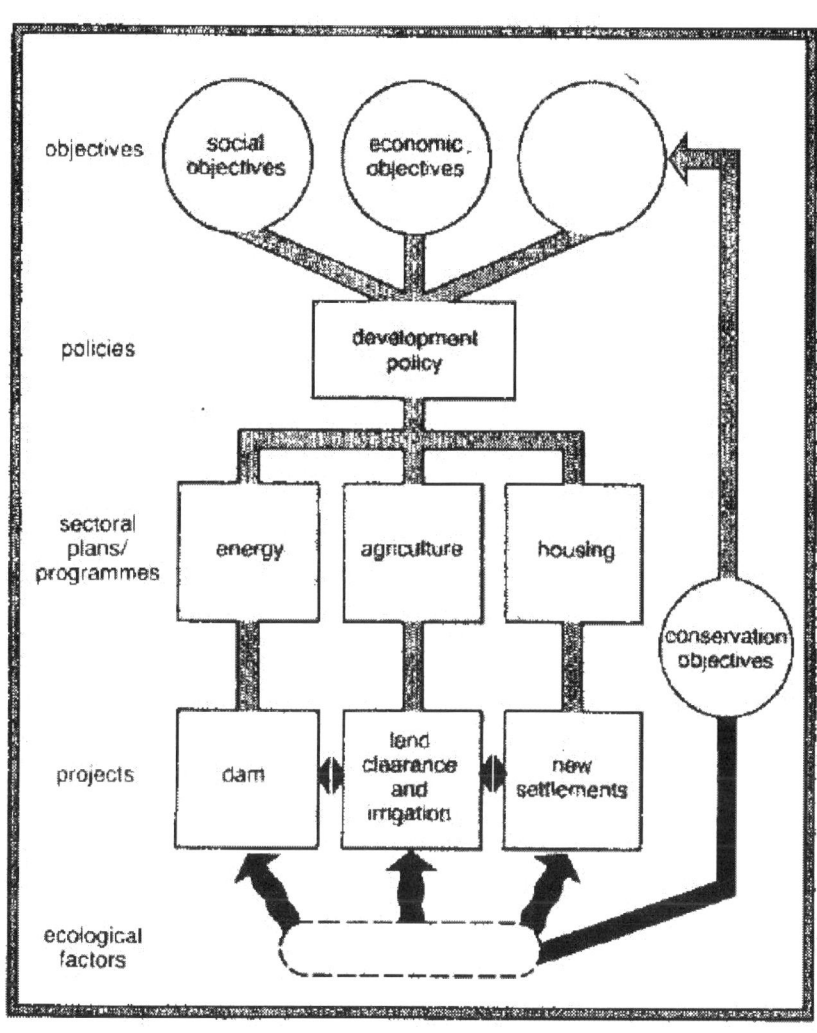

> Clearly, the prime need is an integrated approach derived from a combination of the ecological, sociological, cultural, economic and political aspects to make solutions viable. These solutions must balance urgent, current needs with long-term sustainability (Edwards *et al.*, 1993).

The World Conservation Strategy was published by the International Union for Conservation of Nature and Natural Resources (IUCN) (currently the World Conservation Union), United Nations Environment Programme (UNEP) and the World Wide Fund for Nature (WWF) in 1980 with the objectives of:

(a) maintaining essential ecological processes and life support systems,

(b) preserving genetic diversity, and

(c) ensuring the sustainable utilization of species and ecosystems.

The mission to help the world find pragmatic solutions to its most pressing environmental and development challenges was and is a huge step forward in the history of sustainable practice. There is a tension between environment and growth. The premise is that too much of one will damage the other - the task is to find an appropriate balance (Swindale 1988).

Note that there are two subtle variations in the balance. The first concept is that sustainability is a balance of human needs and environmental protection. A second variation on this balance is that sustainability is in opposition to economic development. The Jakarta Post (29th July 2011), for example headlines "Balancing sustainability with economic development". Sustainability is treated as synonymous with conservation.

While international and national strategy, and indeed public perception during the 1980s, was focussed on finding this balance, there was also considerable scientific exploration of the characteristics of the relationships between the environment and social systems. Ingold (1980), for example, took a social anthropology approach to the dynamics of relationships between social and ecological systems. This model was used to explore different models of utilisation of reindeer (hunting, pastoralism, ranching), despite similar environments and ecology in Arctic tundra.

The notion that sustainability is a balance of human needs and environmental protection has persisted. In the diagram **on the left, the need for a balanced approach between environment and growth** is characterised as a balance with human needs (synonymous with industry) on one end outweighing the environment on the other. Balance is widely used as a metaphor in talking about sustainability, whether it is ecological balance, the balance between rich and poor or the need for balance between environmental systems and business growth. **This simplistic view of balance is offset by a more complex view that presents sustainability as a set of dynamic and adaptive objectives (right, Ingold 1980).**

balance with harmony

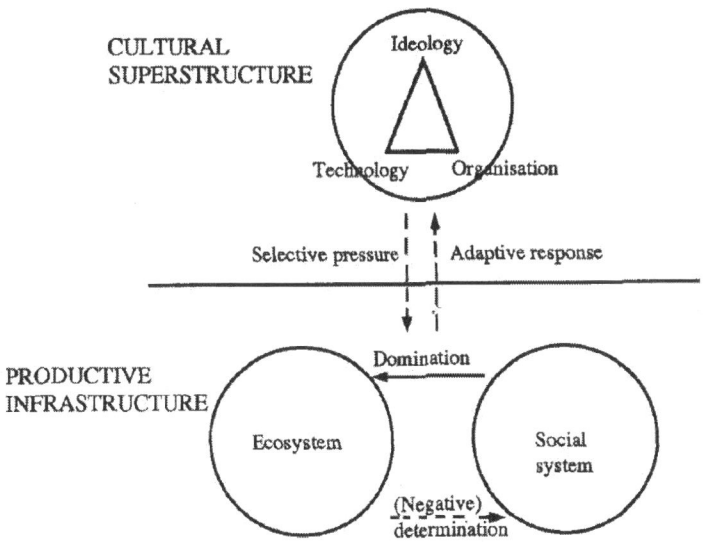

> *Sustainable development is development that meets the needs of the present without compromising the ability of future generations to meet their own needs (WCED 1987)*

The definition of sustainable development in the box above is taken from the World Commission on Environment and Development Conference (1987) - *Our Common Future*. It is widely cited as the Brundtland definition after the chair, then Norwegian Prime Minister Gro Harlem Brundtland.

In the preface to her report, Gro Brundtland comments:

> *When the terms of reference of our Commission were originally being discussed in 1982, there were those who wanted its considerations to be limited to "environmental issues" only. This would have been a grave mistake. The environment does not exist as a sphere separate from human actions, ambitions, and needs, and attempts to defend it in isolation from human concerns have given the very word "environment" a connotation of naiveté in some political circles (WCED xi)*

A key feature of the Brundtland definition is the potential seen by its proponents to integrate environmental and economic concerns, along with a concern for the well-being of all. Sustainable development not only implies greater equity and continued growth, but also growth of a more environmentally, socially, and economically sustainable kind.

> *Until recently, the planet was a large world in which human activities and their effects were neatly compartmentalised within nations, within sectors (energy, agriculture, trade), and within broad areas of concern (environment, economics, social). These compartments have begun to dissolve.*

The Brundtland definition has been widely debated, contested, and criticised. Yet, all other definitions stem from it and most have at the core three components; environment, society and economy, along with the recognition that "the well being of these three areas is intertwined, not separate" (McKeown, 2002).

The **Roman Doric columns in the image give an architectural form to the classic definition of sustainability that has become known as the three pillars – society, environment and the economy**. Each pillar is independent and given equal importance in size and load. Notice that the three pillars together do not represent sustainability; rather their function is to carry the roof "sustainable development". Apart from its form as a triangular pediment, the nature of the roof is not indicated. Does it protect the house? Is it structurally expensive? Would removing one column result in its collapse?

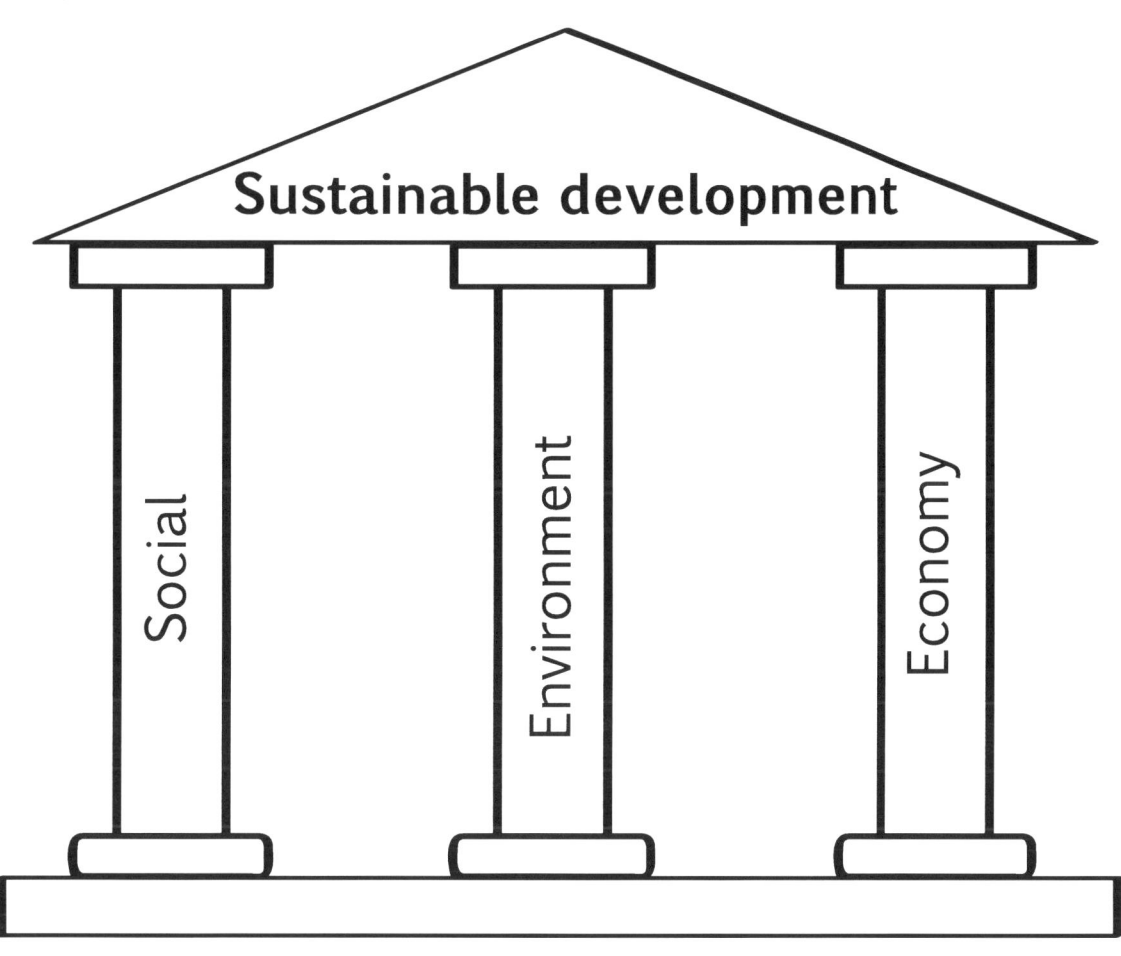

The pillars of sustainability are often visualised as a three legged milking stool - bringing a degree of wholesomeness to contemporary views of sustainability. Like the architectural pillars, the three legs of the stool support a structure; in this case the seat as in the first graphic. Despite their key role as supporting structures of sustainability, no links between the legs are indicated; their implicit function is to keep the stool balanced. Failure to achieve balance (due to a broken leg, as in the second image; or having one leg longer than the other two, as in the third) presumably leads to either dangerous or calamitous outcomes.

These pillars of sustainability are often visualised as a three legged milking stool - bringing a degree of wholesomeness to contemporary views of sustainability. Like the architectural pillars, the three legs of the stool support a structure; in this case the seat as in the first graphic. Despite their key role as supporting structures of sustainability, no links between the legs is indicated; their implicit function is to keep the stool balanced. **Failure to achieve balance due to a broken leg, or having one leg longer than the other two, as in this image from Storck (2006) presumably leads to either dangerous or calamitous outcomes.**

The three 'pillars' device was not specifically referenced in Our Common Future, nor was mentioned in the Rio Earth Summit (Agenda 21, 1992. However, it has become the default metaphor for sustainable development. The Johannesburg Declaration of the Earth Summit (2002), for example, states:

> *These efforts will also promote the integration of the three components of sustainable development — economic development, social development and environmental protection — as interdependent and mutually reinforcing pillars.*

The United Nations 2005 World Summit Outcome Document also refers to the "interdependent and mutually reinforcing pillars" of sustainable development as economic development, social development, and environmental protection.

the three legged stool

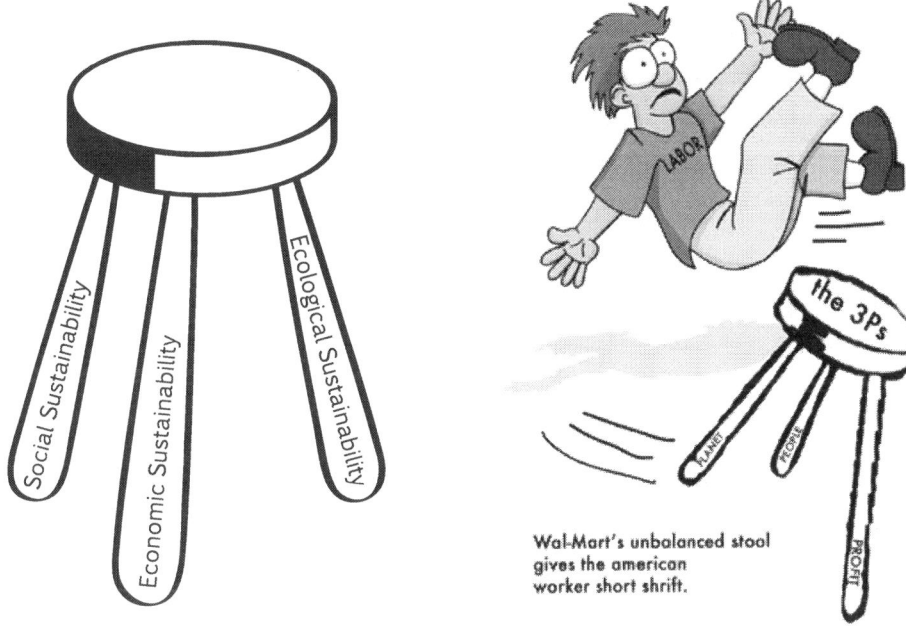

Wal-Mart's unbalanced stool gives the american worker short shrift.

the shape of things

> A Venn diagram shows all the logically possible combinations between a finite collection of sets or aggregation or things. Venn diagrams were conceived around 1880 by John Venn. Since the pillars of sustainability were seen to comprise of three systems, the use of three circles has become a very popular way of representing sustainability. Crucially, sustainability is found only at the intersection of the circles.

Edward Barbier's (1989) article *The Concept of Sustainable Economic Development* would perhaps have gone unnoticed had it not been for the figure shown opposite. Barbier's figure has become as equally famous as Brundtland's three-fold definition of sustainable development. **Barbier was (and is) an economist, who argued for a 'completely new analytical approach' to modeling economic sustainable development.** This approach argued the need for the continuous assessment of benefits and costs across the dynamic nature of development and diversity of social, economic and ecological conditions. Barbier explains:

> *One basic analytical approach is to view this process as an interaction among three systems: the biological (and other resource) system (BS), the economic system (ES), and the social system (SS).*

These systems can be considered in terms of human-ascribed goals. Biological system goals include genetic diversity, resilience and biological productivity. Economic system goals are satisfy basic needs are equity-enhancing and increase useful goods and services. Social system goals involve cultural diversity, institutional sustainability, social justice and participation.

Barbier represented these systems as a Venn diagram. The original caption for the diagram states:

> *Sustainable economic development maximises the goals across the biological and resource system (BS), the economic system (ES), and the social system (SS), as illustrated by the shaded area. In contrast, conventional development approaches maximize only ES goals, and Marxist economies maximizes only ES and SS goals.*

Unlike the literal pillars diagram or the three legged stool, Barbier's Venn shows that the three pillars are interlinked, interrelated, and inseparable. Hence, none of these systems can be sacrificed if sustainability is to be maintained.

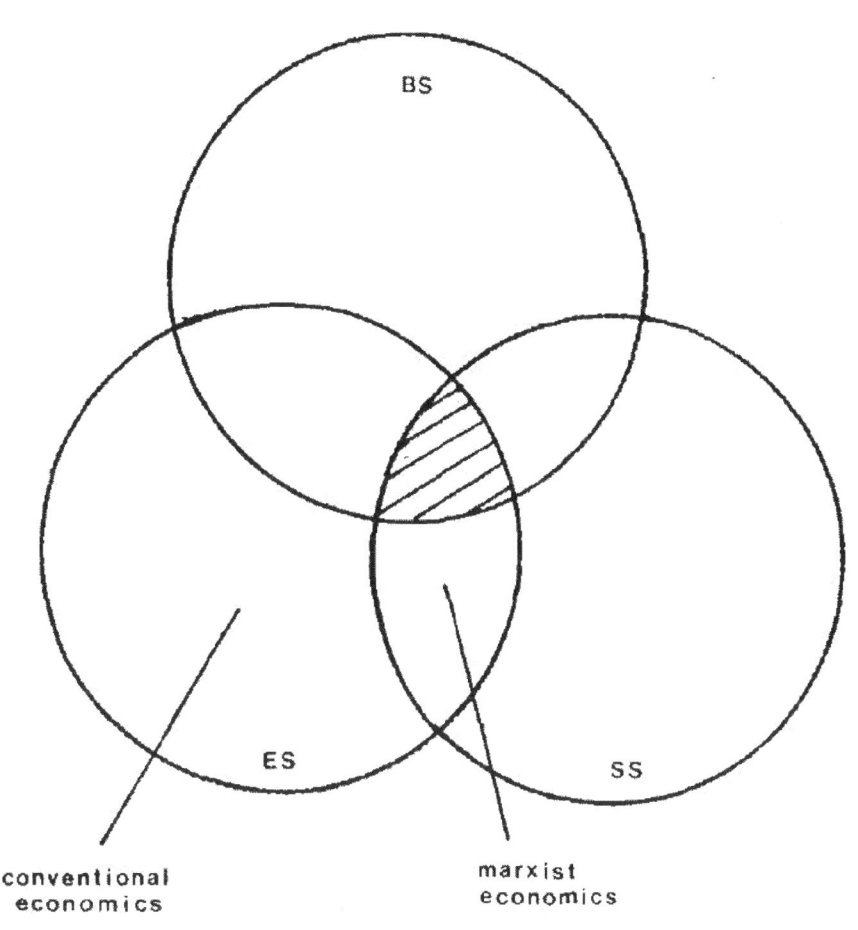

> Without further elaboration, the Venn diagram provides an incomplete picture of sustainability. Barbier recognised that there were missing elements from his original three circle diagram, but made no attempt to represent them visually. I consider here one of the few attempts that I have come across to incorporate something of the bigger picture that Barbier had suggested was necessary for this purpose.

In order to confront and overcome the challenges of economic, environmental and social objectives that he saw at the heart of sustainable development, Barbier suggested that we need to consider processes, priorities and effects that he labeled as 'adaptivity, variability and scale' respectively.

As individual preferences, social norms, and ecological conditions change over time, human beings need to be adaptive because what is considered important and how it gets prioritised will change. Priorities among goals are also likely to vary in different locations and situations and according to scale effects that can impact locally, regionally, nationally and globally. Barbier also recognised that "absolute sustainability may not be physically possible for any particular pattern of industrial development, but one must still find a pattern that is relatively more sustainable than are others". Unfortunately, the three circle diagram on its own is not much help in determining this relative positioning.

The Dalal-Clayton *et al.* (1994) diagram opposite incorporates the three mainstay concepts of sustainability as a single entity within a larger circle. This circle is subject to local, national and global objectives that are mediated through political ideologies and systems. The effect of these systems is dependent on achieving relative political stability in conjunction with established institutional bureaucratic arrangements and mechanisms. Full integration of the three pillars presumably means that sustainability will be achieved with equal input from each system. Notice that the shaded area representing this type of integration is very small (the central intersection). Partial integration on the other hand looks much more likely, but with what kind of contribution from each or all of the systems? What form might such integration take and with what consequences? Represented in this way, sustainability seems somewhat elusive.

not the whole story

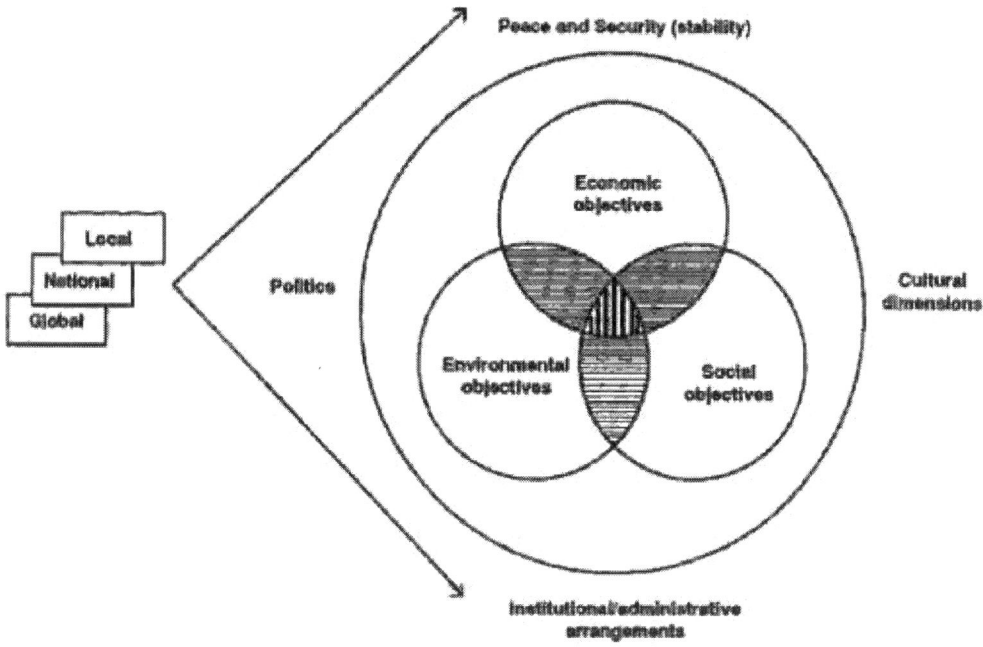

the shape of things

> Visually displaying sustainability as the intersection of three circles is one way of representing the relationship between society, economy and environment. This representation is not without its difficulties. Is the size of the circles incidental? What does the body text tell us about sustainability? Do the three pillar elements generate different types of sustainability, whether socially, economically or ecologically?

The problem about representing sustainability in the form of a Venn diagram is perhaps best described in relation to colours. In a two circle Venn diagram showing blue and red, everyone knows only the intersection is purple. But the diagram is not entirely purple - there is still blue and red. Where is the sustainability equivalent of blue and red? In the same way that red is not purple, economics is not sustainability. Nor for that matter, is the environment.

Unfortunately, this error is perpetuated in most representations of Barbier's Venn diagram. Venn diagrams are often considered to show only positive elements: "a viable natural environment" in the rump of the environmental circle for example. The entire three circle model is considered by many to represent sustainability and each of the circles forms the separate pillars - hence we hear of "economic sustainability", or ecological sustainability". **The sustainability Venn diagram is increasingly being interpreted as the whole set representing sustainability rather than just the intersection.** While the core message from *Our Common Future* is that the three pillars are inseparable, the common use of the sustainability Venn has an unfortunate twist, which I characterise as 'together but separately.'

To understand the limitations of the common use of Barbier's Venn, we need just a little bit of maths theory. The circle on a Venn diagram represents a class (set). The interior represents the elements of the set, the exterior represents elements which are not members of the set. All possible logical relations of these classes can be indicated on the same diagram. A Venn diagram consists of "set, or not set" so the position within the circle is not relevant. As a set schematic, the sizes of the circles are also extraneous.

The Venn diagram (left) shows the three pillars on the same space. Here we have Society, Economy and Environment. Sustainable (development) occurs in the centre of the diagram. While Barbier was concerned with "maximising" each of the three systems, this is not represented on the diagram. We are forced to assume a dichotomous binary sustainability/unsustainability.

Barbier named the centre area "sustainable development" and the intersection of society and economy as "Marxist economics", but the other two intersections are not named. Following his terms, they could perhaps be considered "Allocation" and "Conservation biology". Since Barbier's original diagram, representations of the Venn diagram (such as the one on the left) show the "Systems" dropped, with most representing "Social" or "Society" rather than "Social system". Barbier's "Biological and resource system" has undergone a change to "Environment". The intersections are named, not for the branch of economics that studies them as Barbier did, but for the living conditions they describe: hence the centre is Sustainable, and the Social/Environment is "Bearable", Environment/Economic is "Viable", and Economic/Social is "Equitable". So far this is consistent with the Venn diagram formalism. This though is where the Venn diagram comes unstuck. In the terms of these "___ables", what should be in the rump of the circle? The labels "Social" (and so on) are in the wrong place - they refer to the whole circle.

The right-hand diagram shows an interpretation where the entire diagram purports to show sustainable development, each of the circles represents the nonsensical separate pillar sustainability. Again, where on this diagram would we put something negative? How would we consider child labour, for example?

blue, red and purple

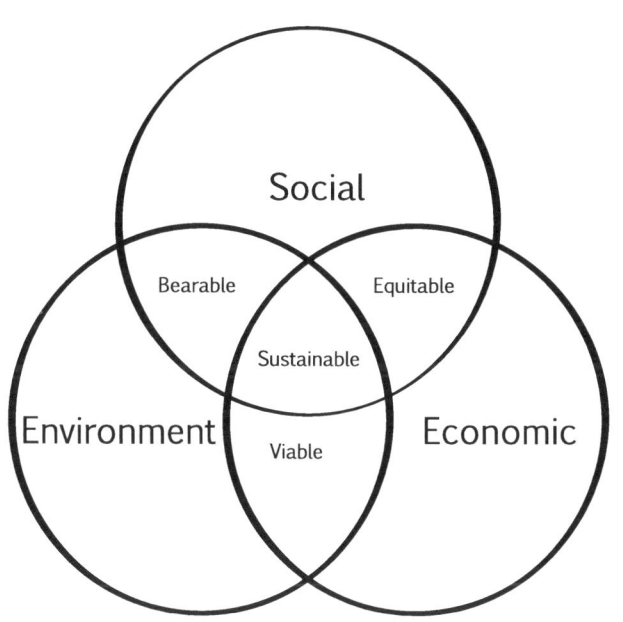

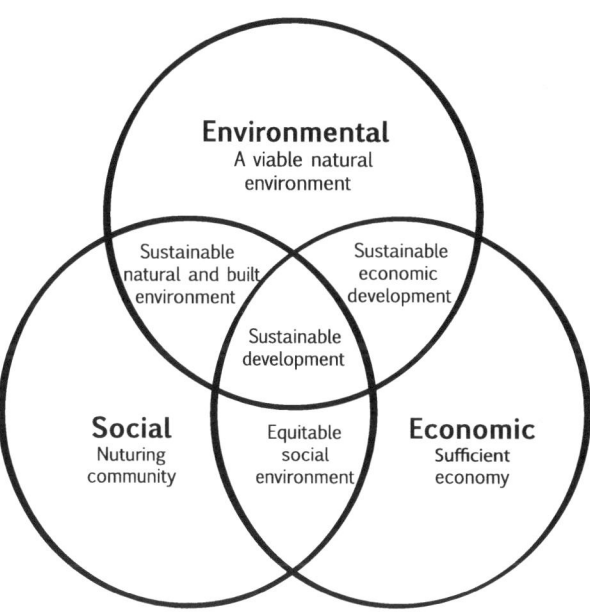

> Trying to capture the meaning of sustainability is one thing, explaining its context another. Here are three versions of how that context can be represented, including the incorporation of decision making processes.

The **circle of people provides the context for Flint's (2003) version of sustainability (top-left)**. Are they protecting sustainability? Is sustainability at the core of the community? Being on the periphery, perhaps the people are distanced from and perhaps even afraid of sustainability? Could sustainability be a treadmill which requires continuous ongoing action by human beings on a global basis? There are many questions that could be raised as a result of this encirclement of the Venn. The issue from our perspective is that if people are the context and solution for the issues that surround sustainability – do they understand what it is they are confronting?

Judith Morrison (2010 - middle-right) focuses on building capacity for participation in collaborative multiparty decision-making or problem-solving processes. She argues that in addition to skills in managing natural resources, there are another "set of sustainability skills that are just as crucial...to work toward developing common ground as we try and negotiate a sustainable way forward with one another". In her diagram, Morrison uses an adaptation of the Venn diagram that focuses on overcoming some of the barriers to sustainability. In doing so, she is clearly attempting to articulate the fundamental relationship between the pillars and how they interact. Morrison uses this diagram as part of a course (Certificate in Understanding and Negotiating Sustainability Issues). She says "these exercises in turn consolidate a capacity to convey how different components need to come together in an integrated approach, as well as some of the factors that make this a challenge" (*pers comm* 30/11/11).

In this model of "sustainability driven entrepreneurship", **Schlange (2009; lower-left) presents sustainability as integrating concept. With no intersection, sustainability becomes the context.** It is not possible to consider, say "socially driven" without the context of an integrated sustainability; though possibly one could consider socially driven without recourse to economics or environment. The diagram is a little confusing - what is the significance of the intersections? Why are the three-pillars of sustainability visualised as an intersecting point?

venn variations

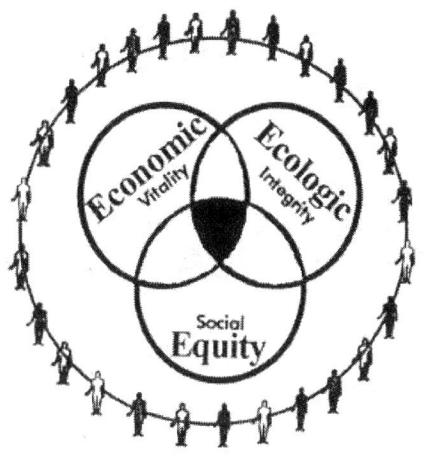

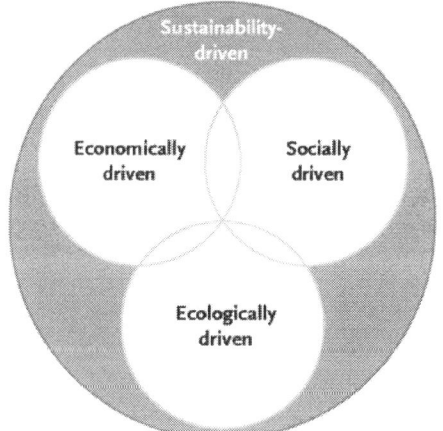

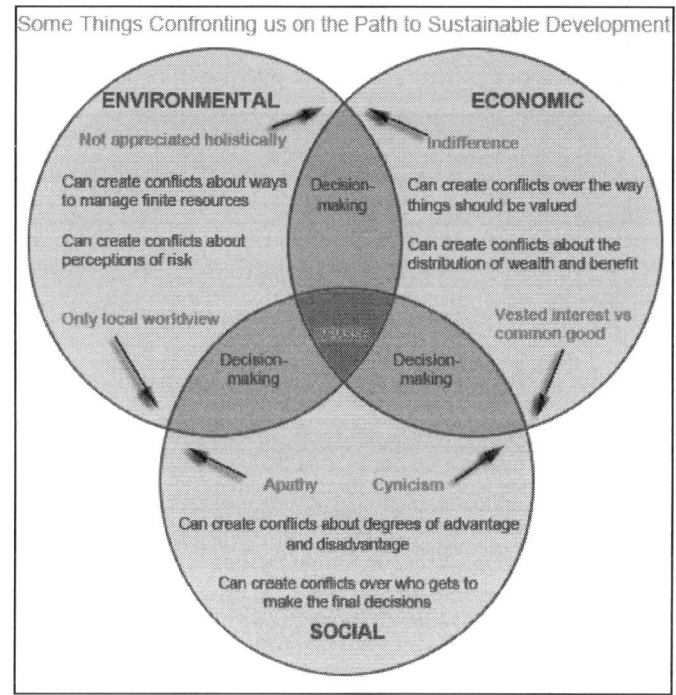

> A Venn diagram does not represent the form or extent of the intersection between sets - merely that there is an intersection. Venn diagrams provide little insight into how to model the complex and reflexive interactions between domains giving the "false picture that each pillar can be organized and measured independently" (Stanners *et al.* 2007).

Within the pillars school, some authors have explored the nature of the relationship between the pillars by questioning how and in what ways three otherwise separate domains can cooperate.

The diagrams opposite explore the nature of the relationship between the pillars. The **diagram (top-left) positions sustainability as a cyclic flow through the three pillars**. The pillars are still three separate elements though. Should colours blend together? Would that be a more realistic expression/interpretation? All the pillars affect each other, but the arrows are only in one direction. Does society affect the environment or the environment the economy? If this model was to be applied in the real world, the speed of the cycle would be important. It would be unfortunate if this led to an understanding of sustainability that was along the lines of "we'll get the economy sorted...that will feed into the ecology...which will feed into society... problem sorted".

The **diagram (top-right) stretches the pillars around the rim of a wheel**. This image shows connectivity between the three pillars and communicates the idea of an active, maintained balance. One can never be at a single point on the widened circumference without also being in contact with another area of sustainability. Unlike the Venn, however, there is not a position where the three pillars are equally represented. The usual sustainability sweet spot has been sacrificed for a representation that considers the pillars simultaneously and dynamically (Greenwood 2010).

Finally, the **never-ending triangle of sustainable development** (after Välimäki 2002, in Stanners *et al.* 2007) is represented as a Penrose Tribar that appears to be composed of three straight beams with three right angles (invented by Oscar Reutersvard in 1934 but popularised by Penrose). As a problem in topology, the image raises questions about the nature of sustainability. Does the image show three interwoven or just three connected bars? Are any of the bars more significant than the others? Whichever bar you focus on stands out, but only makes sense if you look at the bigger picture. Is it possible to capture sustainability in this way?

separate domains, equal dimensions

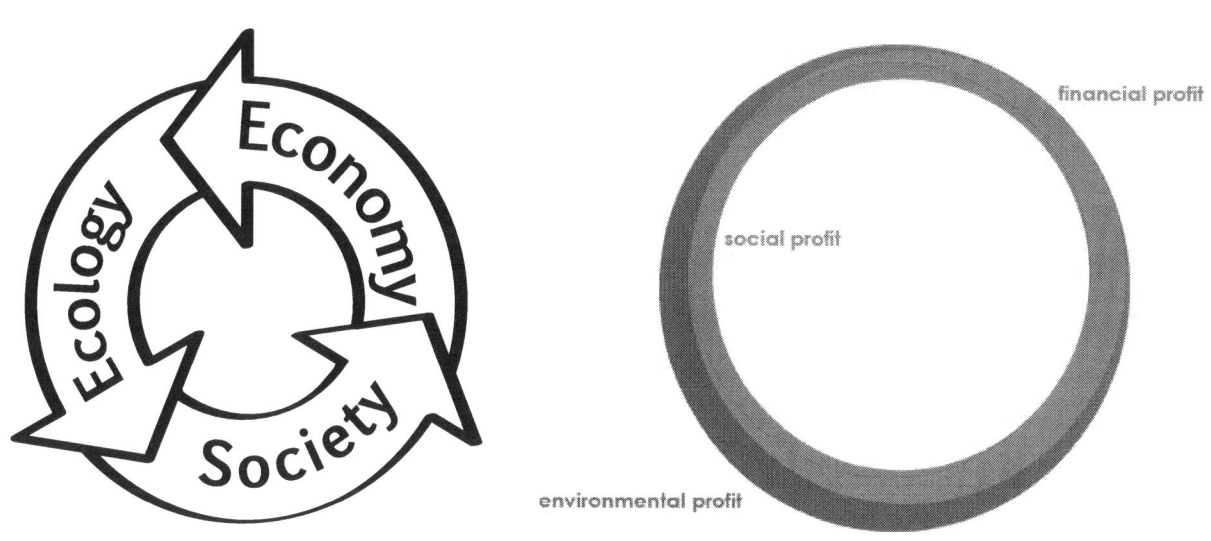

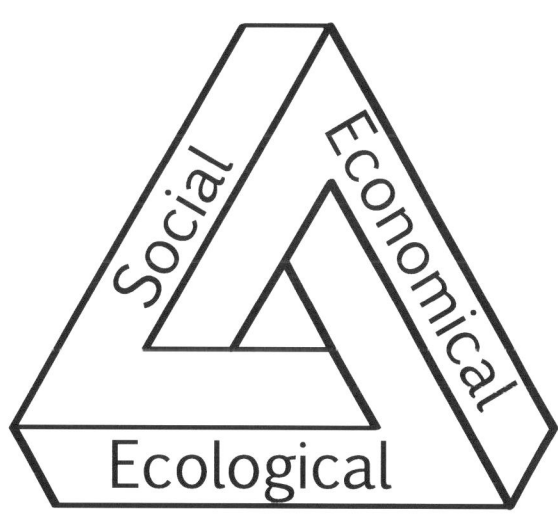

> In order to understand the complexity of sustainability, some authors have created a fourth pillar. This pillar is often labelled 'culture'.

Jon Hawkes wrote *The Fourth Pillar of Sustainability: Culture's essential role in public planning* in 2001. Hawkes added his fourth pillar to environmental responsibility, economic health, and social equity. He argued that culture is "the whole complex of distinctive spiritual, material, intellectual and emotional features that characterize a society or social group". He also argued that culture is 'more than the arts' and includes: "modes of life, the fundamental rights of the human being, value systems, traditions and beliefs; that it is culture that gives man the ability to reflect upon himself". This capacity for reflection assists human beings in developing an understanding of the quality of life, in relation to their goals, expectations, standards and concerns.

Adding a fourth pillar is problematic for the Venn model, since an extra circle (or circles- like the Olympic rings logo) affects the topology. An intersection of all sets with each of the other four sets is not possible using circles. More sets can certainly be added (think of the Venn diagram with a superimposed sad-clown face), but I did not find any examples that visualised sustainability this way. More organic shapes are needed for this purpose. Hence, the diagram that is top-left.

The New Zealand Local Government Act 2002 (Section 10) defines one of the purposes of local government as being to "… promote the social, economic, environmental, and cultural well-being of communities, in the present and for the future". In the **graphic (top left), these forms of well-being are interconnected through an overall notion of well-being, are given equal weight, are interdependent, and are central** (NZ Ministry for Culture and Heritage 2002). Contrast this image with the Venn drawn by Kat Runnalls (2006).

Runnalls argued that culture touches all aspects of sustainability. She represents this in a Venn form (top-right) that has culture emerging out of the intersections of the three pillars. Notice that while it provides a context for the pillars, the cultural dimension does not reach the sustainable core.

Extending the stool models seen earlier **Francesco di Castri (1995, lower left) likened sustainable development to a chair with four legs - economic, social, cultural and environmental.** His chair's four connected 'legs' of sustainability must all be included in sustainable policy and management. If one leg is over-emphasised, (usually the 'economic leg'), then the chair won't be flat or comfortable. Notice also the Renaissance styling of the chair:

> *This is not only because it is a particularly robust chair and its four legs are united by strong linkages, but also because I believe that we are pointing towards a new human development, a new Renaissance, where science and arts, nature and culture should by necessity intimately interact as a whole.*

Representing sustainability as woven flax (lower right) provides a unique and culturally distinctive visual image. Landcare Research (nd) is a New Zealand governmental research agency that structures their annual reports around an integrated Triple Bottom Line approach: "We believe every Key Performance Area (KPA) has interlinked social, environmental and economic dimensions, which are difficult to separate. Hence we do not advocate reporting on KPAs under the three delineated bottom lines". In representing sustainability in this way, the agency is making a strong statement about how the pillars are intrinsically interconnected. The woven flax also links the concept of sustainability and with sustainable practice.

and then there were four

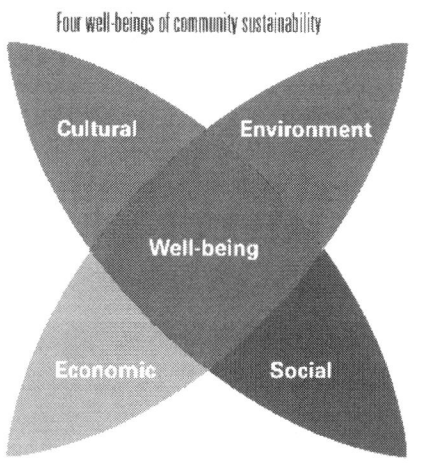

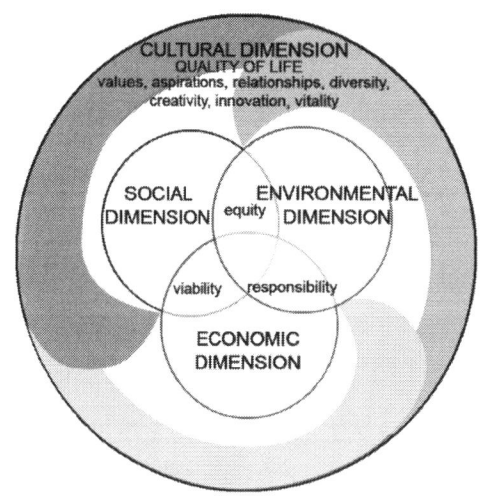

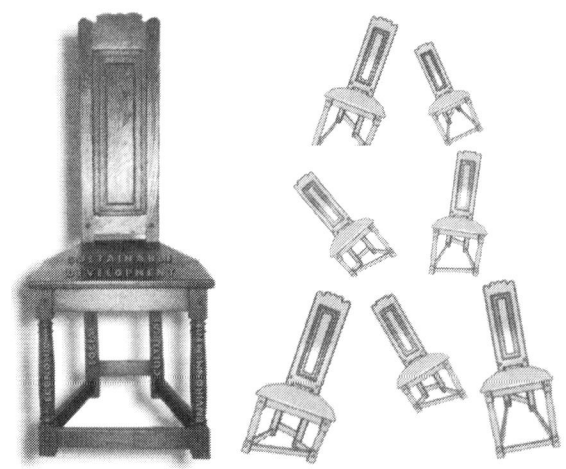

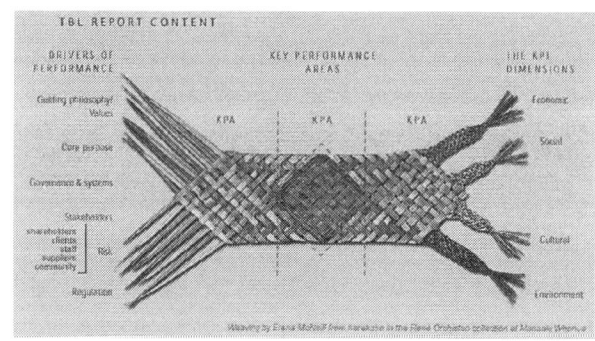

the shape of things

> The Venn diagram approach to visualising sustainability is constrained by the dichotomy of Venn sets - something is either in the set, or out of it. On a three circle Venn diagram there are only seven possible positions for representing concepts or information (eight if you include the outside). This arrangement limits the utility of the model for representing what each pillar can contribute towards a sustainable whole. By arranging the three pillars on a ternary plot, it is possible to graph the intersection of the variables in two dimensions.

A ternary, or triangle, plot uses a triangle to display the proportions of three variables that sum to a constant. The word "ternary" comes from the Latin adjective "ternarius", "having three parts".

In the 1990s at least two schools of thought produced a ternary version of the pillars: Nijkamp et al. (1990) and Munasinghe (1992). They are subtly but crucially different. We consider the Munasinghe version overleaf. Nijkamp presented his model to a conference of the World Bank in 1990:

> *The idea of sustainable development reaches far beyond environmental protection, as it means a process of change in which exploitation of resources, direction of investments, orientation of technological development, and institutional changes are made consistent with future as well as present needs. Consequently, sustainable development is not a fixed state of harmony but rather a balanced and adaptive process of change. This would then be characterized by a dynamic Pareto-optimal trajectory in which progress in one system that is, either the economic or the ecological would not be to the detriment of the other system.*

The **top diagram shows how Nijkamp conceived the plot as a coming together of the three pillars.** He expresses the pillars as separate planes that, in the short term at least, are often seen as conflicting. By integrating the three separate planes into a single plane of sustainable development "a situation of mutual complementarity, or coevolution, can emerge". The ground plane, the "sphere" refers to the undifferentiated knowledge space, into which the planes bring order.

The **lower-left figure shows the three pillars as three dimensions summing to 100%** (forming the edges of the triangle in two dimensional space). In the "Sustainable Development" zone in the centre of the triangle, the value of each dimensions is approximately 33% (the values are read on the angle of the axis that crosses at 100%). Of note is the process focus of the subtitles for the pillars. This process hints at sustainability as a practical progression. This progression is also seen in the "area of possible reconciliation" in the centre.

Thus sustainability is defined by the relative contribution of the three pillars, giving a point on the triangle. While Sustainable Development is the area in the centre of the triangle, other zones can be described. **McDonough and Braungart (2002) expanded the triangle (lower-right), characterising zones and placing sustainable development in a business context.** The questions around the outside are prompted by the more detailed examination of the pillars the triangle allows.

plotting the pillars

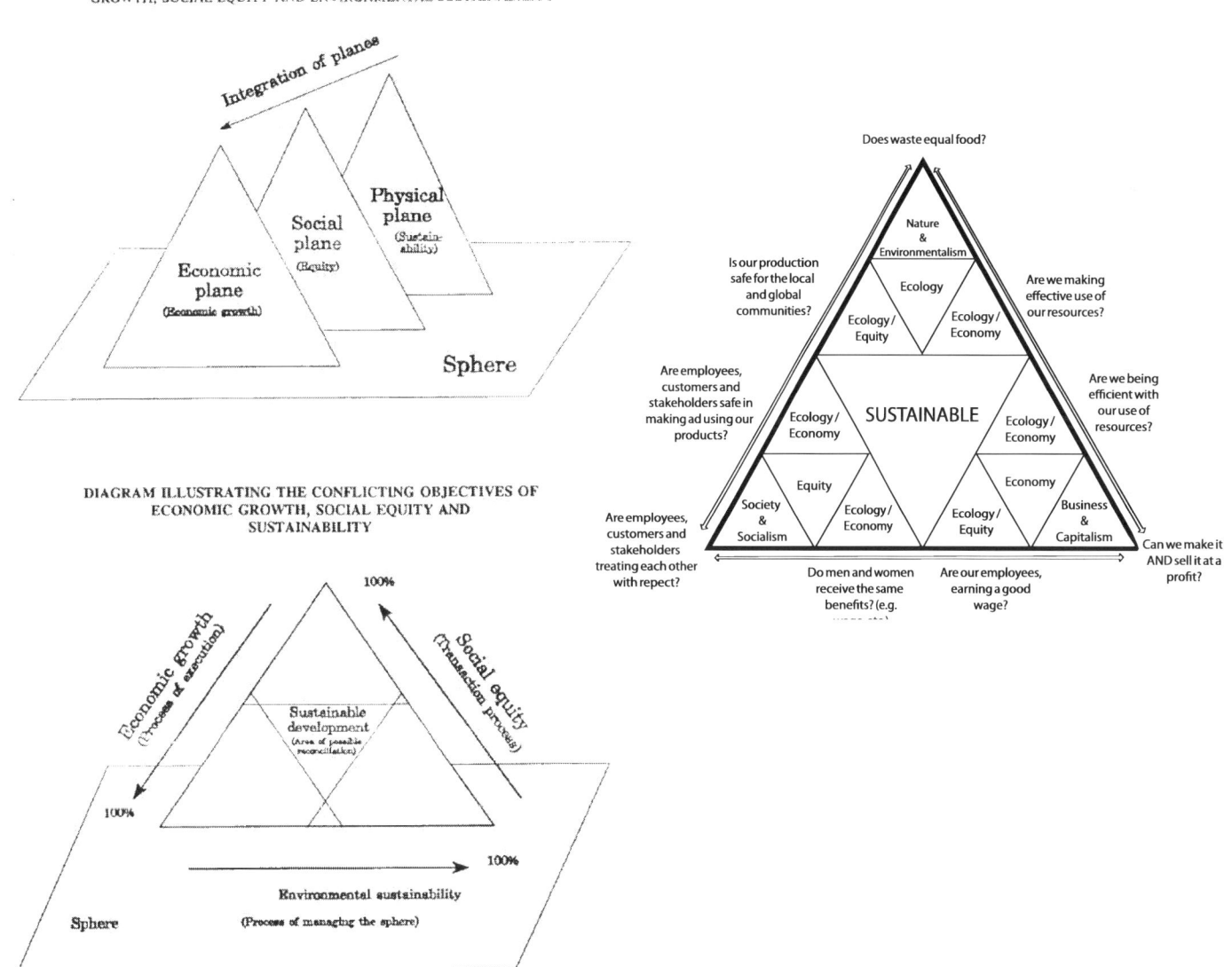

the shape of things

> In Munasinghe's variation of the triangle, each pillar separately scores to 100%. Instead of points within a fixed triangle, different possible states are represented by differently shaped triangles. An outcome of this is to further separate the pillars.

Mohan Munasinghe (1992, 2001, 2010) has a different conception of the triangle. Where Nijkamp has sustainability constrained by a sum total 100% for the three pillars, Munasinghe considers each on a separate axis. So while Nijkamp positions sustainability for a given situation within a triangle, Munasinghe reshapes and resizes the triangle.

Munasinghe's "Sustainanomics" triangle (top left a and b) has the pillars at the vertices - each pillar separately sums to 100%. The degree of each pillar is determined by distance from the centre (rather than position along the edge). The edges represent the interaction of the pillars.

Releasing the pillars from the constraint of having to combine to produce a score summing to 100% means each axis can independently score to 100%. This has the advantage of producing differently shaped and sized triangles for exploring options. **By plotting (lower-left) the current and desired states on the axes gives two triangles.** Notice that the environmental pillar has expanded to include health, nutrition and "other".

Munasinghe gave examples of using the triangles to analyse issues such as poverty and economy-wide policies to "underline the economic, social and environmental dimensions". **Wijayadasa (1997, upper right) refers to Munasinghe's triangles in his discussion of making strategic decisions about drinking water.** While economic value of water might be measurable, it is less easy to place a monetary value on the contribution to social and environmental goals. A full multi-criteria analysis would support decision making as outward movements along the axes trace improvements in the three indicators: economic efficiency (not monetary benefits); social equity (service to the poor) and environmental pollution (water quality).

A disadvantage of this approach is that it worsens the together-but-separately notion of the pillars. Yes, you have to do all three, but there is no integration of the pillars (except in the shape of the resultant triangle).

edgy triangles

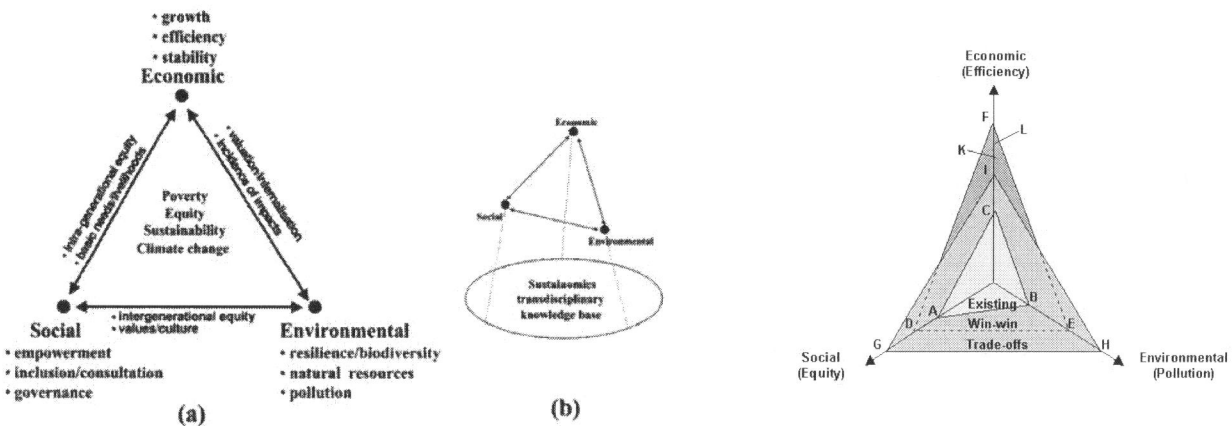

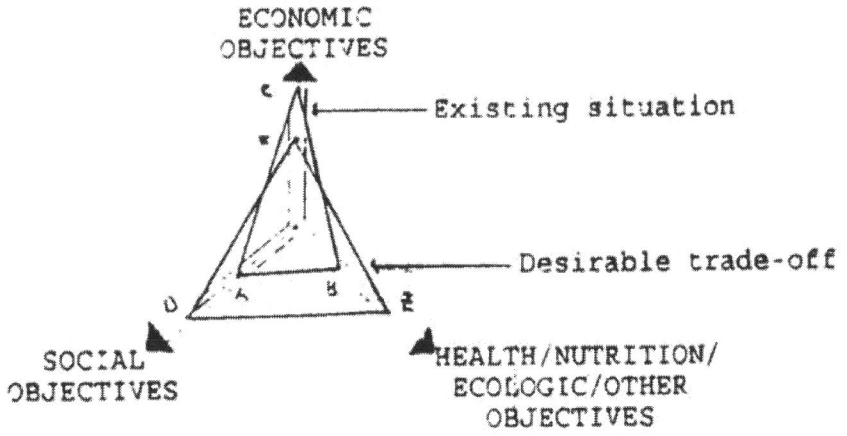

the shape of things

> The Strong Sustainability model does not have an area representing sustainability. Instead it is the hierarchical relationship of the pillars in concentric circles that defines the Strong approach to sustainability. This is in contrast to the Barbier Venn diagram that shows sustainability at the intersection of the pillars - environment, society and economics - where it is possible (though not desirable) to consider each pillar in isolation

The strong sustainability model was developed by ecological economist Herman Daly. Strong sustainability asserts that all of life, including humans is contained within the biosphere. This model recognises that the economy is a subset of society (i.e. it only exists in the context of a society), and that many important aspects of society do not involve economic activity. Similarly, human society and the economic activity with it are totally constrained by the natural systems of our planet. As then US Undersecretary of State Timothy Wirth stated in a 1994 speech **"The economy is a wholly owned subsidiary of the environment".**

> *Our deficit spending of environmental capital has a direct, measurable impact on human security. Simply put, the life support systems of the entire globe are being compromised at a rapid rate--illustrating our interdependence with nature and changing our relationship to the planet.*

This is represented by the "bullseye" diagram on the left (it is also sometimes simplified as an "egg" Prescott-Allen 1991 in Guijt *et al.* 2001).

A Strong Sustainability view argues that the stock of natural resources and ecological functions are irreplaceable. Daly (1996) specified:

1) rates of use for renewable resources that do not exceed their rates of regeneration;

2) rates of use for non-renewable resources that do not exceed the rate at which sustainable renewable substitutes are developed; and

3) rates of pollution emission that do not exceed the assimilative capacity of the environment.

To these three, the OECD (2001 in 2004) has added a fourth: avoiding irreversible impacts of human activities on ecosystems.

The **Strong Sustainability concentric circles can be seen in cross-section in Daly's conceptual pyramid framework.** The pyramid, later improved by Meadows (1998) and shown opposite, draws attention to the main socioeconomic components and processes essential to ensure the viability of a system. This is different to other triangles we have considered which have been in same plane as Venn, with pillars at the centre. Essentially this triangle expresses that there's no way human ends can be realised without healthy, functioning natural and economic systems. The hierarchical structure portrays a grading: from ultimate means at the base (natural capital, or the resources out of which all life and all economic transactions are built and sustained), followed by; intermediate means (human and built capital, which define the productive capacity of the economy), then by; intermediate ends (human and social capital, or the goals that economies are expected to deliver, such as consumer goods, health, knowledge, leisure, communication and transportation), eventually leading to the ultimate ends of society: (happiness, identity, freedom, fulfilment, etc.).

The Strong Sustainability diagrams show dependency, but not integration. The pillars are still there, as separate elements. Any representation of sustainability that relies on three separate ideas only weakly integrated can only ever portray a restricted conception of sustainability.

wholly owned subsidiary

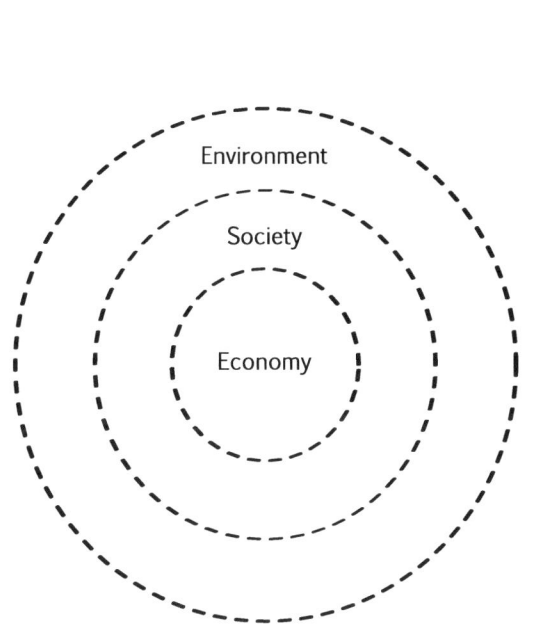

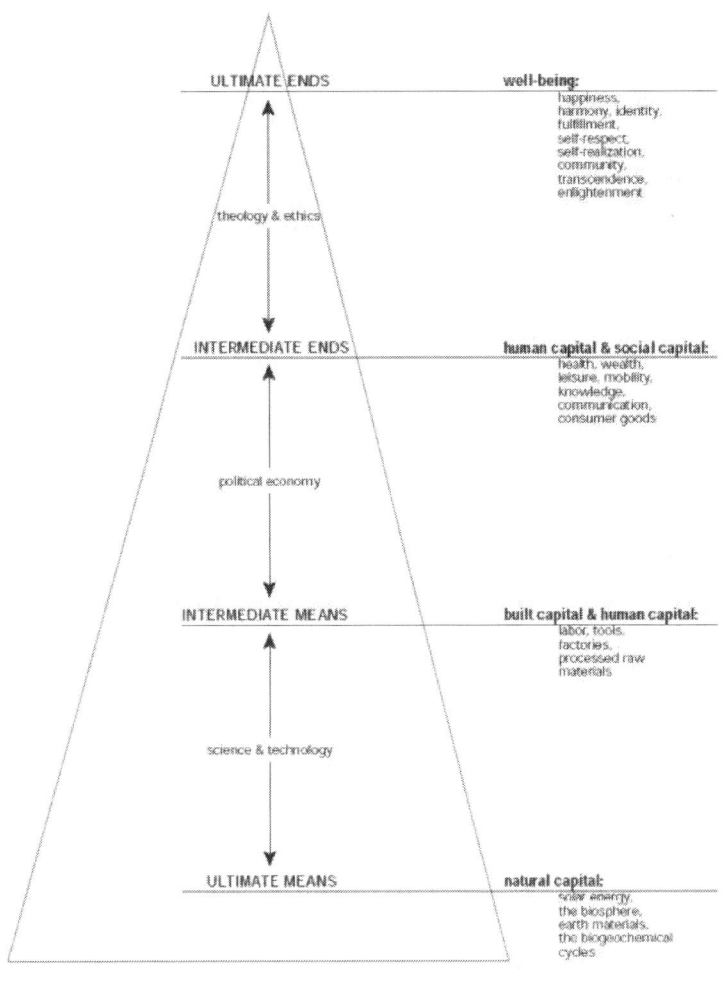

> The message from Brundtland is clear: we live in a world in which our economic and social systems are interdependent upon one another, and both of these systems are completely dependent on the ecological systems upon which all life and all social and economic activity depend.

These three constructs - variously called domains, systems, dimensions, areas, disciplines and pillars - have been visually represented as columns, circles and triangles. Different diagrammatic devices have been used to indicate integration of the pillars, but without really examining the nature of that integration. Different models talk about the need for balance, or the importance of what it is for present and future generations to rely on the environment, but they tend not provide the conceptual frameworks that can lead to decision making and action.

The challenge of the pillars models is fundamental. We are required to consider the three separate pillars as a single element, but with little or no guidance about what constitutes a sustainable whole. Sustainability after all is a holistic concept, where the whole is greater than the sum of the parts. It is more than a set of pillars, or a compendium of constituent bricks: peace, justice, economic vitality, social equity, universal opportunity, stability, human health, ecological health and so on. It is the integration of these things that defines sustainability. Is it reasonable to assume that sustainability is a property that can be found simply by incorporating the different dimensions together, or is sustainability more like an emerging property and one that is not easily detected from the properties of different dimensions?

Can sustainability be achieved? Possibly, but I suggest that a *Sustainable Lens* is not going to enhance our understanding by taking a pillars approach to visualising sustainability.

The series opposite places the Barbier Venn model and a version of the 'Strong Sustainability' model in a progression that leads to "sustainability achieved" (Dodds and Venables, 2005).

Dodds and Venables suggest:

> *Sustainability can be thought of as the region in the centre (of the left-hand component of the diagram) where all three sets of constraints are satisfied, while sustainable development is the process of moving to that region. Alternatively, sustainable development can be thought of as the process of moving the circles together so that they almost completely overlap but with the societal and techno-economic circles sitting within the environmental circle, at which point all human activity is sustainable.*

They recognise that the diagram is simplistic, but argue that it "reminds us that sustainability means living within all three types of long-term constraint: technology cannot be deployed as though it has no environmental or societal implications. Engineers must therefore be key players in sustainable development".

It is not entirely clear what the x-axis represents; in the text, it is just "development". However, I wonder if that represents physical change, professional understanding, sensitivity, maturity or perhaps simply time?

The right-most component is perhaps the most illuminating. This is "Sustainability Achieved" and absolutely where we want to get to as well. But the graphic gives little indication of how we get there and what it will be like when we arrive. If the sequence was about red and blue, but represented in black and white, we would be left with a circle at the end with a label saying only "Purple". Useful in labelling a endpoint, but ineffective in describing the meaning encapsulated in that label.

in or out of circles

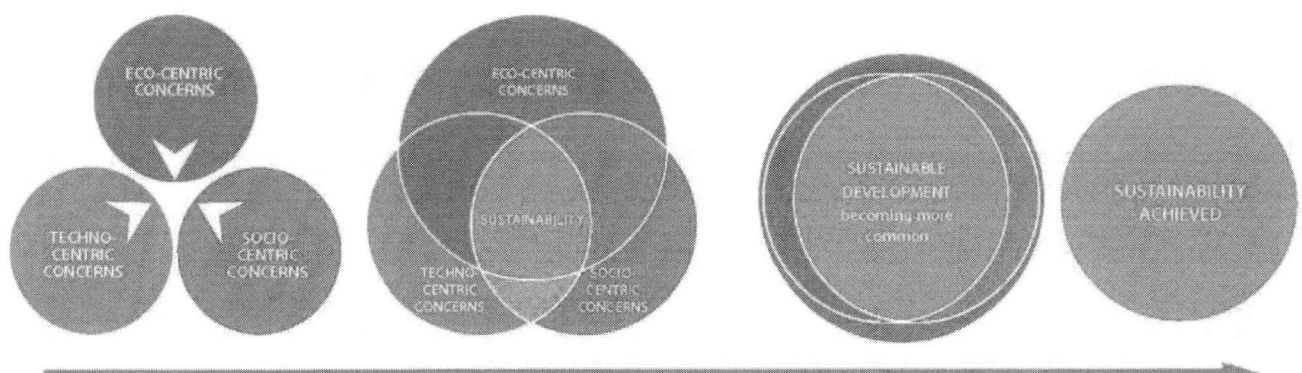

> Considering the pillars as capitals emphasises that they are stocks that should not be run down.

The **World Bank (1994) developed a 'capital stock model' (top-left).** The definition of ecological capital for the planning process includes bio-diversity, landscape, mineral resources, clean air and healthy water. Human and social capital equates to health, social security, social cohesion, freedom, justice, equality of opportunity, and peace. The representation of the pillars as "capital" reinforces the importance of not consuming the substance. World Bank Vice President Ismail Seregeldin saw the Social capital as important in its own right and developed this pyramid representation (Spangenberg 2007).

The **capital stock model (lower-left) was developed in association with a "pressure-state-response" model**. This PSR model is based on causality: humans exert pressure/this pressure changes the state of the environment/society responds. This affects how we think about the relationships between the pillars. Spangenberg (2007) argues that this leads to an "end of pipe thinking" with little room for proactive polices.

In 1995 the UN Department of Policy Co-ordination and Sustainable Development addressed these problems by expanding the PSR model to become a Driving force- state - response scheme (DSR). Spangenberg and Bonniot represented that in this triangle where rather than representing the capitals as static (or as stocks) they focussed on the processes that affect these capitals - action verbs. **Spangenberg and Bonniot (1998; top-right) aimed to produce a model for sustainability indicators that considered the capitals (on the vertices of the triangle), but also the flows between the capitals.** For example the transport intensity can be considered as a socio-environmental disturbance indicator. The gain from transport, considered as a service acts as a enviro-economic link indicator.

The **Sigma project (2003; lower-right) argued that the five capitals are "interrelated and, therefore, need to be managed, protected and enhanced in an integrated fashion"**. The five capitals emphasise the underpinning nature of natural capital, as well as the fact that "financial capital is simply an expression of the value of the other capitals".

Sigma is clearly influenced by Strong Sustainability as natural capital encompasses the other capitals: "natural resources and ecological systems form the basis of life, on which all organisations (and wider society) depend". Within the organisation however, Sigma sees a more complex relationship: "All of the capitals are heavily interlinked and there is some overlap between them". Social, human and manufactured capitals are valued for their roles in delivering "value to both organisations and society, not to mention improving the quality of life of stakeholders". Financial capital, crucial to the ongoing survival of an organisation, is "simply derived from the value that the other four capitals provide" (note that this is superimposed rather than integrated with the others).

This whole system is then encircled by the principle of accountability representing the relationship that an organisation has with the outside world – with its stakeholders and for its stewardship of the five capitals.

the pillars as capital

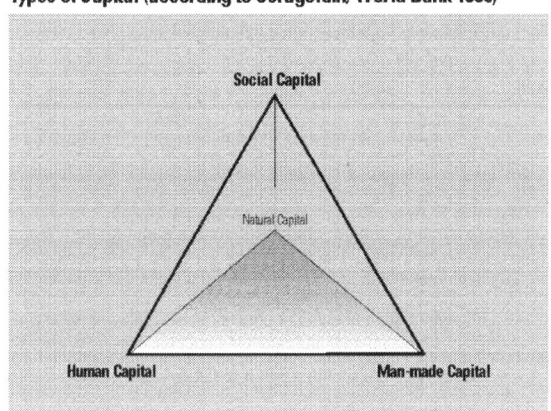

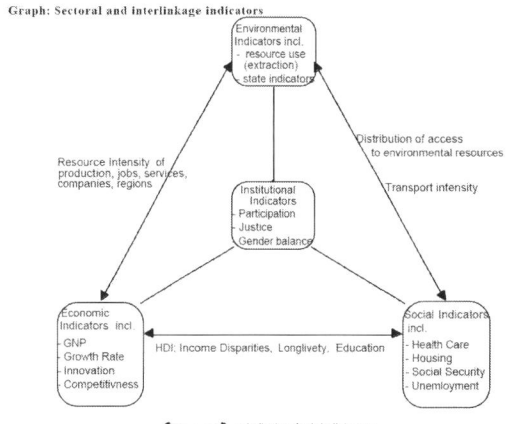

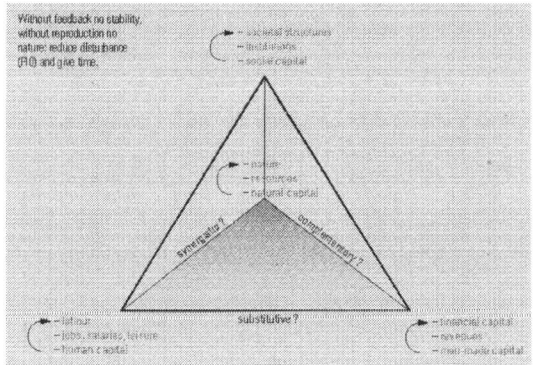

> Creating a visual image that captures and explains the concept of sustainability is challenge enough; you may wish to compare your own efforts to draw what sustainability means for you. But if we extend the exercise to incorporate practical ways for visualising and drawing how sustainability, the architecture of our three pillars begins to crumble in complexity.

The **pattern map (left) represents "…57 elements for greater economic, social and environmental well-being"** (Ecotrust, nd). These elements combine to create "reliable prosperity", which "…inherently serves the self interest of individuals, communities, and nature".

While the map presents an overall picture of what "reliable prosperity" and some notion of a network of parts and connections, it also fragments the three pillars. It therefore becomes difficult to see what relationship holds between 'household economy' and "biodiversity" for example.

The **South Gloustershire Council diagram (right) shows no explicit sustainability pillars. It presents a two-way relationship between eight strategic priorities and the core issues they involve.** Notice the the vertical nature of the arrows and their lack of horizontal integration. Following the arrows though begins to give a sense of how 'strategy' and issues are interwoven.

The issue of 'Improving Health and well being', for example, is presented underneath three priorities – 'Promoting safer and stronger communities', 'Being healthier' and 'Modernising health and community care services'. It is notably absent from 'Valuing the environment' and 'Maintaining economic prosperity'. 'Delivering growth' is a top line issue for the strategy 'Valuing the environment', 'Managing future development', and 'Maintaining economic prosperity', but only a third tier priority for 'Investing in children and young people'.

When complexity is added, the pillars start to crumble.

crumbling complexity

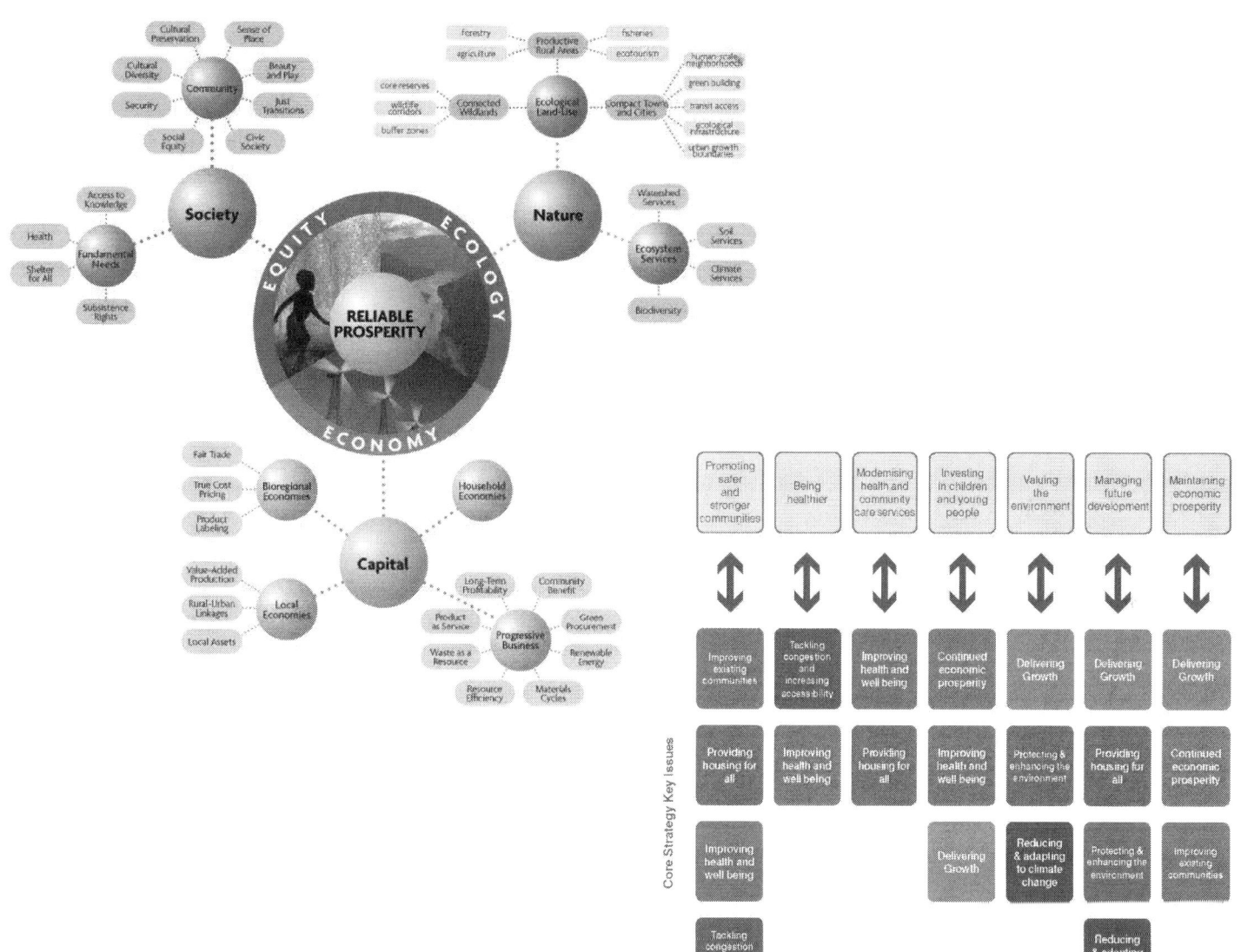

> Wheels are another way of representing the three core pillars. By adding spokes, it is possible to increase the informational content of the wheel. However, the nature of this information and its connection to the pillars loses something of its explanatory potential, because the spokes are connected to a hub that is an amalgam of the pillars. The number of spokes is presumably limited by the size of the wheel and the hub.

The **image from Auckland City Council (2008; top-left) is used to explain how they operationisalise the four well-beings** of the New Zealand Local Government Act 2002 (Section 10: "...promote the social, economic, environmental, and cultural well-being of communities, in the present and for the future"). There is no hub. The four well-beings are represented in the inner circle without divisions; though notice that culture and society are combined. The outer section of the wheel is used for selected elements that are divide into sections around the circumference. But how do these sections relate to one another. It is difficult to establish the connection between social, environment and economics, and to see how air relates to economic development.

The **image (middle-lower) is an assessment tool for cities (Ecostep nd). It is based on W. Cecil Steward's (nd) five domains** - the three mainstay pillars, plus 'Technology' (eg transport) and 'Public Policy' (eg regulatory context of a habitat). Steward argues (Ecospheres nd):

> *Whether we individually value these conditions, or not, is not the key consideration. A fact of modern life is that technologies exist, that they are influential, and that they will continue to accelerate through human ingenuity. So, too, will the rules and regulations for relations among us, and our access to the bounties of the earth. Both domains are pervasive, affective, and the cause and effect relationships to the other three domains are inseparable from them.*

The diagram places the 5 domains in sectors around a circle. Each is then divided into a further three axes for sub-domains. Moving out from the centre there are three concentric rings representing short-term, mid-term and long term. Within each zone and on each axis a small circle represents the community's positioning on that sub-domain. Each circle is sized according to priority, and coloured according to the coded 'severity' of the issues. Six different dimensions are shown on this diagram.

The **Egan Review (UK Office of the Deputy Prime Minister, 2004; top-right) wheel graph is based on an investigation of the skills needed to support the development of sustainable communities.** The review focuses on the professional needs of planners and government official, rather than the general population. The Review defines sustainable communities as:

> *…those that meet the diverse needs of existing and future residents, their children and other users, contribute to a high quality of life and provide opportunity and choice. They achieve this in ways that make effective use of natural resources, enhance the environment, promote social cohesion and inclusion and strengthen economic prosperity.*

These needs are represented as seven key components, which are expanded in the form of broad operational definitions. The image has the same problem as the other two circular figures, primarily that there is no integration of the pillars, and this only worsens as one progresses outwards. What, say, is the interaction of transport and public health? Notice it uses adjective phrases rather than nouns on the outer circle, which describe the conditions needed to achieve sustainability, rather than phrases of the 'environmental influence' that attempt to define the concept.

too many spokes

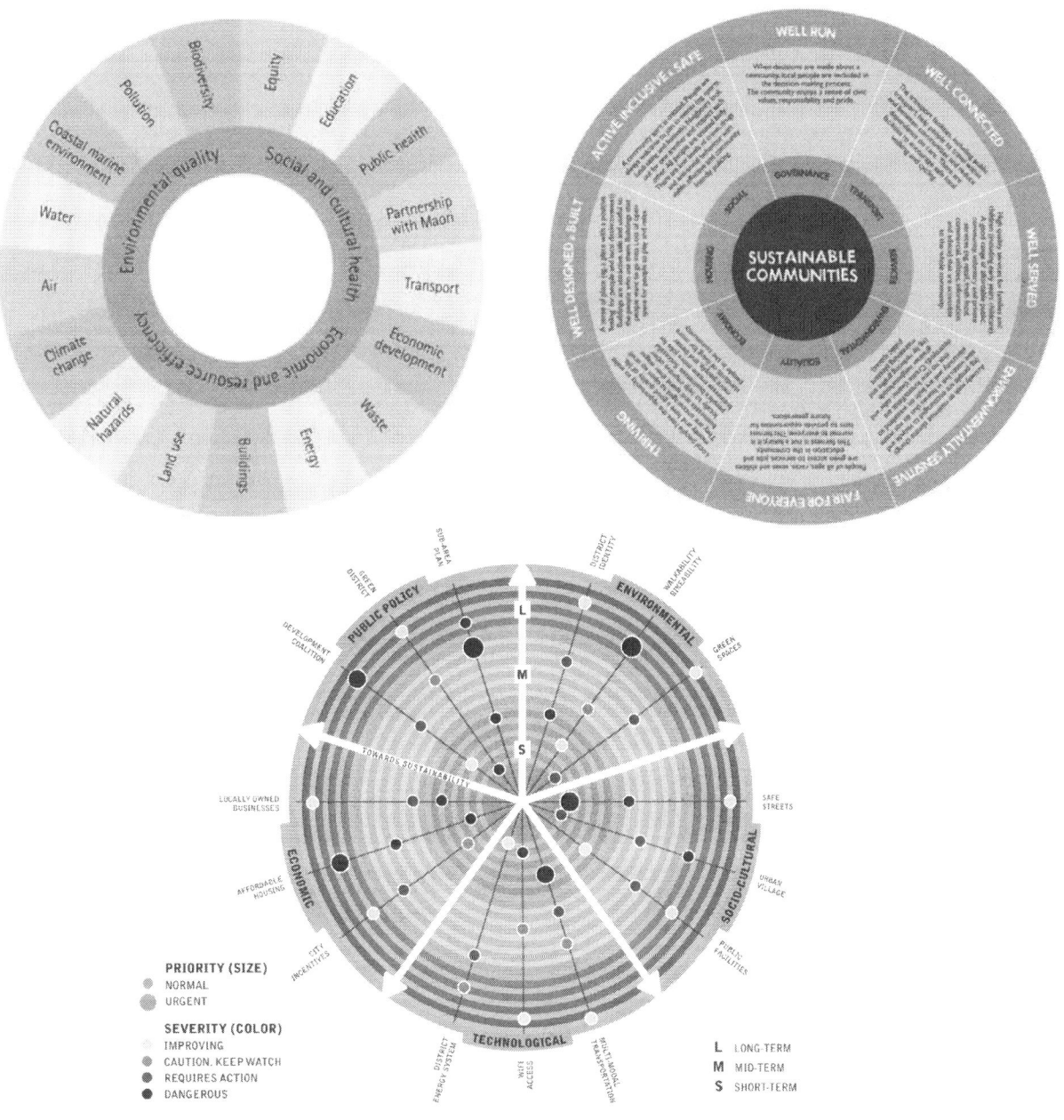

> In order to understand and represent sustainability, we must learn to live in a complex world of interdependent systems with high uncertainties and multiple legitimate interests (Stagl 2007). These complex and evolving systems require a new way of thinking about risk, uncertainty, ambiguity and ignorance and require us to think of the drivers and impacts of our action; where these extend across scales and barriers of space, time, culture, species and disciplinary boundaries.

The image opposite is taken from the Encyclopedia of Life Support Systems (2004) and **represents six major systems of the anthroposphere and their major relationships.** These six sector systems can be aggregated to the three subsystems: Human System, Built System (Human Engineered System) and Natural System In order for the total system (the human system embedded in the natural system) to be viable, each of these essential subsystems must also be viable. The six subsystems correspond to potentials that must be sustainably maintained.

Notice that the diagram does not include the word sustainability. This is the clue, the signpost that points us in the right direction. Rather than attempting to define the concept as combinations of pillars, this diagram shows us that sustainability is about the operation of systems. This realisation that sustainability is about systems is the first point of entry to seeing the word through a *Sustainable Lens*. A second point is to recognise that our thinking needs to be transformed.

Maiteny (2009) summarises our sustainable efforts to date as "ever more urgently and uselessly, to rearrange deckchairs on the ecological Titanic as it sinks deeper into the ocean". Maiteny again: "What we prefer to see as the 'problems' are actually ways of unconsciously avoiding these deeper causes within ourselves. These are the real problem, but this is just too excruciating to admit".

By not explicitly showing "sustainability" but by hinting at a system, the EOLSS diagram points us in the right direction: sustainability is about the operation of systems. A first step in seeing with a *Sustainable Lens* is seeing systems.

interdependent systems

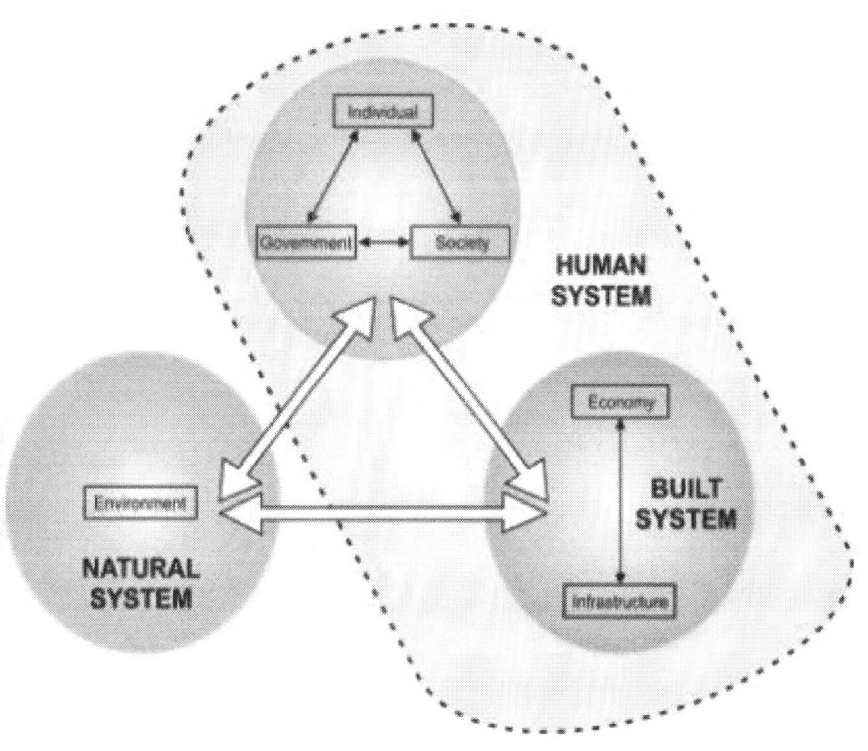

> The "sustainability is a journey" metaphor is common (eg Anderson 1998). In the introduction to Rowledge *et al.* (1999), John Elkington (of Triple-bottom-line fame) acknowledges that some talk of journey is "a way of putting off the evil day when they have to set out on the hard road", but, he says, "others embrace the challenge and are eager to be off". Rowledge's book describes case studies of businesses recognised for their environmental and /or social achievements yet "they are not - and most would not claim to be - anywhere near their final destination".

I often use the line: "sustainability is a journey and we might never reach the destination". Di Castri (1995) writes

> There is no doubt that we will be confronted with turbulence, extreme events, bifurcations and dangerous reefs in navigating towards a sustainable human development. Our helmsmen and helmswomen, mainly ourselves according to the principle of individual responsibility and commitment, will have to sail between two opposite yet complementary streams, that of globalization and that of diversity. To be at the helm will mean frequently correcting the course in order to finally reach a moving target. But this is precisely, cybernetically speaking, the 'art of governing'.

There are similar thoughts in Goleman's *Ecological Intelligence* (2009). In exploring Life Cycle Analysis, Goleman describes the impact of the manufacture of glass and finds an incredibly complex process with a multitude of impacts. This leads to a really insightful observation:

> This transforms our notions of "green" from what seems a binary judgment—green or not into a far more sophisticated arena of fine distinctions, each showing relatively better or worse impacts along myriad dimensions.

I particularly like Goleman's conclusion: "*Green is a process, not a status—we need to think of "green" as a verb, not an adjective*".

That the transition towards sustainability is an ongoing responsibility has implications for the way we manage the change (Stephens *et al.* 2008). Most change management process literature describes a one off change – a single implementation, or a transition to a changed state – and while it might take a while, there is the clear implication that you'll get there eventually. Yet sustainability is not a binary state – the goal might never be reached.

Rowledge *et al.* (1999), proudly features, even "honours", organisations on the sustainability journey, likening them to "explorers charting an unknown course through raging torrents". These organisations are seen as "pathfinders…mapping the territory, finding the hidden trails, and gaining the critical knowledge for creating sustainable industrial system". The focus of Rowledge's book is not on the path , indeed, "clearly the entire path is not visible". Instead they focus on the characteristics of the leadership: "what vision, courage and team spirit and strength of character sustained them through the hardships" - how it is done as much as what is done.

Benford *et al.* (2009) considers interactions as a continuity of experience – as journeys. This leads to the realisation that interactions can be interwoven, steered and captured. Each of us is also having multiple continuous trajectories. While these journeys may pass through different places, times, roles and interfaces as I discuss below, they maintain an overall sense of coherence; of being part of a connected whole. These journeys are steered by the participants, but are also shaped by narratives that are embedded into spatial, temporal and performative structures by authors. What you see through your *Sustainable Lens* will be different to what I see.

destination unknown

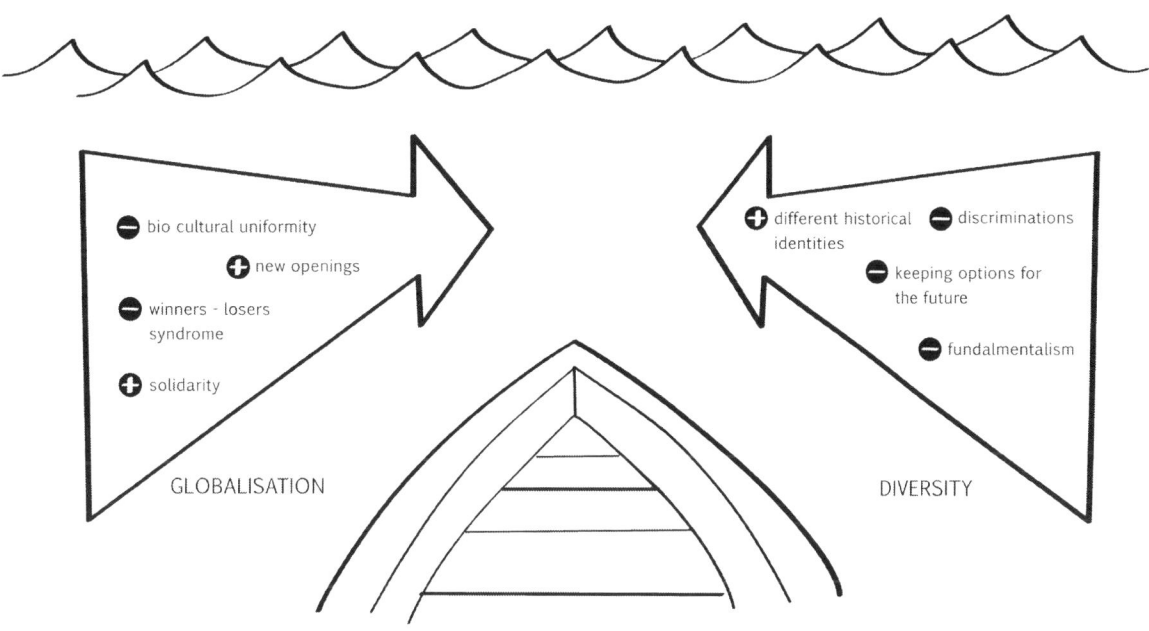

> Blackburn's Sustainability Operating System (2007) is a pathway with an underlying transformation but Milne *et al.* (2006) found that the journey metaphor was more often used as a cover for inaction.

A journey appropriately defines sustainability as forward looking, blending people, profits and planet; but (and it's a big but) without questioning growth. Invoking the journey metaphor permits organisations to emphasise that they may be just beginning their engagement with sustainability, but without spelling out what this means. Going on a journey can simply mean the act of travelling from one place to another, from point A to point B for example. It is not always clear what these points are, nor what we might find to be unsustainable en route or what could be changed as a consequence.

Milne *et al.* (2006) explored the use of sustainability as a journey in the professional and business literature. They found that the journey metaphor is applied to both commitments and sometimes actions (behaviours, decisions, etc.) that might be considered to lead towards sustainability, and to the process of reporting on the triple bottom line . There are benefits of the journey approach - the promotion of camaraderie in business, and the sense of action. These benefits, though, do not counter the many disadvantages of the metaphor:

There is little acknowledgement of unsustainability. Instead businesses "have embarked" on the journey, suggesting that they are therefore 'doing sustainability' without any real degree of specificity. Others claim a "Journey With No Destination, But One in Which Progress is Made Towards Sustainability". While this brings an interesting juxtaposition with navigating and exploration, Milne argues:.

> On the one hand, we are told sustainability is not a destination: it is a journey. Yet on the other hand, we are told it is possible to measure progress towards sustainable development. Without a defined end point, future state of affairs or future condition of (or for) sustainability, though, how is it possible to know one is making progress towards sustainability? It seems to us that to deny sustainability a destination is also to deny one the logical possibility of arguing that progress is being made towards sustainability.

Contradiction of change being presented as the heroic journey of a brave leaders to some far off distant shore yet the business not addressing the inherent paradox of organisational change. Journey has a positive connotation so long as it does not upset the balance of power, or run counter to management and business interests.

Faith in progress affirming what happens anyway without required transformative change. Because journeying offers no grand vision, yet paradoxically hints at such a possibility, it "precludes the disruptive and radical leap in imagination".

Journeying, Milne *et al.* , conclude "offers paradox and complexity on the one hand (as a potential excuse for relative inactivity and lack of substantive progress) while also expressing a notion of progress, if not actual achievement even in the embarkation on the journey itself". The concept of journey, they suggest, and its associated imagery in organization and management writing that appears not dissimilar to Alice's aimless wanderings. The journey describes a functionalist line of business as usual, perhaps with a bit of tweaking – the "business case" for sustainability - usually in the form of eco-efficiency. Strong sustainability goes beyond efficiency to a fair distribution of resources, opportunities between the current generation and between present and future generations, and a scale of economic activity relative to ecological life support systems (e.g. Daly, 1992). It has a goal state, and a transformation to get there. So, our **Sustainable Lens** needs to **support a transformation on the journey such as that represented by Blackburn (2007).**

pretending to journey

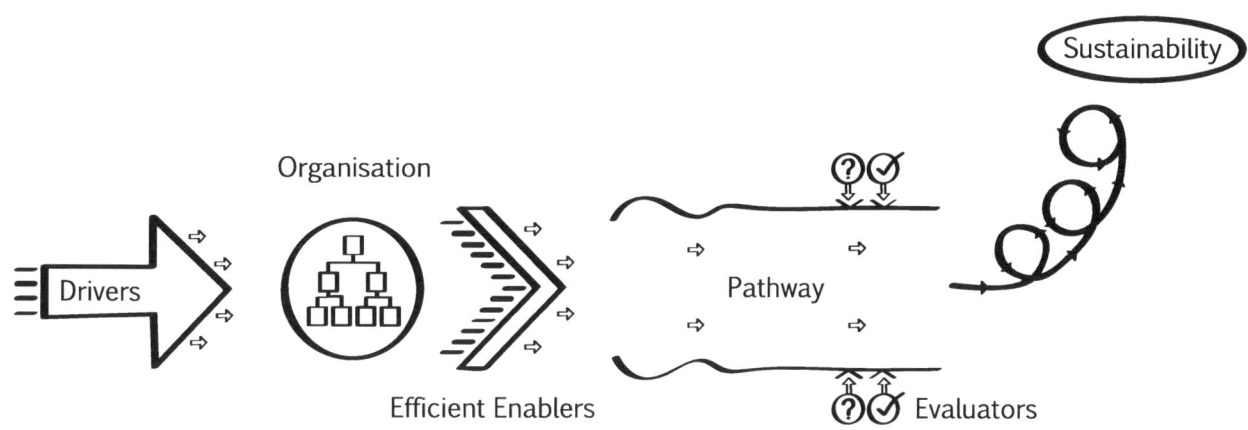

Drivers	Efficient Enablers	Pathways	Evaluators
Top management /support	Organisational structure	Vision, values and policy	Indicators and goals
Approach for selling management on sustainability	Deployment and integration	Operating system standards	Measuring and reporting progress
Accountability mechanisms		Strategic planning for aligned priorities	Stakeholder engagement and feedback

> The journey metaphor was given a challenging twist by Buckminster Fuller in the 1950's and 1960's earth in his conception of the earth as a spaceship with a limited set of resources that cannot be resupplied, save for energy from the Mothership Sun. A key element of his 'operating manual', which is pictured, is that the ship only consists of crew – there are no passengers (1965 in Vallero 2005. 367). Hence, different thinking is required if the problems facing the earth and its systems are to be addressed because "…we have been mis-using, abusing, and polluting this extraordinary chemical energy-interchanging system for successfully regenerating all life aboard our planetary spaceship". Looking through a *Sustainable Lens* it would seem that ground control has truly lost touch with Major Tom (and all of his crew).

In 1879, Henry George, a critic of Malthusian economics, argued that "it is a well provisioned ship this which we sail through space":

> If the bread and beef above the decks seem to grow scarce, we but open a hatch and there is a new supply, of which before we never dreamed. And very great command over the services of others comes to those who the as the hatches are opened are prepared to say. "This is mine!" (2005 reprint).

This nautical (and journeying) metaphor was turned on its head and made famous through the 1950s and 60s by Buckminster Fuller (1969). Rather than George's ship with seemingly endless supply hatches, **Fuller considered the earth as a spaceship with a limited set of resources** (the book is still in print, this new edition 2008). He described how Spaceship Earth operates as a closed system that has served us well: "Spaceship Earth was so extraordinarily well invented and designed that to our knowledge humans have been on board it for two million years not even knowing that they were on board a ship". Fuller's Spaceship provided a framework which encompasses many of the problems of sustainable living we are currently grappling with:

- The earth and its systems – both natural and human are seen as one general system.
- Everyone on board has a role as the crew in the successful voyage of the ship. This means we expect sustainable behaviour from everyone because everyone has both a vested interest in a sustainable future, and is entirely complicit in the need for sustainability.
- We need a new way of thinking: "What we want everybody to do is to think clearly", we must ask, "How big can we think? (Fuller is enthusiastic over humanity's extraordinary and sometimes very timely ingenuities, but gives the example of being in a shipwreck, a piano top comes along making a fortuitous life preserver. But this is not to say that the best way to design a life preserver is in the form of a piano top).

Others added to the metaphor. In "*The economics of the coming spaceship earth*", Kenneth Boulding (1966), for example:

> …Once we begin to look at earth as a space ship, the appalling extent of our ignorance about it is almost frightening. This is true of the level of every science. We know practically nothing, for instance, about the long-run dynamics even of the physical system of the earth… at the level of the biological sciences, our ignorance is even greater…and when it comes to understanding the world social system or the sociosphere, we are not only ignorant but proud of our ignorance.

> The moral of all this is that man must be made to realize that all his major problems are still unsolved, and that a very large and massive intellectual effort is still necessary to solve them. In the meantime we are wasting our intellectual resources on insoluble problems like unilateral national defence and on low-priority achievements like putting a man on the moon. This is no way to run a space ship.

just crew

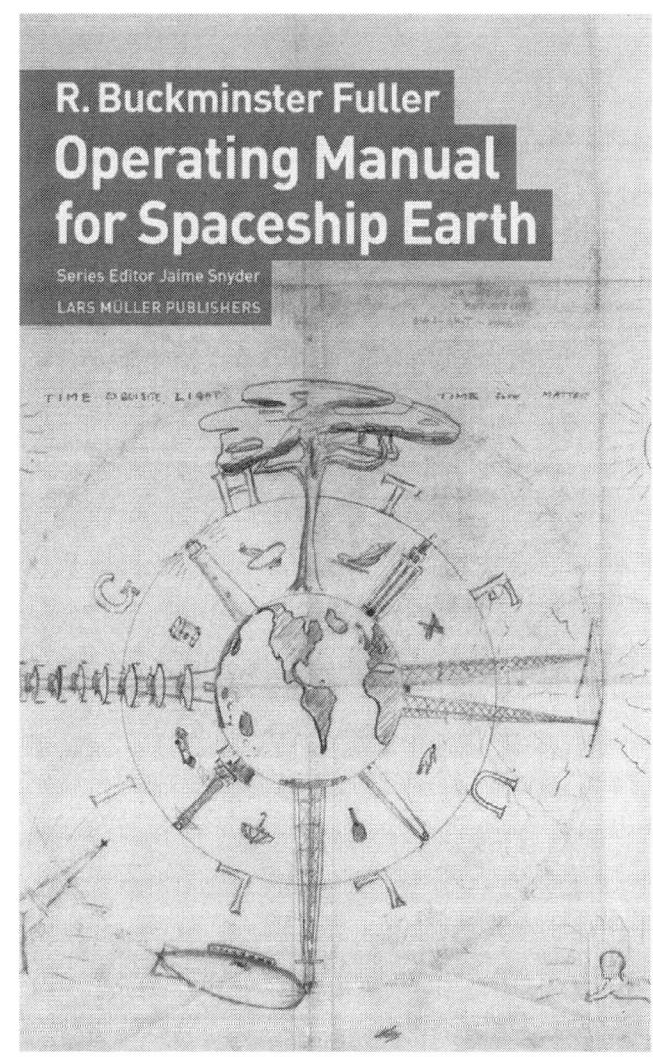

> In designing a **"Life Support System" for astronauts living in space (Johnson and Finn 1963) attempt to replicate a climax or steady-state ecosystem with the carrying capacity for only a few astronauts.** The cabin ecology presents a closed ecosystem via technological means, a 'neo-biological civilisation'. (Ankler 2005). The framing of nature in terms of space ships has enabled an ecological ethic for humans on earth modelled on the scientifically manageable astronaut. However it is this belief in technical prowess which dogs the spaceship metaphor today and "…risks pushing us in the wrong direction" (Freyfogle, 1996). Despite some early opposition, from some who viewed a love of wilderness as the core of authentic environmentalism, the spaceship metaphor persists.

The Spaceship metaphor can be seen to capture the fragility and connectedness of the earth:

> We travel together, passengers on a little spaceship, dependent on it's vulnerable reserves of air and soil, all committed, for our safety, to it's security and peace. Preserved from annihilation only by the care, the work and the love we give our fragile craft.

This quote from Adlai Stevenson's 1964 speech to the UN reflects the fragility and the attention we need to pay to the Earth. The quote also reflects the context in which it was given. The Spaceship arose during the Cold War and Space Race. This context can be seen in the belief in technical prowess of mankind and in the mention of security. While Boulding saw unilateral defence systems wasted effort, others such as Stevenson and Ward saw the Spaceship as justification for focussing on world order. Deese (2009) writes of the Spaceship as a locus of cold war gamesmanship - a ship can have only one captain, after all.

The framing of nature in terms of space ships enabled an ecological ethic for humans on earth modelled on the scientifically manageable astronaut.

In Anne and Paul Ehrlich's (1987) "Earth", they suggest:

> No sane person would want to travel on a plane whose airline did not have a "progressive maintenance" program . . . and only a lunatic would want to ride on Spaceship Earth if the components of its ecosystems were being dismantled so fast that maintenance could not begin to keep up with repairs. Yet here we are—and we have no other spaceline offering transport.

It is, though, this belief in technical prowess which dogs the Spaceship today.   Largely because of this, Freyfogle (1996) argued that "the spaceship image risks pushing us in the wrong direction".

Fuller argued: Spaceship Earth was so extraordinarily well invented and designed that to our knowledge humans have been on board it for two million years not even knowing that they were on board a ship and that the Earth needed to be cared for as "we have not been seeing our Spaceship Earth as an integrally designed machine which to be persistently successful must be comprehended and serviced in total".

Even if we look past the creationist overtones, this presents the Earth as an artificial system that can be understood and controlled - the real rocket powered spaceship is a symbol of human cleverness. Using the metaphor suggests a system that is logically predictable and where ignorance is eliminated. As Frefogle (1996) argued "on earth, where we really live, life is not like this. The earth is far more complex than a spaceship; we didn't create it, and we don't understand it". This can be seen in the Life Support diagram where there is Environmental Control and plants and animals are solely resources.   As Freyfogle continues, ""on a spaceship, humans count, all else is a tool" (although, as Myers (1963) argued, even the human was really just "part of the instrumentation". Ankler (2005) challenges us to "abandon the intellectual space capsule".

the wrong direction

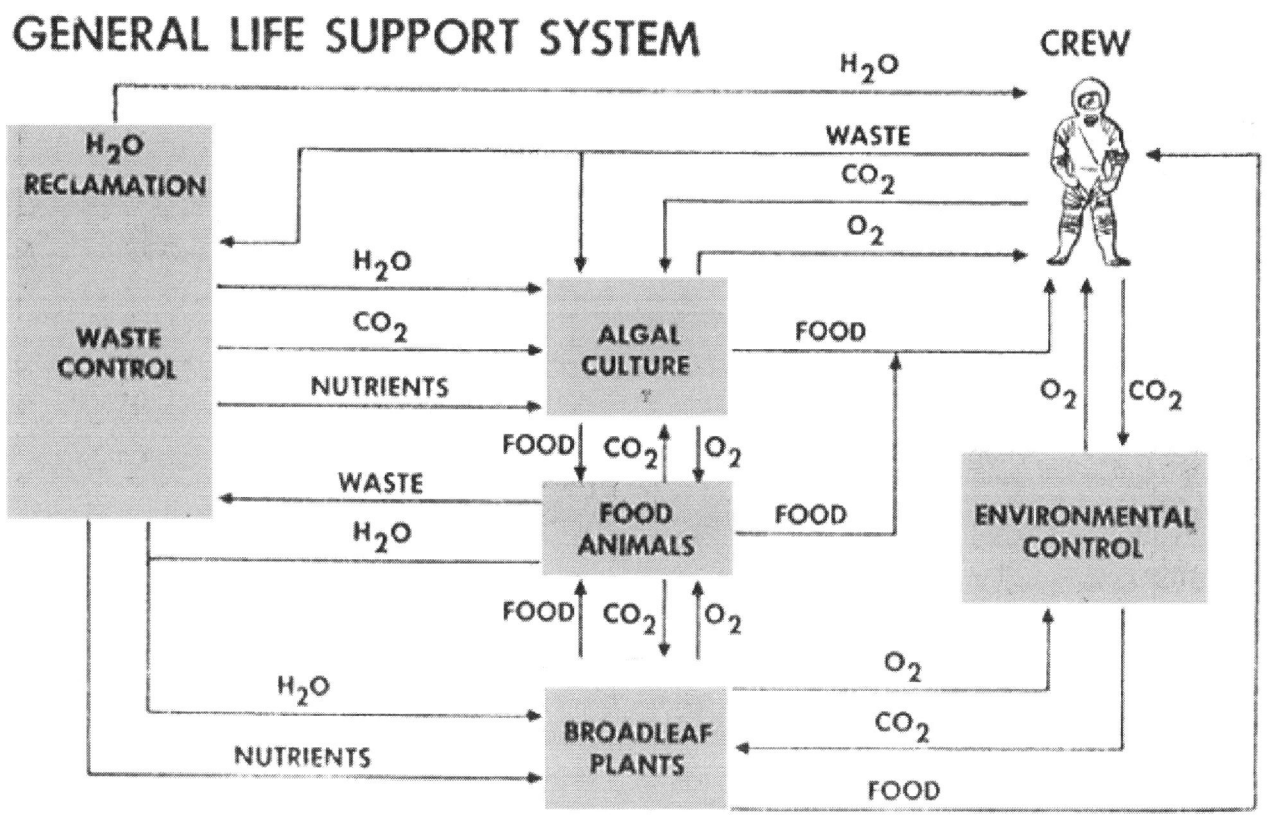

all the world's a stage

> In contrast to the spaceship with a crew who control its systems, Gaia Theory argues that the earth is a single planetary organism of which we are a small part. The theory was developed by James Lovelock (1965), who was an atmospheric scientist working with NASA considering how to detect life on Mars. Lovelock describes the Earth as a single, highly complex organism with numerous sub-systems and feedback loops. This is an earth-centred perspective that challenges the mechanistic view that humans are separate entities and hold dominion over nature.

Mankind has long harboured an ancient belief of harmonious interconnectedness among natural phenomena. This organic view holds that people are part of nature, that every habitat possesses a soul and is filled with organisms and thus requires respectful treatment. This idea of nature having holistic unity reached contemporary thought as James Lovelock's Gaia (1965). Earth, seen from a Martian perspective could be seen to be acting as a super organism.

Lovelock described the Earth as an organism. Not just like an organism, but is an organism. This is the notion that "the surface of the earth behaves as a highly integrated organism capable of controlling its own composition and its environment." Lovelock describes the Earth as a single, highly complex organism with numerous sub-systems and feedback loops. The "Gaia Theory" holds that important elements (carbon, nitrogen, oxygen, phosphorous, calcium) in Earth's major environmental compartments are in constant motion within and between compartments. This biogeochemical interaction between all of Earth's processes serves as a buffer system, lessening the effects of minor perturbations upon important physical/chemical properties, such as temperature, oxidation state, and acidity, in the various environmental compartments. Instead of an inanimate rock, with the addition of life, in combination with the Earth's other subsystems, the Earth's various aspects constitute a feedback system that seeks an optimal environment to sustain life.

This is elegantly captured in Harding's (2006) diagram showing non-gaian and gaian views of the relationship between life and the environment.

Humans are clearly part of Gaia. If we become too harmful to our habitat the system will automatically bring us to our extinction. Gaia, then, is both nurturing and controlling. Indeed the very name Gaia (suggested to Lovelock by William Golding of *Lord of the Flies* fame) is the goddess of earth in Greek mythology who had dual characteristics: maternal and nuturing but in contrast, a harsh destroyer of lives who do not obey her governance. Gaia had significant impact. Here's a quote from the second paragraph of *Our Common Future*:

> *From space, we can see and study the Earth as an organism whose health depends on the health of all its parts. We have the power to reconcile human affairs with natural laws and to thrive in the process. In this our cultural and spiritual heritages can reinforce our economic interests and survival imperatives.*

Originally Lovelock described an unashamedly telological superorganism. That is, one that has purposeful behaviours. This was widely criticised on the basis of all things having a predetermined purpose and that to implement it requires forethought and planning by biota. In 1988, Lovelock abandoned any attempt to argue that Gaia consciously or intentionally maintained a balance. He used a series of conceptual and computer models ("Daisyworld") to demonstrate stability through homeostatic feedback (rather than thought).

This Gaia is now more widely accepted whereby the climate and environment are actively regulated by organisms. It is an earth-centred perspective that challenges the mechanistic view where humans are separate and hold dominion over nature. People are significant because we are conscious and self-reflexive and have impacts disproportionate to our physical presence, but are in no way special. We cannot both treat the earth as a machine and simultaneously immerse ourselves as participants without considering our social and cultural processes as part of the organism, not separate from it or merely acting upon it.

one organism

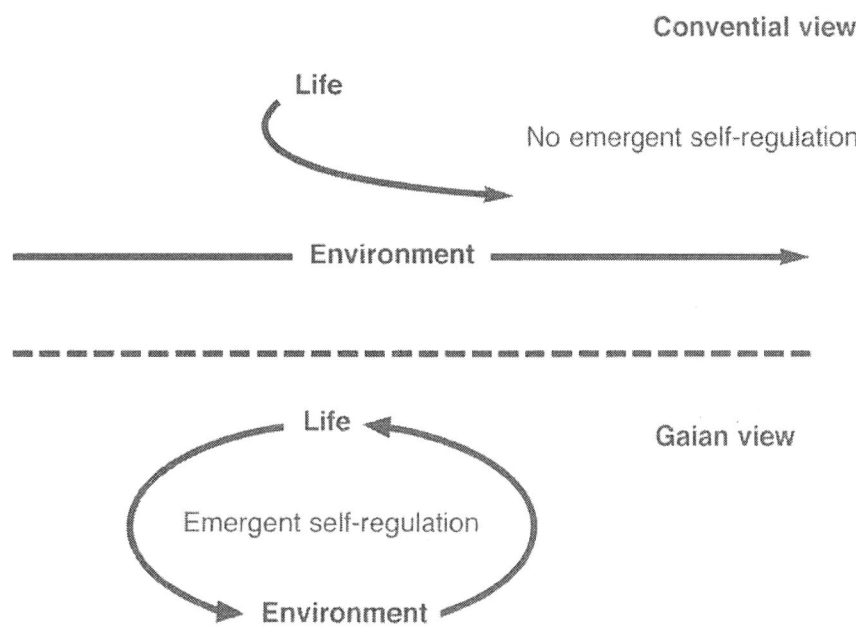

> Imagine you had a pair of glasses that had a sustainability mode. This mode meant that you looked at the world through a *Sustainable Lens*. What would you see?

The premise of this book is that as we go about our lives we need to develop a sixth sense. As we work, live or play, we all need to be able to "see" sustainability. In order to see through a *Sustainable Lens* we need to improve our capabilities to see *sustainably* - hence an exploration of visual depictions of *sustainability*.

The image on the opposite page is overlaid with a diagram of sustainable thinking – not obscuring the original, but hopefully giving the message that everything can be viewed through a lens of sustainability. In this case the diagram is one of Strong Sustainability. These concentric circles was carry an important message that is quite different from the more common Venn diagram overlapping circles approach (The Shape of Things. Chapter 2).

A *Sustainable Lens* operates on multiple scales. It is the result of layers of context, and combines history, the present and the future. This very structure – the multiple scales and the layering – gives some notion of *sustainability*: every story has a back story, every image can be viewed with a *Sustainable Lens*. The augmentation provided by the lens needs to carry the essence of sustainability in a few lines. The goal is to add value to the primary image, not detract from it.

Imagine you had a pair of glasses that had a *sustainability* mode. This mode meant that you looked at the world through a *"Sustainable Lens"*. What would you see?

These lenses wouldn't merely be green tinted glasses like the ones from the Emerald City in the Wizard of Oz. Instead, think about the analytical eyes of the Predators (robots) in the Terminator movies. These eyes scan the landscape, identifying threats, analysing options and proposing actions.

As we go about our daily lives we are good at avoiding threats - we can see the pothole and drive around it. We are also good at recognising impacts and taking action - we can see when our child has cut her knee and offer care and sympathy. We can also see the relationship between our actions and the consequences - when I push on a pile of blocks I can see them tumble to the floor. We're not so good when the threats are hidden - when invisible (such as poison in a stream). We're not good when the action and consequences are separated by time or space, or when the effects are cumulative or bedevilled by a myriad of complicating factors. Such factors are inherent in sustainability - we cannot easily see the impact of our actions on generations to come, or how our situation is affected by decisions made on the other side of the world, or how seemingly innocuous behaviours multiplied across society result in possibly irreparable damage to our connected socio-ecosystems.

Augmented reality holds much promise in making the invisible visible. Indeed, in many applications it is starting to deliver. Engineers can "see" the arrangement of underground pipes and other services superimposed on the ground. Doctors can be similarly guided to affected areas. Perhaps more mundanely, standing on a street in a foreign city I can be guided to the nearest subway (and Subway!). Ubiquitous augmented reality is some way off however, and even if it weren't the question would remain - what would you sustainably see?

So this book is not about achieving sustainable augmented reality by technological means. Rather, the *Sustainable Lens* asks how might we conceive our internal heads-up display to make the invisible visible to help us better live, work and play in a sustainable manner.

supra-spectral specs

> Perhaps you have a nice sleek laptop computer on my desk. It is a triumph of our age. In a remarkably short time, computing has progressed from room-sized power hungry monsters to machines limited in smallness primarily by the restrictions of human interaction. Using this computer has revolutionised business as it has our leisure time. The trouble is, though, that this shiny marvel does not come for free.

Whatever else it may be, the sleek machine on your desk is a still an appliance. It uses power to run and its manufacture resulted in considerable carbon emissions. These embodied emissions can be elucidated with a life cycle assessment.

Deng *el al.* (2009) conducted a full life cycle analysis on a laptop, focussing on energy intensity calculations. They computed the energy required to manufacture and run a computer. Manufacturing energy is calculated by combining the energy required to produce (usually extract) the bill of materials (various plastics, glass, copper, aluminium, steel, gold, silver, epoxy, palladium, zinc, tin, lead, nickel, neodymium and so on) with the process sum energy (production of semiconductor, circuit board, LCD, wafers and assembly etc). This gives a range from a conservative 3364 MJ to 4696 MJ.

Adding life cycle use phase energy (using normal patterns of use, sleep, off) adds a further 2000 to 3000MJ (depending on processor size, use etc). They didn't consider transport, either of components or the finished laptop.

This gives a life cycle total of between 5247 to 7826 MJ (a desktop machine is 25% higher). Over an average laptop life span average 3-5 years this annualises to 3500MJ per year. Despite being concerned about carbon footprints, however, this information means little to me. Even knowing this number I can't "see" the amount, nor estimate its impact.

Converting the energy use to the coal needed to produce that much energy conservatively comes out at 400 grams of coal per day. This is something I can see - an actual lump of coal burning, a considerable amount of smoke in my office.

If our computers were dirty and emitted smoke, would we perceive them differently? Would I be more vigilant about turning it off when not in use? Would I use it less? Would I value it more? Hopefully I might reconsider decisions about upgrade cycles and try to extend its functional life. I might seek a laptop designed for upgradeability rather than planned obsolesce. I might even investigate a different model of computing ownership - a lease/take back where I buy computing service rather than the equipment and thus the manufacturer has a greater incentive to lower impacts.

Actually, if the computer really emitted smoke, what we would probably do is devise an extraction system - we wouldn't want the smoke in our offices. But this would be to address the symptom and not the cause. Perhaps, somewhat perversely, a virtual (augmented reality) or conceptual (*Sustainable Lens*) visualisation would be better than to actually generate smoke.

Also, it is important that we do not interfere unduly with the actual experience - a cloud of smoke whether real, virtual or conceptual would remove the functionality of the computer - and then how would we find our friends on facebook?

my coal fired computer

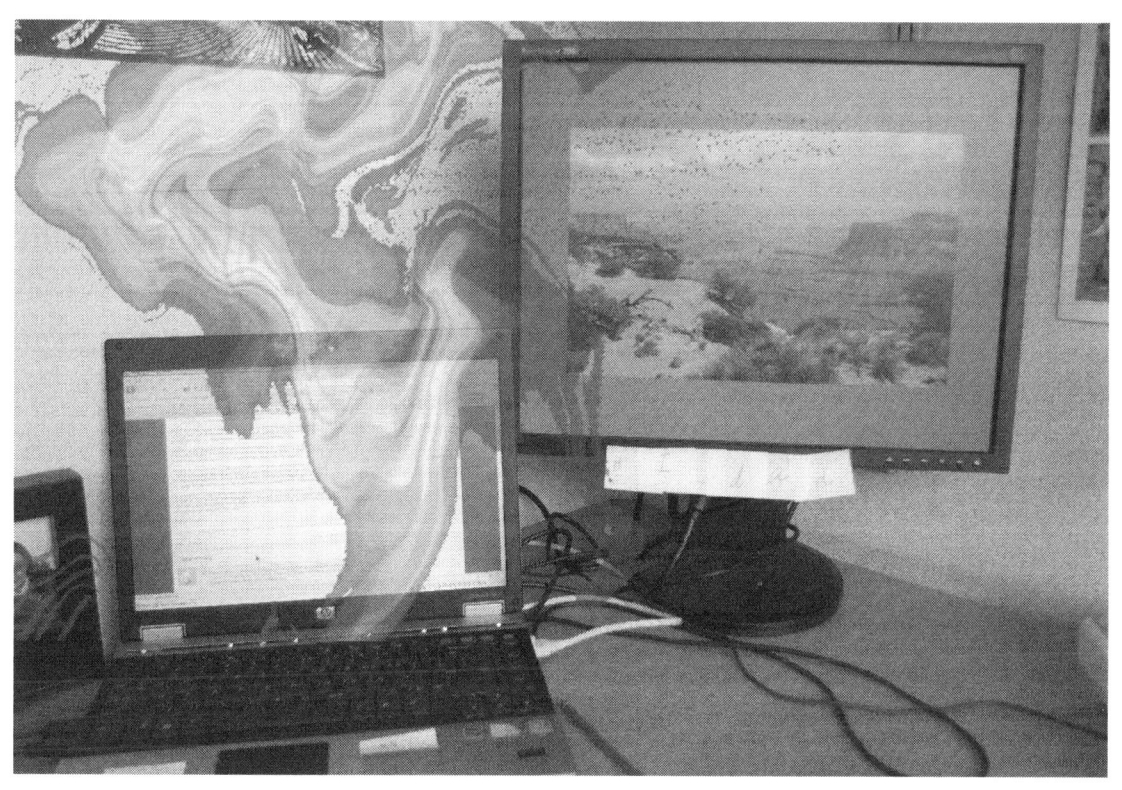

> *Behind every gold wedding ring lies a genuine gold mine, and the possibility of a massive cyanide spill. Behind a tuna steak is a decimated tuna population. Behind a comfortable car is a strip mine, a hundred toxic chemicals leaching into nature, and war in the Middle East.*
>
> AtKisson (2008)

The image opposite is from Bonanni *et al.'s* **(2010) work on open source supply chain mapping. In this example Bonanni gives the sources of the components of a typical laptop (from www.sourcemap.org).** Their approach takes life-cycle analysis in a different direction - instead of focussing on energy independent of geography, they examine transparency of the supply chain with disclosure of materials and processes and where they occur.

An interesting challenge is to try and find a source component that isn't described somewhere as being linked to unsustainable practices: "Cobalt Congo". Put that phrase in your favourite search engine and see what you find (or read Butcher's 2008 Blood River).

For some components on Bonanni's map you don't have to look very hard to find the sustainability issues, for others you can speed the search by adding key search phrases such as environmental degradation, human rights injustice, war, pollution and so on.

The smoking laptop on the previous page provided a direct visualisation of one component of sustainability. While energy/smoke is admittedly useful as a integrator, it does not provide a visualisation of the millions killed in the Congo, nor the environmental and social effects of the copper from the huge open cast pit and smelter in Chuquicamata Chile (nor the contribution of the mine to Chile's economy) and so on through the list of 43 components.

The previous page considered only energy consumption in the production of the laptop, the *Sustainable Lens* needs to operate on a much wider range of impacts and drivers. The supply chain mapping approach of Bonanni provides a way of visualising and sharing the sources but it only goes a little way to make the sustainable invisible visible. At best it provides us with the beginnings of an understanding of the complexity of modern industrial supply chains but this is only a small part of the possible sustainability related issues.

This is an issue of perspective. Most definitions of sustainability include poverty, and vice versa. Poverty is an (morally) unsustainable reality if we consider that we have a duty to alleviate suffering when we can (Singer 2007). Poverty can be caused by: a lack of education, dependence on cash crops with low remuneration, and monocultures that might force people into marginal land. Poverty can only be dealt with when people have environments and social systems (cf failed states) that can meet their needs. How might we represent these considerations on the *Sustainable Lens* looking at a computer? How might we go beyond the impacts and threats, and also include possible responses?

What we can learn from this is that there is more to a *Sustainable Lens* than visualisations of single elements. Instead we need to represent complex systems of both impacts and drivers. These systems require more than a literal unmasking of the invisible.

the invisible whole

> Our way of seeing the world frames our behaviour, as does the context of our skills, knowledge and occupation. No matter what our discipline, we need everyone to act in a sustainable manner. So what could a *Sustainable Lens* contribute to your discipline? to your understandings? to the behaviours expected of being a sustainable practitioner in your discipline? The answers lie beyond the trivial, the things that every worker should do (recycling office paper, walking up stairs etc), but with harder questions about the nature of the trade or profession.

Imagine a forestry worker - let's call him David - attending a chainsaw maintenance course. As part of that course the chainsaw operators are taught all about being careful when changing the chainsaw oil, not spilling it and collecting it for recycling. The first task for the *Sustainable Lens*, then is to see the opportunities to practice such skills. Perhaps even more important, though, is what our David does on his first day on the job when, after a morning of carefully changing oil, he is roundly abused – 'just chuck it in the stream, you're holding up the whole gang'. How might a sustainable view of the world help here? How would he respond if told that his selfishness is preventing a colleague earning money needed for a child's lifesaving surgery?

And what do we expect our David to do when told to go and chop down the last Kauri (an NZ native tree - let's assume our David's *Sustainable Lens* recognised it!). The answer isn't as simple as saying no (he'll get fired and someone else will chop it down), nor is as simple as saying 'yes' (surely unsustainable). Nor is the answer something about integrated catchment management – such material is perhaps considerably outside the scope of our chainsaw operator. Instead the answer is something about polite questioning and discussing alternatives. Perhaps the *Sustainable Lens* could help here.

David's problem can be further extended by considering that most problems are not of the "last Kauri tree" variety, rather, the 999th Kauri tree (i.e. a tragedy of the commons problem). Recognising the significance of the tree is also something not going to happen by accident.

Equivalent scenarios abound in every discipline. Take, for example, the role of procurement within computing. Every year major organizations purchase hundreds if not thousands of computers. How will the *Sustainable Lens* help when the IT manager is told to 'get them off the back of a truck this year', or to choose between several competing suppliers, all touting apparently green credentials. Clearly one of the things we expect our *Sustainable Lens* to be able to do is to recognise if something is unsustainable, or distinguish degrees of sustainability. This has two aspects, they need to recognise and deal with greenwash, and they need to understand the implications of the potential purchase in terms of systemic thinking. Another expectation for the *Sustainable Lens*.

I explored this chainsaw scenario with a group of building trades lecturers. They agreed with the premise that their graduates should act as sustainable practitioners, but that this would not extend to changing any behaviours that they considered unsustainable. It is, they say, vital to the safety of the building process, that you do exactly as you are told on a building site. Fair point, but this is in itself a value position – that of safety. We further explored the ramifications of safety. What would we expect our David to do if instructed to climb on an unsafe structure? He would be expected (required even) to object to this immediate threat. Clearly, in the area of safety everyone on the building site is empowered to manage their own safety. The same applies if they see someone else doing something dangerous – they are required to object. So, let's say they are instructed to do something unsustainable – maybe hide some heavy metal in material destined for landfill, or to order rainforest timber – the time scale or spatial scale of the threat might have changed, but it is still there.

I don't have actual answers for what people should do in these situations, clearly the line is blurred, and sustainability does not possess the same urgency as a wobbly ladder, but the point is that everything has a basis in value positions. The *Sustainable Lens* is not black and white.

chainsaw massacre

> **The world is not in a good shape. The *Sustainable Lens* needs to make that clear. This diagram from Rockstrom (2009) highlights multiple threats.**

Food security (including depleted fish stocks, higher food prices, degradation/loss of agricultural land (some of it in huge volumes of dust) reduced fertility. Superabundance contributes to some diseases of affluence.

> *"if we want more fish on the table, the shortage isn't fishing boats, it's fish"*   Farley (in Barnes 2006)

Biodiversity Loss (including indicator species such as frogs and insects vital to pollination = bees) This can be due to the spread of Western eating habits. This loss can have negative effects on our wellbeing not to mention what it does for species becoming extinct. Includes habitat loss e.g. Godwits migratory path disturbed by developments in China – habitats mightn't respect borders.

> *The current extinction rate one thousand times higher than fossil record (MEA 2005)*

Pollution including mercury (from coal burning often), Pacific trash vortex, noxious fumes in countries without adequate legislation or public involvement in decision making.

Conflict/preparation for conflict: Civil wars tear countries apart and also causes land degradation and lost food production. Amongst more affluent countries expenditure on real or potential conflict is a distraction from more pressing issues.

Water/Sanitation: Natural reservoirs melting. Waterways polluted. Aquifers exhausted. Rainfall patterns disturbed. Adequate sanitation vastly improves quality of life.

Energy Security: Fossil fuels. Peak oil may have been reached. New sources (e.g. oil sands) can be very costly to retrieve oil from. Coal is the nightmare for some climate scientists. Production of disposable goods takes petrol away from more important applications. Alternative sources also demand lots of inputs of fossil fuels in the construction e.g. Lovelock points out the vast amounts of concrete used in wind farms produces a lot of emissions. In developing countries the burning of wood (sometimes as charcoal) leads to deforestation, soil erosion, health concerns and loss of time in gathering wood. Haiti is left with 1% forest cover.

The status of women: a lack of education and status can deny a woman's rights to make decisions in regards to her fertility. Much suffering due to abuse.

Education: In poor countries there is insufficient access and so human capital is not realised. People can then only contribute their muscle power to the economy. Economy is not always about growth and wealth it is also about how food and essential resources are acquired. Education also lifts the aspirations of woman which delays child bearing, reduces the number of children born and increases the length of interval between births. In wealthier countries an emphasis on one's economic contribution detracts from educating people about real world concerns.

Health In developed countries, affluenza, obesity and depression = problems of too much. In developing countries war trauma, malnourishment, infectious diseases.

> *Nature can survive without humanity but society is dependent on the biosphere for crucial services. Society's systematic destruction of the biosphere threatens nature's health and its capacity to sustain human society (IDSA 2001)*

one page of gloom

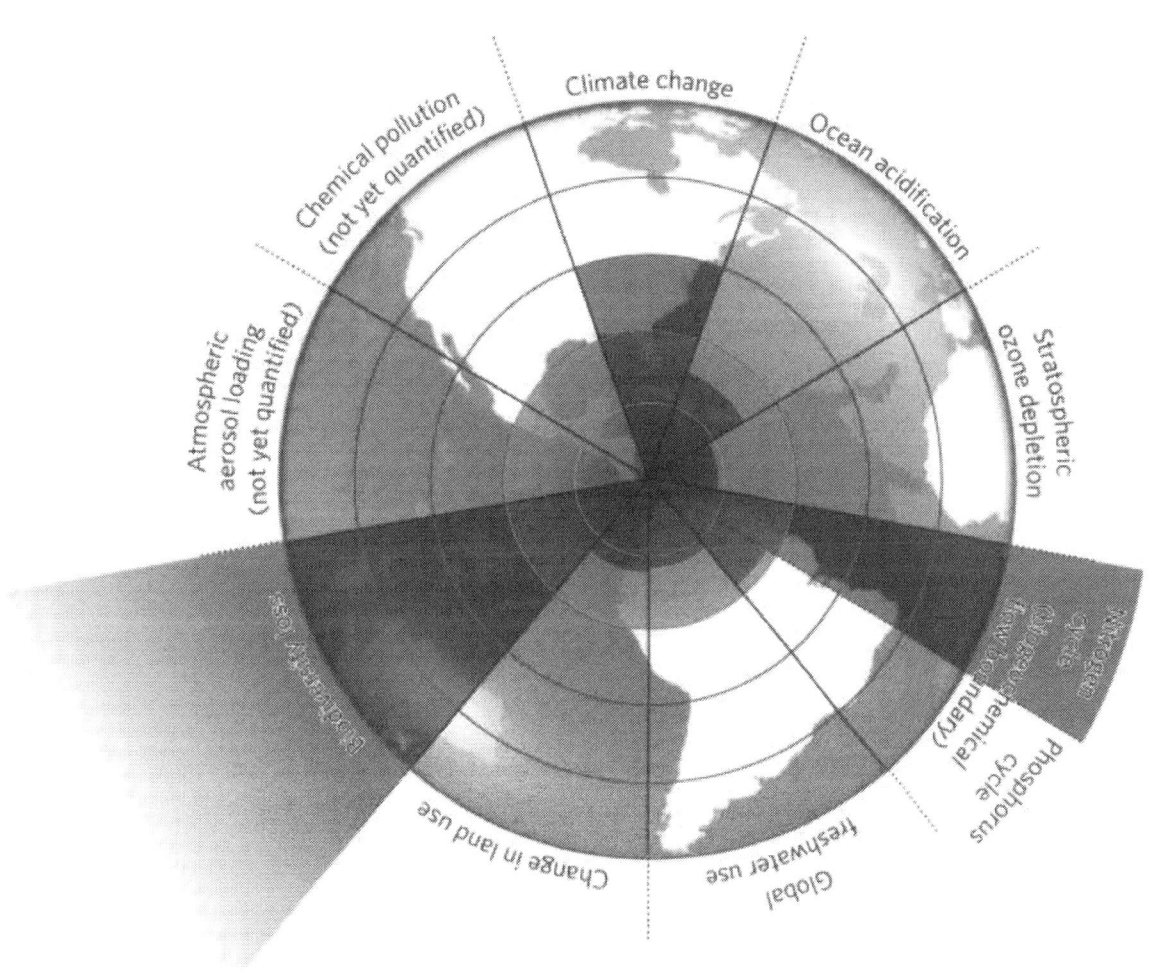

> Critical and creative thinking are essential to unfogging a *Sustainable Lens*. The *Sustainable Lens* challenges us to examine the way we interpret the world and how our knowledge and opinions are shaped by those around us. Critical thinking leads us to a deeper understanding of interests behind our communities and the influences of media and advertising in our lives.

The study of environmental problems is an exercise in despair unless it is regarded as only a preface to the study, design, and implementation of solutions.   (Orr 1992)

There are several different approaches for a Orr's solution focused approach, but all require a balance of critical and creative thinking.

Schendler (2009) makes an important distinction. He says it is vital that we do not see the challenge (in particular climate change) as the end of the world. Instead we can see "an opportunity on the scale of the Enlightenment or the Renaissance, a rare chance to radically change the face of society forever".

For Senge *et al.* (2006) critical and creative thinking are paramount to sustainability. They described a process where the first question is to unearth all the assumptions underlying strategies for the future. They then ask, "How do our current strategies serve us if these assumptions change?" The third question is "What options could we create and invest in over time that would improve the robustness of our overall portfolio of strategies in the event that these assumptions change?"

Martin (2005) described the backcasting approach (top, widely used e.g. by Natural Step). Backcasting can be contrasted with the usual way of approaching the future through forecasting.   While forecasting starts from where we are and works forward, backcasting starts with the current situation and a desirable future state based on defined parameters, and then deduces possible future paths:

The idea is to think imaginatively about the business or organisation to which you belong and seek to explore a range of fundamental changes that will make it more closely fit the sustainability framework. From each alternative future created, you then work your way backwards from the future towards the present in stages, asking such questions as—what barriers did we overcome; who helped us; who did we need to persuade?

This process engages people in conceiving and capturing a vision of their ideal future and in uncovering the steps required to get there.   It clearly relies on both critical and creative thinking.

In pathways to sustainable industrial societies Morioka *et al.* (2006) and Osamu Saito (2007) describe eight transition principles (bottom). Drivers "technology development" and "innovation" are seen in six types of transition: Upgrading and Upscaling ; Downscaling and Downsizing; Replacing and Substituting; Coupling, Combining and Synergising; Networking and Linking; and Enabling Wise Management and Use.

Critical and creative thinking are not a dichotomy. Users of the *Sustainable Lens* are critical thinkers. They are also caring, creative, systems thinkers (to name a few).

beyond an exercise in despair

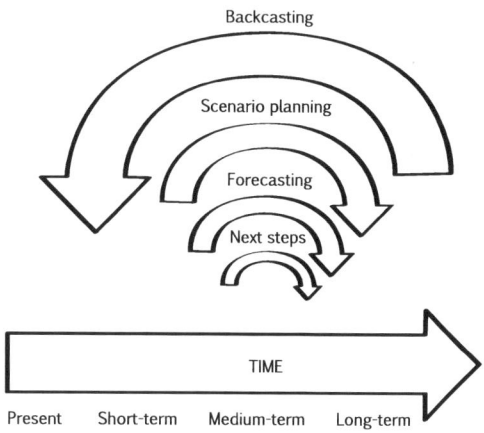

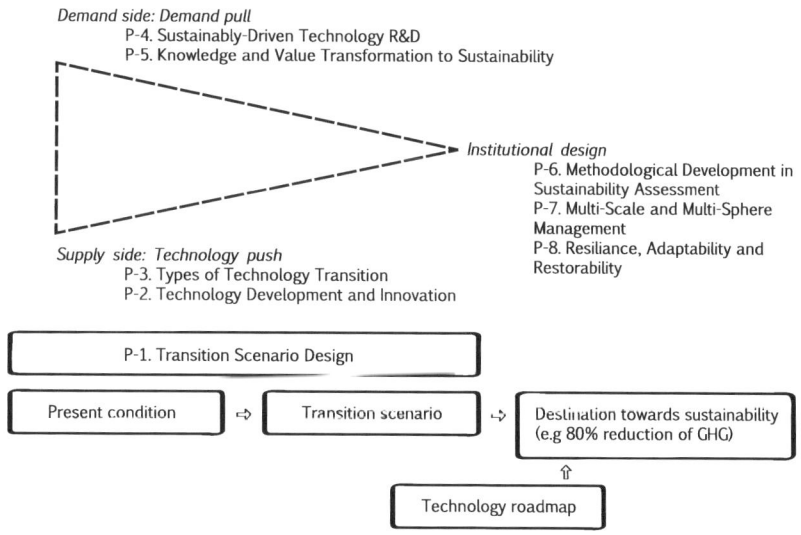

The top diagram represents a society that is based on maximizing the flows of energy (open arrows) and matter (solid arrows) (Taylor 1994 after Miller 1985). This process results in rapidly converting the energy and products of the ecosystem to an entropic state: to waste heat, trash, and pollution. The maintenance of such a society requires infinite supplies of natural resources and energy and an infinite capacity on the part of the environment to absorb the resulting heat and waste by-products. **The bottom diagram provides an alternative that seeks to balance a sustainable society with the environment.**

Green at Fifteen? (OCED 2009) explores how 15-year-olds perform in environmental science in the PISA international study of student competence.

> *An environmentally competent generation of young people will need both to understand the science of the environment and to have the interest and willingness to address the problems that it raises.*

Rather than testing the students on the findings from science (how many electrons in carbon? etc), the report focuses on competence of science: can they extrapolate? can they separate scientific information from non-scientific aspects? can they distinguish between competing explanations? and so on.

Importantly, science is not seen as something for the elite, while we need well-trained geoscientists, biologists, environmental scientists, and environmental policy-makers to take a leading role in confronting environmental challenges in every country, the rest of us also have a role:

> *Equally important are informed and motivated citizens that understand and can interpret sophisticated scientific theory and evidence and act upon this knowledge.*

In order to be a useful contributor to a sustainable society, the crucial part of science is not the knowledge of science (earth and space, physical and living) but rather scientific competencies:

- identifying scientific issues

- explaining phenomena scientifically

- using scientific evidence

- knowledge about the processes of science as a form of enquiry.

Perhaps the most important finding of the report is that students' optimism regarding environmental issues is negatively related to the environmental science performance index. The lower students perform in environmental science, the more optimistic they are that the situation will improve over the next two decades.

A limitation of the PISA report is the exclusive focus on physical sciences - the humanities are not considered. What might be the elements of a sustainability science? How would this translate to a *Sustainable Lens*?

greener than a 10th grader?

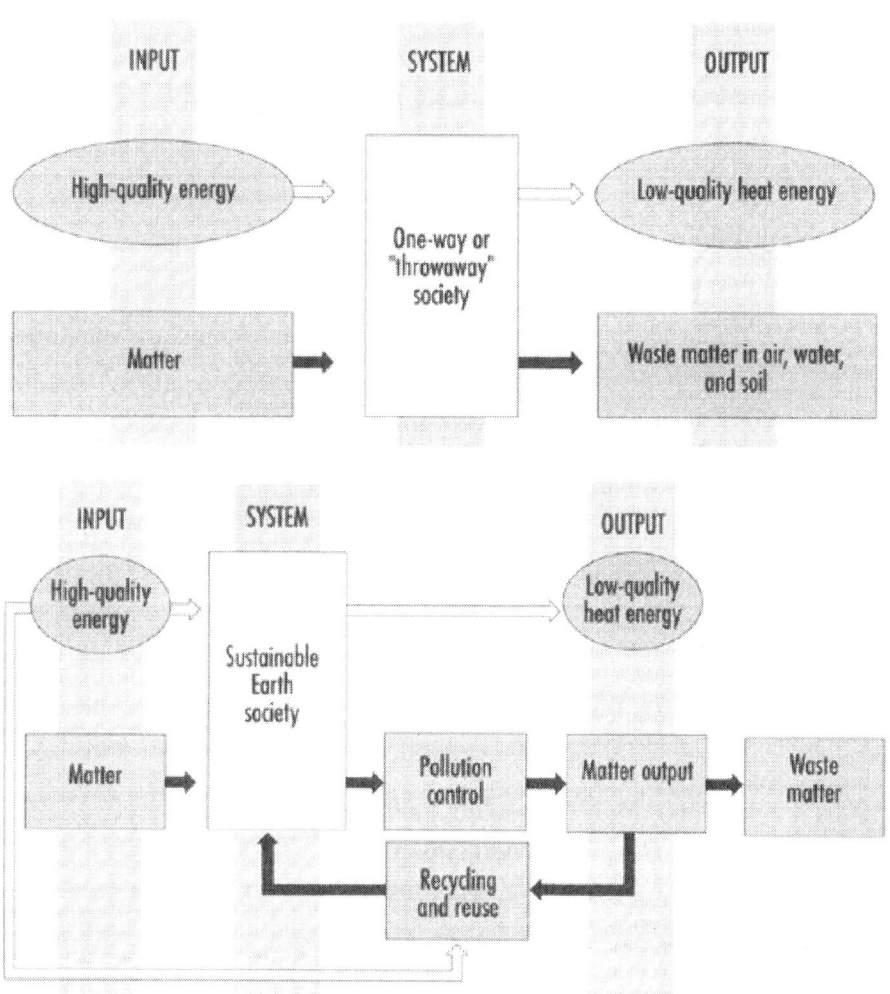

visual thinking

> In order to see the world through a *Sustainable Lens*, it helps if we can *think sustainably*. The tendency is to view *sustainability* in a way that has become largely habitual as a static object of study; the three elements or pillars perspective. **What happens if we view sustainability in an action based way, as a way of seeing the world; as a mindset? Aleh Cherp's diagram provides some ways of engaging our thinking.**

In order to see with a *Sustainable Lens*, we need to be able to *think sustainably* (we can then put back the dimensions and visual structures in the following chapters). So as not to constrain our thought - or our seeing - the challenge is to do this thinking without reference to Brundtland's definition or its pillar-based visual representations.

Cumming (2007) *In Art Explained:* For seeing is not the same as looking, just as hearing is not the same as listening, seeing only involves the effort it takes to open your eyes; looking means opening your mind and taxing your intellect. So, what constitutes sustainable thinking without relying on Brundtland/Venn (or similar)? I propose the following attributes:

- Systems thinking

- An understanding of the connected nature of our socio-ecological system

- Critical and creative thinking

- Ability to act as change agent

- Understanding of ethics

- Sense of participation and action

I explore each of these in the pages that follow, starting with Systems Thinking. Rather than sustainability being a thing to study, it is an action based way of seeing the world - a mindset.

Others have similar lists. These are Aleh Cherp's five mindsets (Cherp nd):

- Earthly – focusing on the interplay between environmental and developmental agendas in the short- and long-term both globally and locally;

- Analytic – based on 'systems thinking' and encompassing assessment, planning and management;

- Careful – based on respect for complexity and uncertainty;

- Collaborative – focusing on the interplay of interests, values, cultures and capacities of various actors;

- Action – guiding strategy formation to manage change, continuity and learning for sustainability.

thinking without pillars

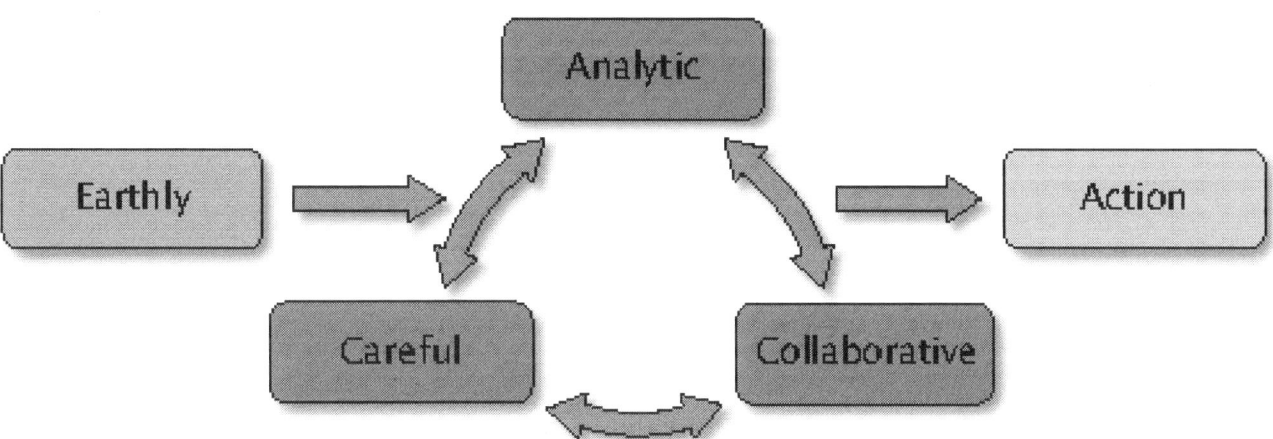

visual thinking

> Systems thinking can be characterised as a belief that the component parts of a system can best be understood in the context of relationships with each other and with other systems, rather than in isolation. The systems of E.P. Odum's Fundamentals of Ecology (1971) were described by an energy circuit language borrowed from his brother (H.T. Odum 1974).

The systems of E.P. Odum's Fundamentals of Ecology (1971) were described by his brother H.T. Odum's energy circuit language.

> *A generalized world model of man and nature based on one-shot fossil fuel usages and steady solar work. Pathways are flows of energy from outside source (circle) through interactions (pointed blocks marked 'X' to show multiplier action) to final dispersion of dispersed heat. The tank symbol refers to storage. Here world fuel reserve storage helps build a storage of structure of man's buildings, information, population, and culture.*

Using these cybernetics models based on energy flows and nutrient cycles H.T. Odum (1974) showed a transition from growth to low-throughput steady state through a succession of ecosystems. Hart (1984) identifies organisms that have an impact on the system disproportionately larger than the amount of energy they consume. These are referred to as the information processors, making decisions that control material and energy flows. In the non-natural state humans take on this role almost entirely.

In *"Redesigning Industrial Agroecosystems"*, E.P. Odum and Barrett (2004) ask why conventional agriculture practices frequently result in environmental problems. They ask whether a model of a natural ecosystem can be used to describe a reduced-input agroecosystem. **They describe a model (top left) of a natural, unsubsidised solar-powered ecosystem.** This has two chains, the grazing energy flow path (plants, herbivores, carnivores); and the detritus microbial loop. It is characterised by recycling of nutrients, internal pest control and a low rate of organic output. **This model is similar to the pre-industrial model (top right). Farm animals replace wild ones, and there is active management of the residue loop.** The diverse system shows little erosion or loss of nutrients. There is a limited amount of food available for export out of the local system.

In **Industrial Agriculture (lower left) the system is supported by inputs of fossil fuel driven machinery, fertilisers, pesticides and irrigation water.** This increases yields per unit area of the monoculture but also increases chemical and nutrient pollution. Without crop residue and export of foodstuffs, the residue return loop is reduced. There is loss of soil quality and soil erosion, and habitat loss.

The **Low-Input Sustainable Agriculture (lower right), reduces the amounts of human subsidies.** Less inputs are balanced by a return to a diversity of biota, integrated pest management and a increased rates of nutrient recycling.

Bergandi (2000), though, is critical of this style of models being considered systems models as the narrow focus on thermodynamics in Odum's energy circuit language not only "misses the emergences" but also is "hyper-reductionist".

At the other end of the system thinking paradigm from the energy balance of approach are those who focus on the connectivity - even without concern for the vector or currency. This is a recognition of the interdependence of objects and their attributes - independent elements can never constitute a system.

A *Sustainable Lens* that adopts any systems thinking approach implies several core beliefs. Thinking this way brings about several habits. The core tenets are focuses on the interdependence of objects. Together objects form complexes whose emergent properties could be detected from the constituent parts. Processes transform inputs into outputs. Feedback mechanisms ensure regulation of the system. In closed systems inputs are determined once and constant; in open systems additional inputs are admitted from outside the system. Hierarchies of systems mean complex wholes are made up of smaller subsystems.

a systems approach

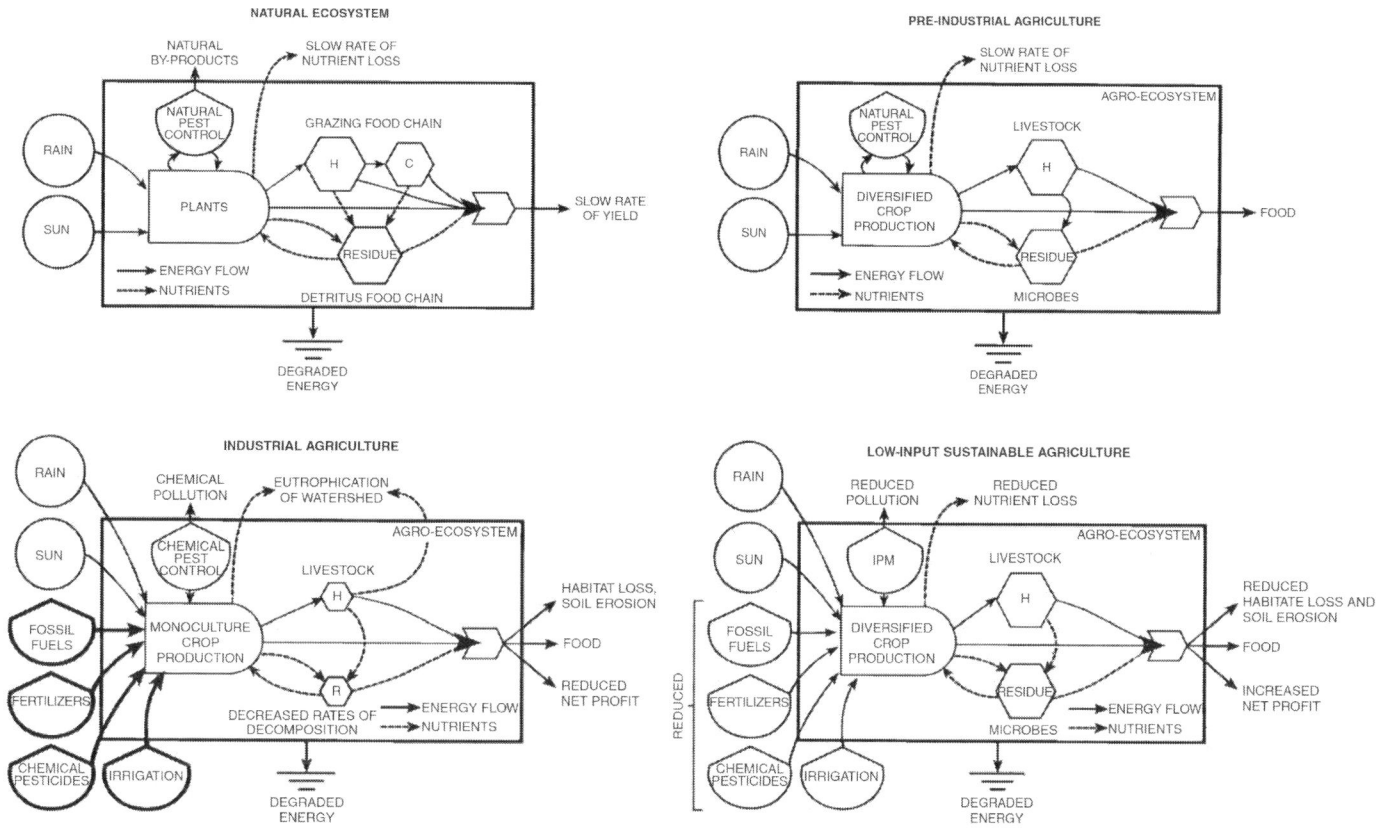

> For many people, recycling is a word that is taken to be synonymous with sustainability. However, I suggest that recycling is the least preferred of the "three Rs" (reduce, reuse, recycle). As McDonough and Braungart (2002) pointed out in *Cradle to Cradle: Remaking the Way We Make Things*, most of what we think of as recycling is more accurately described as downcycling. This means it is not a true cycle, as Anderson's diagram suggests. The process is more like a downward spiral as waste is converted to new materials or products of lesser quality and reduced functionality.

In terms of public recognition of sustainability diagrams, **Gary Anderson's Recycling arrows are perhaps only second to Barbier's Venn diagram.** In 1970 the first Earth Day prompted the Container Corporation of America, a large producer of recycled paper-board to sponsor a contest for art and design students at high schools and colleges across the United States to raise awareness of environmental issues. It was won by Gary Anderson, a 23-year-old college student at the University of Southern California, whose entry was the image now known as the universal recycling symbol.

Anderson (reported in Jones and Powell 1999) described his symbol as

> *Designed as a Möbius strip to symbolize continuity within a finite entity. I used the [logo's] arrows to give directionality to the symbol. I envisioned it with the small edge or the point of the triangle at the bottom. I wanted to suggest both the dynamic (things are changing) and the static (it's a static equilibrium, a permanent kind of thing). The arrows, as broad as they are, draw back to the static side.*

For many, recycling is synonymous with sustainability. However, it is worth remembering that recycling is the least preferred of the "three Rs" (reduce, reuse, recycle). As McDonough and Braungart (2002) pointed out in *Cradle to Cradle: Remaking the Way We Make Things*, most of what we think of as recycling is actually downcycling. This means it is not a true cycle, as Anderson's symbol would suggest, instead it is a downward spiral as waste is converted to new materials or products of lesser quality and reduced functionality. While this downcycling reduces the consumption of fresh raw materials (and hence energy use etc) as compared to virgin production, it is not as good as a truly closed loop.

Incidentally, I recently looked for the "fourth R". Here's 26 of what I found: Repair; Refuse; Remove; Respect; Rot; Restore (meaning repair); Restore (meaning inner self); Recover (eg extract energy); Recycle (meaning buy recycled goods); Rethink; Replacement; Renew; Remanufacture; Responsibility (meaning producer responsibility); Recreation (meaning make recycling fun); Read (meaning increase awareness); Restock (meaning find a new supplier); Recharge Residual management (better manage what you do have to dispose of); Rainwater (meaning rainwater harvesting); Resell (meaning eco-chique); Reinvent (meaning have a good look at your processes); Return; and Rejuvenate.

Naveh and Lieberman (1994) described how the Total Human Ecosystem is a combination of the natural and human environments that involves complex structures and includes many feedback paths, both positive and negative (and combinations of these). An example of such feedback is the death of forest trees. Trees in a forest are increasingly vulnerable to wind-throw as their degree of isolation increases as trees are blown over (Hubbel and Foster 1986). In a land management sense, a system includes many forms of feedback: phtyomass will accumulate unless ecological factors limit growth, and bare ground gives rise to more bare ground unless other feedback effects become active, not the least of which being the landholder's procedures.

A *Sustainable Lens* must focus on seeing flows, and on seeing process - on verbs not nouns.

down cycling

> Processes can be seen as functions of pattern. The *Sustainable Lens* must be able to see how these fit together as a whole rather than a series of disjunct components.

In preparation for the Earth Summit in 1992 Anthony Judge prepared this systemic mapping of strategic dilemmas. He identified polarising issues and strategic dilemmas. The intent was to explore ways of building on these 'irreconcilable differences' rather than trying to avoid them:

> To explore and illustrate new possibilities, the focus of the exercise described here is on identifying strategic dilemmas underlying debates on Earth Summit issues. These are the dilemmas which reflect such seemingly irreconcilable concerns as safeguarding watercourses versus exploiting essential hydro-electric energy reserves. The assumption is that the set of these local (namely issue specific) long-term dilemmas may offer clues to new patterns of global (namely inter-sectoral) strategies and bargains.

Judge was responding to a call to obtain suggestions for inter-sectoral images which could best capture the Earth Summit insights and empower people to move forward in new ways. He was endeavouring to "open up new possibilities by portraying sectoral and issue relationships in two and three-dimensions".

In searching for "some meaningful overall pattern", Judge recognised that we "might not yet know how to put all the pieces together" of our "systemic jigsaw puzzle", but this was preferable to a "laundry list" of issues. A tabular view is considered a "conceptual trap" as it encourages a very mechanistic approach to the pattern of dilemmas, reinforcing tendencies to much-contested forms of "linear thinking" and a focus on identifying a singular "most important problem". Judge characterises the outcome of tabular thinking as promoting separate and competing views of different sector groups, each blinkered by its dominant function.

The two icosadodecahedral nets represent two alternate patterns of strategic dilemmas. Each is a pattern of strategic functions clustered around "local bargain areas". When folded the irreconcilable dilemmas become instead complementary triangles and the whole forms a "globally organised network".

Judge also argues that the modelling structure itself can be seen as providing further insights into how local bargains may interlock. "Tensegrity structures are effectively patterns of sustainability...(as)...the spherical structures can be rendered self-sustaining in practice".

The codes are Population, Wellbeing, Learning, Production, Environment, and Regulation (equity)

Each combines into a pair of strategic dilemmas. For example W and E:

WE: Over-consumption and exploitation of non-renewable resources

EW: Reduction in quality of life (+ jobs) to safeguard environment

On the icosadodecahedral nets each pentagon has five of the six functional areas. The triangles formed by the edges are the emergent focus areas. Note that there are 120 possible triangles, each ball would only contain 10 (if the order didn't matter). As can be seen in the right-hand image, however, the order does appear to matter, the LPT triangle appears twice, as "Cultural produce" and as "Proprietary trade (arms)".

dilemmas as focus areas

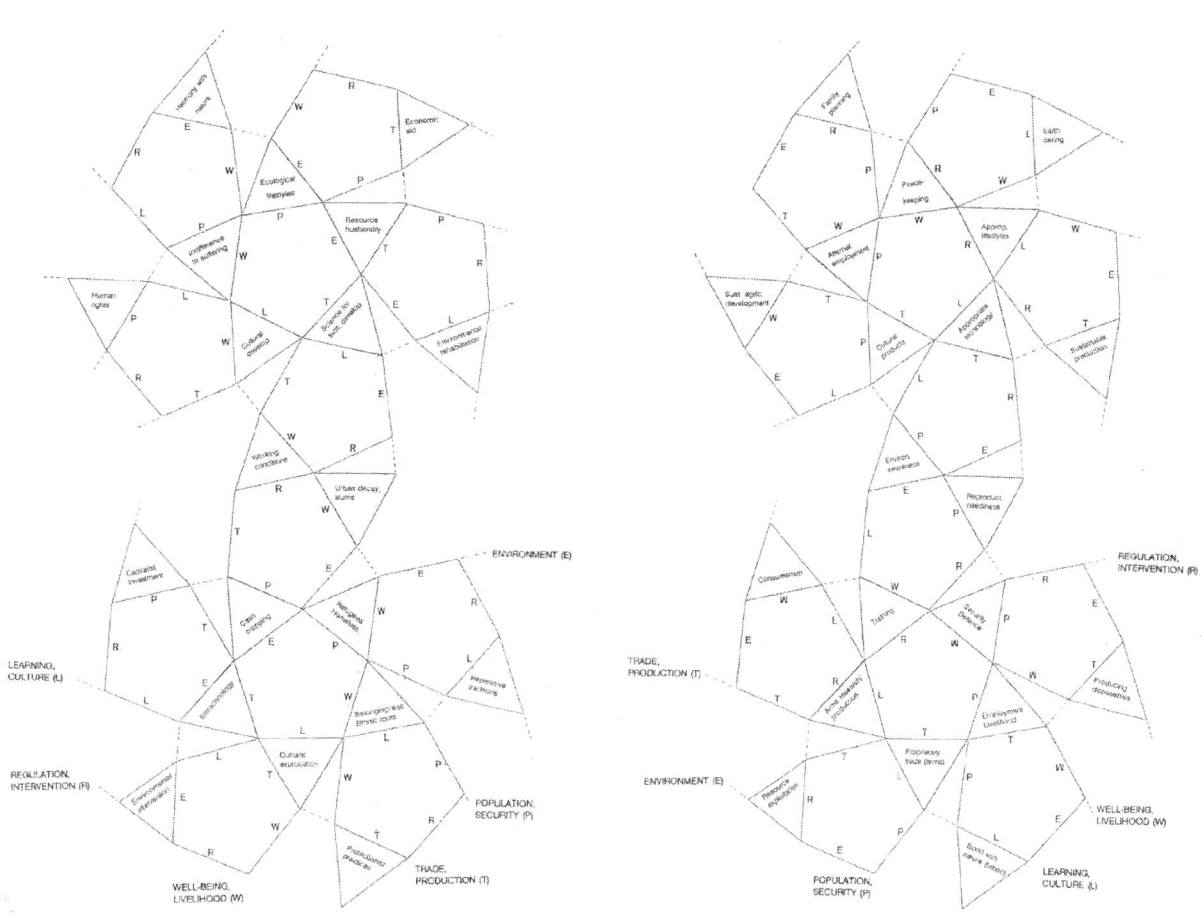

> There was a trend in the early 2000s to put an "e" in front of everything, suggesting a whole system at the forefront of new technologies. Unfortunately in many cases this turned out to be presumptuous. There is much the same danger in prefixing sustainability with "eco…" or with the uncritical use of ecosystem metaphors. Daly (2007 ex 2001) **in an "empty world" state, the ecosystem has room to act as a buffer so that the economy has room to operate. In a "full world", where natural capital has been replaced by human capital, the expectations on the environment are more than it can provide.**

Messerschmitt and Szyperski's (2003) book *Software Ecosystem* renamed the software industry the software ecosystem and examined the complexities of our business in terms of larger systems. Unfortunately, Messerschmitt and Szyperski don't go far beyond the emphasis on the interconnectedness of a variety of issues surrounding software development. In the preface Messerschmitt and Szypersk argue:

> The software industry is itself very complex, with many complimentary products necessary to for a systems solution and complex alliances and standardisation processes needed to meet the needs of numerous stakeholders. Together, the software suppliers, standardisation bodies, content suppliers, service suppliers, and end-user organisations form a complex web of relationships. The "ecosystem" metaphor is truly descriptive.

Metaphors bring many benefits – common vision, a shared vocabulary, architecture and generativity. All of these, especially the last, benefit most from actually using the metaphor – borrowing from the idea to create new understandings. It is pointless to have a metaphor and then ignore it. Messerschmitt and Szyperski do recognise the value of cross disciplinary thought: it is interesting to compare software to other industries, looking for parallels that might offer insights to the software industry and some insights and perspectives on software from the economics profession are described in chapter 9. Nowhere though, do Messerschmitt and Szyperski actually use the ecosystem metaphor. And they are missing so many opportunities. They do take something like a systems approach – they look for simple laws to describe flows of information and then try to consider these in larger systems. They examine Moore's law, for example, and consider how it might operate over different scales "since previous technologies (like transportation or electrification) did not advance according to Moore's law, there must be something distinctive about the material information technologies".

It is a shame, though, that a whole field of environmental science is ignored: landscape ecology. It has much to say about scaling effects. Missed opportunities for new understandings continue:

- there is discussion about heterogeneity without reference to biodiversity;
- specialization and change without evolution;
- networks without food webs;
- value chains without food chains;
- change without disturbance;
- cooperation without relationships;
- interfaces without edge effects.

In addition to missed opportunities, things seem awry from an ecosystem perspective. "Environments" are described that in the various chapters that stop at the boundaries of that chapter (users, hardware or network). A model of the internet is provided where the heterogeneous internet consists of separated (but communicating) homogeneous environments. Other factors crucial to ecosystems are missing entirely: stochastic events, feedback, limiting factors.

A *Sustainable Lens* is not just a green tint, nor it is a simple matter of calling things - business processes and the like - "ecosystems". The opportunity is to consider the implications of this approach. What, for example, might be the business implications of truly considering a business as an ecosystem within Daly's full world?

"e" verything

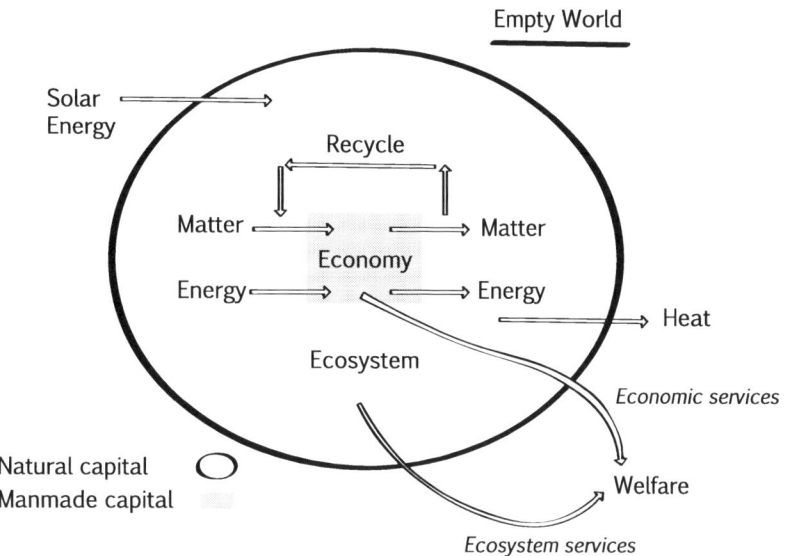

Empty World

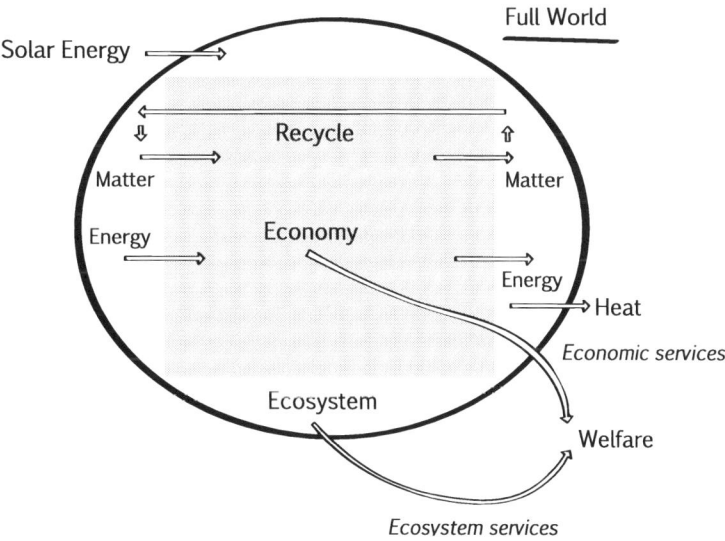

Full World

> In order to think sustainably, one must consider the interrelated nature of human and natural systems.

In 1882 Friedrich Ratzel wrote *Anthropogeographie* which Ellen Churchill Semple expanded in 1911 (Semple 2005).

> *Every clan, tribe, state or nation includes two ideas, a people and its land, the first unthinkable without the other.*

> *A land is fully comprehended only when studied in the light of its influence upon its people, and a people cannot be understood apart from the field of its activities.*

> *The history of the life forms of the world leads always back to the land on which that life arose, spread, and struggled for existence*

In other words, humankind and the environment are intertwined. Stagl (2007) describes social-ecological systems as co-evolving systems. She contends that this co-evolution can be seen in co-evolution of the environment and governance; in co-evolution of technology and governance; and in co-evolution of human behaviour and culture. As a society, she argues, we have to learn to live in a complex world of interdependent systems with high uncertainties and multiple legitimate interests. This has two consequences. First it means "these complex and evolving systems require a new way of thinking about risk, uncertainty, ambiguity and ignorance" (Stagl 2007). Second, it means we should reduce our reliance on "artificial divisions between, on the one hand, the environment and, on the other hand, economy and society" (Koutsouris 2009).

Kesavan and Swaminathan (2006) argue that vulnerability to disasters has social, gender and economic dimensions. This **diagram (top-left) reflects the two-way relationship between the socio-economic system (including physical assets) and the natural disasters.** The human systems are susceptible or resilient to the impact of natural hazards. Human pressures both precipitate hazard events and increase the susceptibility to increased impacts - combining to enhance the vulnerability in a vicious spiral.

This **cause and effect diagram (lower right)** is the result of a workshop modelling session (Stephen Hinton (2010).

> *"The more we discussed, the more we could see how the very fabric of society is imbued with counter sustainability, from deepest held beliefs to physical infrastructure. As an individual, even with years of working with sustainability behind you, you live in a world that is talking and acting as if action on sustainability is not urgent, indeed it is under discussion if it is needed at all".*

The *Sustainable Lens* must see socio-ecological systems as one and the same.

socio-ecological systems

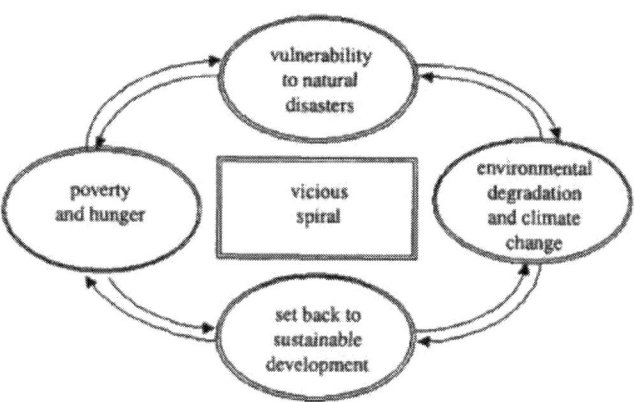

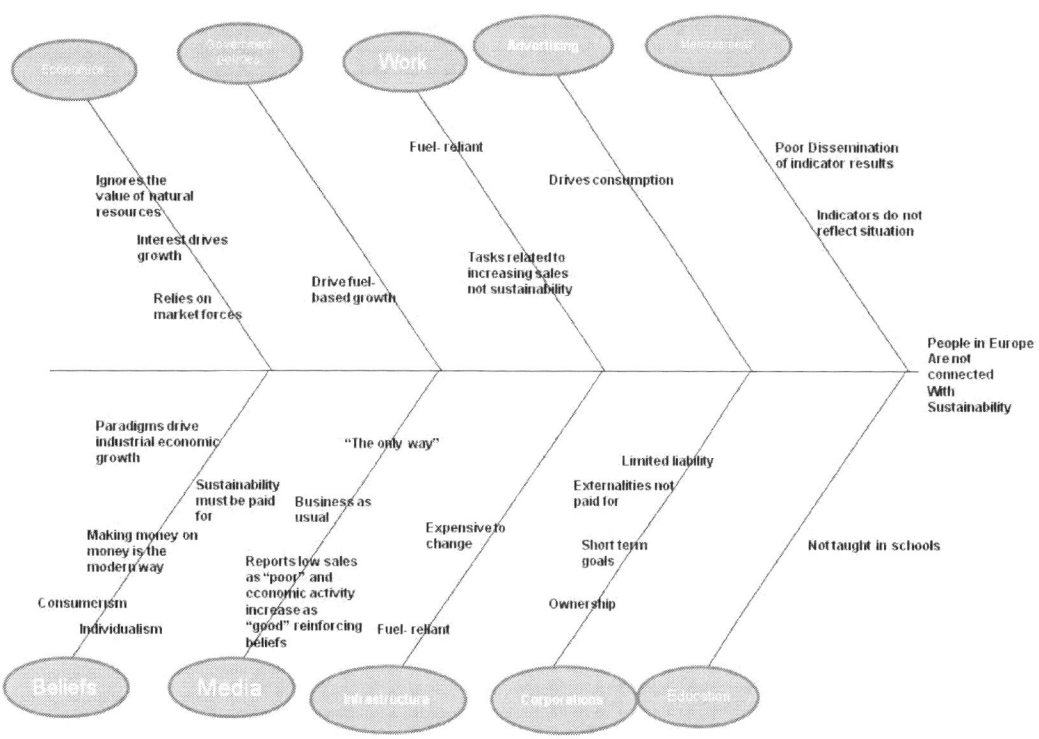

> Total Human Ecosystem allows human aspects and dimensions to be considered as part of the whole integrated human-nature systems complex.

Naveh and Lieberman (1994) argued that "we are living in both a physical-geographic-ecological landscape space and a conceptual space…info-, socio- and psychospheres".

Naveh and Lieberman (1994) described a systems-based theory of landscape ecological processes (SLE). Because of the complexity of interweaving biological, physical and cultural systems in the landscape, an interdisciplinary approach is encouraged in which landscape ecology provides a theoretical framework and information source. Landscape ecology helps guide the understanding of the Total Human Ecosystem (THE) as an ecological system that includes natural and human-made systems.

Naveh (1980, 1982, 2000, 2004) describes how the THE comprises human aspects and dimensions as an intrinsic part of landscape processes and functions. Naveh and Lieberman described how the conceptual framework for this approach is derived from three closely connected scientific theories:

1. General systems theory (GST): A holistic scientific theory and philosophy of the hierarchical order of nature as open systems with increasing complexity and organisation and with living systems and ecological systems as their special biosystem.

2. Biocybernetics: The theory of cybernetic regulation of biosystems, enabling their self-stablisation and self-organisation through deviation-countering (negative) and deviation-amplifying (positive) feedback couplings.

3. Ecosystemology: The theory of a transdisciplinary ecosystem concept with the Total Human Ecosystem (THE) as the highest level of ecological integration and with the ecosphere as its concrete space-time-defined global landscape entity.

"Modern man occupies a dual position, serving as a receiver of vital inputs from the biosphere and geosphere but, through the outputs of the technosphere, concurrently modifying the biosphere and the geosphere. He is thus affected and being affected by these modifications" (left, Naveh 1982).

The right-hand diagram represents a functional classification of natural and cultural biosphere landscapes (Naveh 1982). THE Landscape is classified according to energy and material inputs, throughput and outputs; differences in the amount and kind of regulation by natural or human information; and, the capacity of landscapes to organise themselves in a coherent way (including structural integrity in a process of continuous self-renewal).

All THE landscapes and their ecotopes are presented in a hierarchical model, ranging from the natural bio-ecotope pole to the cultural techno-ecotopes pole along a gradient of increasing degrees of modification, conversion, and replacement of natural elements, controls and functions by human-made, artificial ones. These are closely related with increasing throughputs of fossil energy and materials with much high energetic differences between the regenerative natural and cultural biosphere landscapes and the throughput agro- and urban-industrial technosphere landscape systems.

The *Sustainable Lens* considers human aspects and dimensions to be part of the whole integrated human-nature systems complex.

total human ecosystem

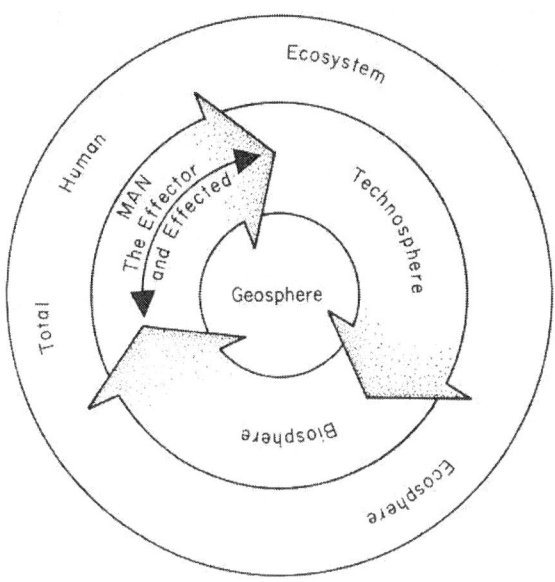
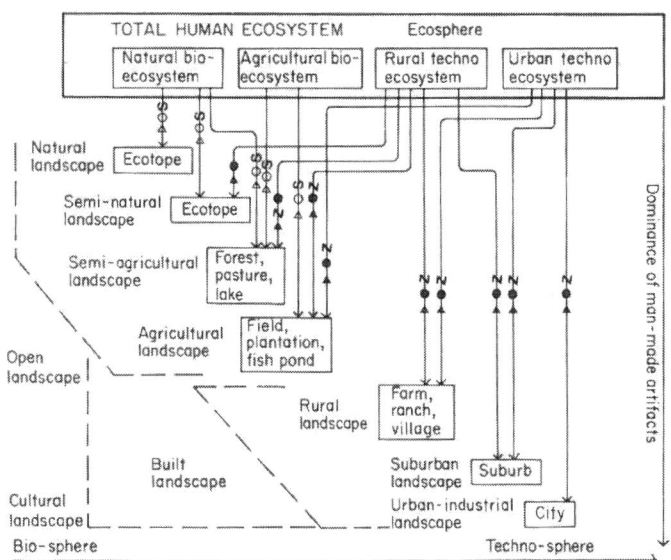

> In recognising the oneness of systems, framing the world through a *Sustainable Lens* becomes a broad concept. It therefore embraces both ecological literacy and cultural literacy (Polistina 2009) indeed, many authors argue that the cultural aspects are preeminent: "Culture includes our whole system of beliefs, values, attitudes, customs, institutions and social relations. The global crisis facing humanity is a reflection of this system and is therefore a cultural crisis" (Svanström *et al.* 2008).

If the systemic thinking is to enable thinking about our socio-ecological system, then a second goal for our *Sustainable Lens* must be to actually apply these connections to the connected nature of our socio-ecological system. In short, we need some ecosystem science. Several questions arise. How much ecosystem science is needed? Is the focus on people or physics or plants? Clearly some information is needed, else how would you recognise the last Kauri tree?

It is not sensible to attempt a list of what people need to know – energy balance, water cycle etc. Instead, the answer must be defined by the context. Fortunately we have made considerable progress here, the answers are embodied in the notion of the *Sustainable Lens*.

The *Sustainable Lens* should promote an inclusive consideration of ecosystem (i.e. one that makes little distinction between natural and human systems). Naveh and Lieberman (1994) called this the Total Human Ecosystem - an ecological system that includes natural and human-made systems.

Similarly, in discussing developments in ecosystem science, Dearing (2007) argues that we should treat humans in natural environments explicitly, as actors rather than stressors and second, that we should assume dynamic rather than static systems. Osbaldiston and Sheldon (2002) argue that merely providing information about unsustainability is not enough I agree. This is a change from the roots of environmental education that was based on "the assumption that people were insufficiently aware of the environment and understood little about it" (Sterling 2004). Thus we do need information, but it needs to be in context - and that context is of a total human ecosystem.

Machlis *et al.* (1994, 1997) presented a model of the human ecosystem as a "coherent system of biophysical and social factors capable of adaptation and sustainability over time" (this later version Machlis *pers comm)*. Human ecosystems rest upon a foundation of abiotic and biotic factors taken as base conditions: a solar-driven energy system obeying thermodynamic properties, biogeochemical cycles of high constancy, landforms and geological variation of great complexity, the full genetic structure of life including biophysical properties of homo sapiens. The base conditions limit, constrain, influence and occasionally direct many human ecosystem processes. Boundaries can be spatially identified through ecological transition zones, administrative and political boundaries, or more fine-scaled analysis of sharp perturbations in system flows.

Ecosystem services are the benefits that humans obtain from ecosystems, and they are produced by interactions within the ecosystem (Millennium Ecosystem Assessment, 2005). There are strong linkages between categories of ecosystem services and components of human well-being. These interactions can take place at more than one scale and can cross scales. This includes indications of the extent to which it is possible for socioeconomic factors to mediate the linkage. The strength of the linkages and the potential for mediation vary according to the specific ecosystem and region. In addition, other factors—including other environmental factors as well as economic, social, technological, and cultural factors—influence human well-being. Ecosystems are in turn affected by changes in human well-being (Rodrigeuz *et al.* 2006).

Considering socio-ecological systems does not mean abandoning the humanities for the biophysical sciences. The *Sustainable Lens* must be able to see interactions with and within social structures such as belief systems, legal systems, social norms and aesthetics as well as individual habits and desires.

human ecosystems

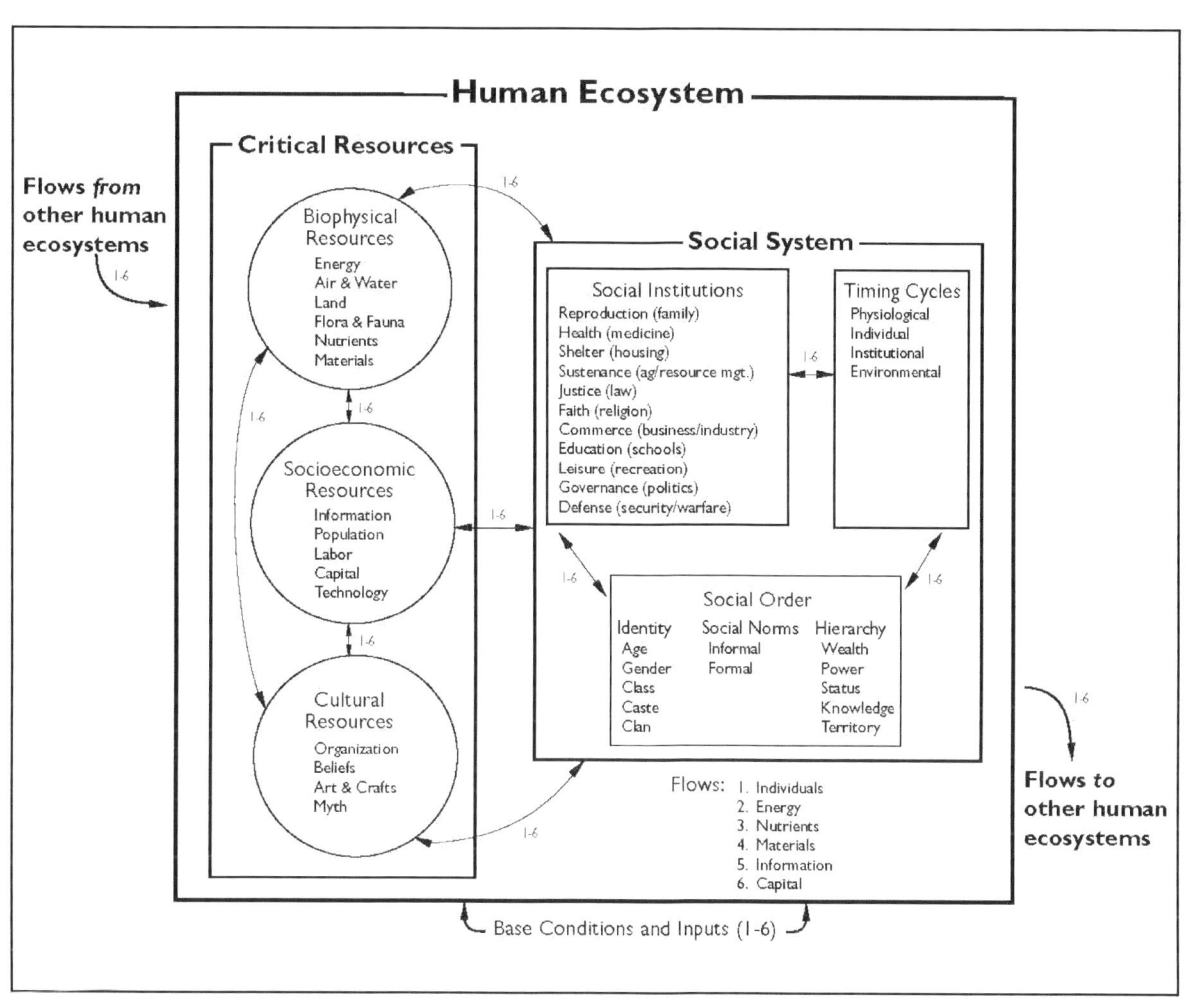

> The *Global Environmental Outlook* (UNEP GEO4, 2007) developed a framework for assessment that considers the "entire environment and the interaction with society".

The GEO4 framework describes a system made up of drivers, pressures, state, impacts and responses (top). These are either encapsulated within "human society" or "environment". The system is depicted graphically with two further dimensions - temporal and spatial scales - but it is not clear how these function.

Drivers refer to fundamental processes in society, which drive activities with a direct impact on the environment. These include demographics; consumption and production patterns; scientific and technological innovation; economic demand, markets and trade; distribution patterns; institutional and social-political frameworks and value systems. The characteristics of each driver varies according to geographic region.

Pressures are human interventions in the environment plus natural processes such as volcanoes. Human interventions may be directed towards causing a desired environmental change such as land use, or they may be intentional or unintentional by-products of other human activities, for example, pollution. The pressures act alone and in combination. The relationships between society and environmental pressures varies according to the society. With high levels of production and consumption, affluent societies contribute more pressures, not only on their own environment, but by transferring environmental pressures onto the environment of other societies through globalised trade.

Environmental state also includes trends, which often refers to environmental change. This change may be natural, human-induced or both. The complexity of the physical, chemical and biological systems constituting the environment makes it hard to predict environmental change. Key forms of human induced environmental change include climate change, desertification and land degradation, biodiversity loss, and air and water pollution.

Impacts refer to change (either negative or positive) in human well-being and in environmental changes.

Responses address issues of vulnerability of both people and the environment, and provide opportunities for reducing human vulnerability and enhancing human well-being. Responses take place at various levels: for example, environmental laws and institutions at the national level, and multilateral environmental agreements and institutions at the regional and global levels. The capacity to mitigate and/or adapt to environmental change differs among and within regions, and capacity building is, therefore, a major and overarching component of the response components.

While the framework does not explicitly model effects, the integrated system does make it apparent human activities result in multiple impacts on the environment because of biophysical interlinkages. Land, water and atmosphere are linked in many ways, but particularly through the carbon, nitrogen and water cycles, which are fundamental to maintaining life on Earth. Feedbacks and thresholds affect the boundaries, composition and functioning of ecological systems. The model also emphasises that many gains in human well-being facilitated by the social and economic sectors have been at the cost of growing environmental changes, and the exacerbation of poverty for some groups of people.

The GEO4 uses the framework as the basis for analysis of issues. **In the lower figure, the model is adapted to highlight the dual roles of economic sectors such as agriculture, forestry, fisheries and tourism** – in contributing to development and human well-being, and also in exerting pressure on the environment and influencing environmental change, and in some cases, to human vulnerability to such change.

Seeing through a *Sustainable Lens* requires a framework to reflect the key components of the complex and multidimensional, spatial and temporal chain of cause-and-effect that characterises the interactions between society and the environment.

under pressure

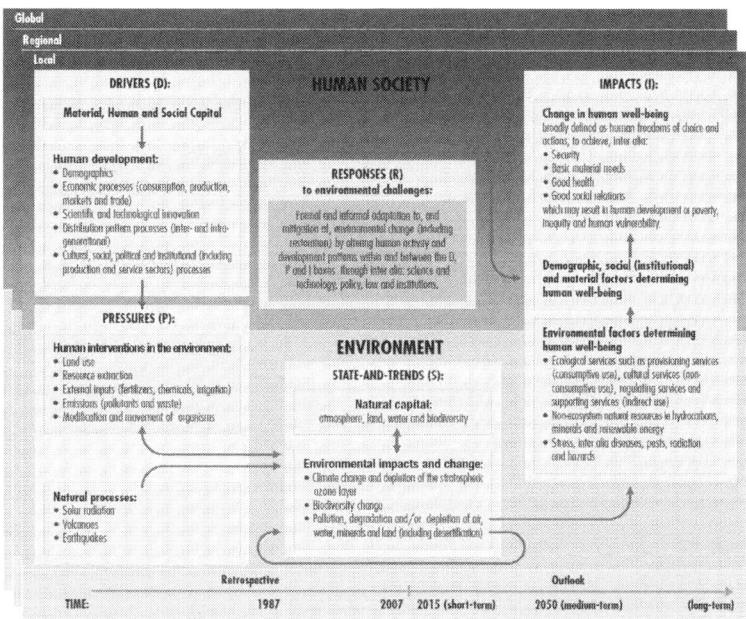

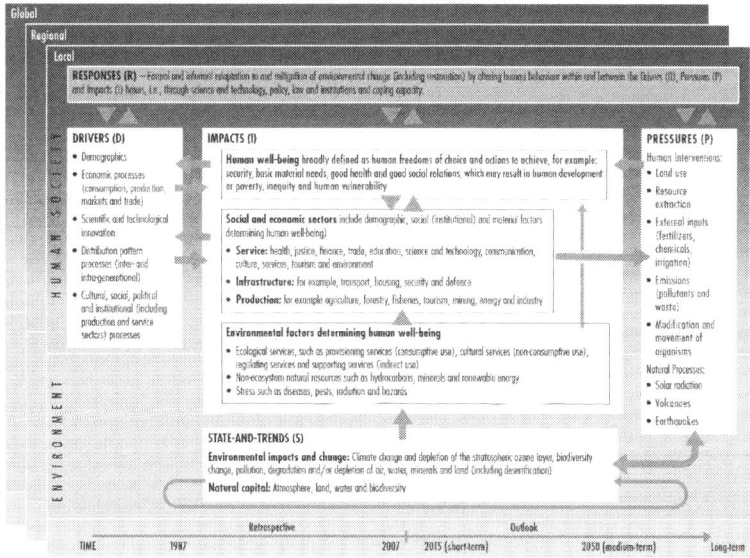

> Integrate local knowledge and modern science.

It is widely recognised that the separation of people and the environment is not so apparent in traditional cultures. Pilgrim and Pretty (2010) see a spectrum of the acceptance of our place in nature. At one end they see a dichotomous relationship, whereby people and the environment are separate and humans seek to assert dominance over nature. This separation is a by-product of industrialised thought shaped by a need to control and manage nature. At the other end of the spectrum, ecocultures see an "biological and cultural diversity as part of the same interconnected whole". Pilgrim and Pretty described this as an "acute sense of oneness".

The beliefs, cosmologies, practices and worldviews vary within indigenous traditions, as do the approaches to ecology, but there are common threads. One is the degree of intertwining of culture and nature- to the extent that a distinction between culture and nature can be somewhat arbitrary. Other common threads include:

- ritual practices and cosmologies with holistic approaches to ethical interaction
- subsistence practices with intimate knowledge of local conditions
- love of the land, often taking form of a feeling of kinship with the land. Described by E.O. Wilson as biophilia- the bond between people and other living systems.
- a recognition of an interconnected whole and a deep and abiding respect and reverence for the natural world... a belief in sacred nature (Robson and Berkes 2010)

Another thread is the ways in which knowledge, beliefs and practices are transmitted. Stories or narratives are important in what is referred to as Traditional Ecological Knowledge (TEK).

This Navajo Hooghan has been developed by Navajo Flexcrete, (also in O'Neill *et al.* 2009)

> *The Hooghan is highly symbolic of the Navajo's spiritual understanding of the interconnectedness of all things through all time. A visitor enters the Hooghan from the East, the direction in which the door of the Hooghan always faces. East is the direction of the sunrise, which begins the day and is symbolic of the beginning of life. The visitor moves clockwise through the four quadrants. The first quadrant belongs to the Mother, who represents work and wealth, which is passed through maternal inheritance. The Father and, when he visits, the Medicine Man, occupy the south-west quadrant. The Father ties the families and clans together through marriage. The Medicine Man is a vehicle for the fundamental beliefs and values of the Diné. The north-west quadrant is for the Children, whose basic needs must be taken care of by the Father and Mother. The north-east quadrant is where the visitor ends and where Visitors gather when in the Hooghan. The Navajo consider all of life to be integrated and sacred, thus the entire structure is the 'Spiritual' whole. The Hooghan thus embodies all of the aspects of life.*

Dickison (2009) points out that as a result of scientific enquiry a great many indigenous narratives are wrong. We need to accept not separate but equal but rather respect the different narratives. Berkes (2009) argues that we should recognise that all knowledge is partial and incomplete, what TEK offers is a knowledge process - ways of knowing - rather than the details of the knowledge. TEK is therefore important, even if, such as in the case of climate change, the scope is beyond the range of experience of the traditional group: they provide a voice of nature that might otherwise go unheard.

A *Sustainable Lens* needs to integrate both forms of knowledge capital (Stephenson and Moller 2009). Wehi (2009) argues that if humans are part of ecology, then sustainable decision making requires all possible sources of knowledge available.

co-evolved socioecological systems

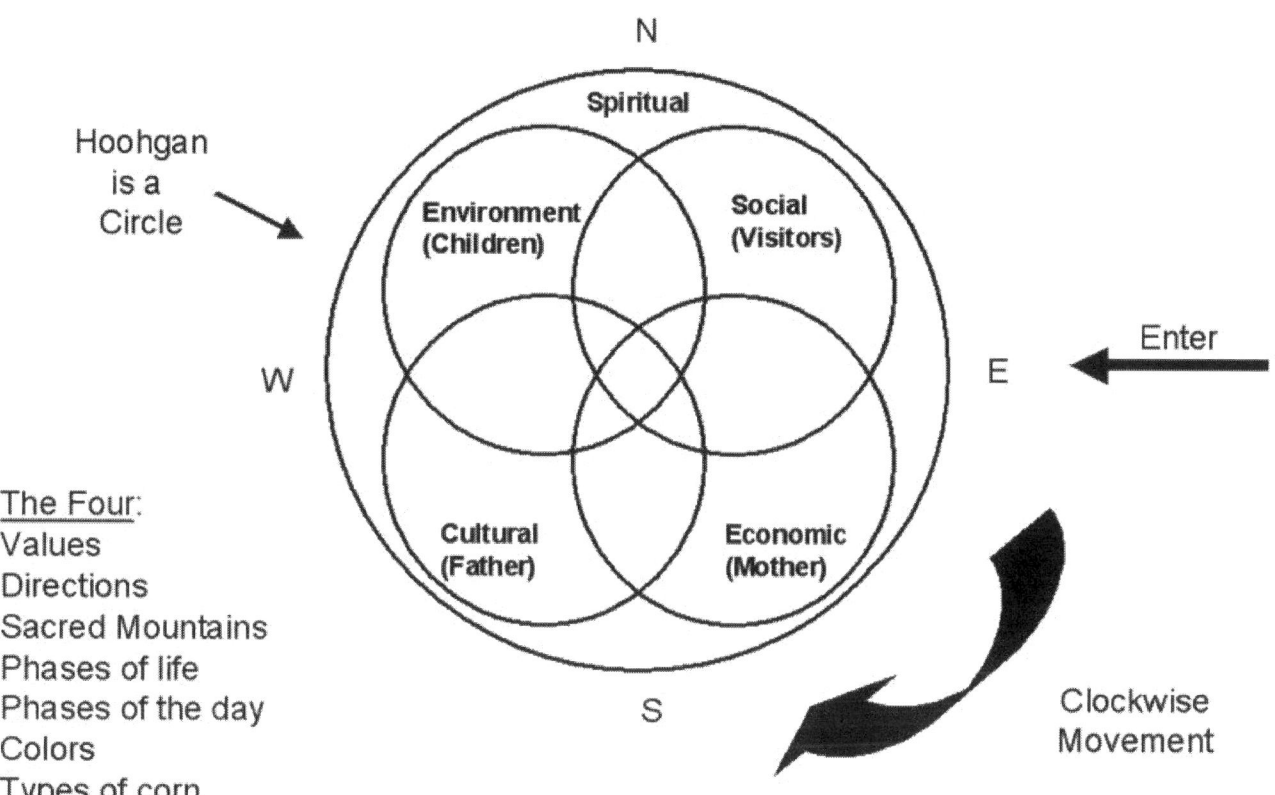

> A *Sustainable Lens* can be seen at multiple levels: a goal for an actual device or as or as a conception for an internal heads-up display. It is both a description for wider efforts in sustainable practice; and a plea to recognise that all practice needs to be considered as part of a sustainability ethic. It is a value statement - we need to care.

Goodwin (1994) refers to a "professional vision". He defines professional vision as "socially orgainsed ways of seeing and understanding events that are answerable to the distinctive interests of a particular social group". Thus any profession learns to see though discipline-specific practices. The *Sustainable Lens*, though, rather than being discipline specific, is by its very nature multi- and interdisciplinary. It requires specific knowledge from each profession but also crosses the professional boundaries.

As a way of seeing the world, the *Sustainable Lens* is in a long tradition. Blevis (2008) writes of a sustainability lens in human computer action (to the extent that he has spawned a new field: sustainable interaction design). Brown (2005) applies the integral framework to a number of areas. AtKisson (2008) describes several sustainability approaches that provide both insight and frameworks: Compass, ISIS and a pyramid. In some cases, sustainability might prompt a change in framework: Jalas' (2006) work on decoupling economic growth and resource use is a case in point. In all of these cases, the model - such as the integral framework - provides a framework for how we perceive the world.

These diagrams both attempt to position Sustainable Development in a context of scientific and political thought. **On the left, Milne et al. (2009, after Colby 1991) describe a graph with social change on the horizontal axis and a continuum of valuation of material wealth through to environment on the vertical axis.** The "dominant social paradigm" (DSP; technology and economic growth will save us) anchors the bottom right quadrant, while the New Environmental Paradigm (planetary demise is caused by humans so we should protect the environment) is in the upper left. A progression based on time, moves from the DSP to a compliance focussed environment as an externality compliance approach. Then it progresses through resource management to "Ecologise Economy". This transitional state is described by Milne as "the contested middle ground of sustainability".

On the right-hand image, Baudot (1993) also describes sustainability in terms of a middle ground. Here it is posed as a middle ground between zero growth policies - achieved by "authoritarian decree and coercion" - and "maximising material production". Interestingly, while this latter option results in environment that is used, abandoned, and destroyed, it is headed by "realm of economic and social reality".

What these diagrams miss though, is probably the most important dimension in sustainability - you have to care. In thinking about what a sustainable practitioner does in any given discipline, it is sometimes easy to focus on only one half of the impact of a discipline. Frequently people say things to me along the lines of "we've sorted the recycling" with the strong implication that "we're done", or at least "we can't think of anything else to do".

Acting as a sustainable practitioner, however, means addressing both reducing my footprint (reducing harm) and increasing my handprint (actions towards sustainability). There are similar terms: McDonough *et al.* (2003) describe "doing more, not just less", while Senge *et al.* described "regenerative sustainability" (2008). This argument of a dual responsibility is not new: it is strongly rooted in the principles of non-malfeasance and beneficence (e.g. in Medical Ethics).

Here our interest is on the reflexivity – in the self reflection aided by a *Sustainable Lens*. Why would we want someone to do that? The answer is simple, we want them to care. "First you have to care" argues AtKisson (2008) as the first step towards sustainability. We need to "embed sustainability itself as a core cultural value of the system".

the opportunity

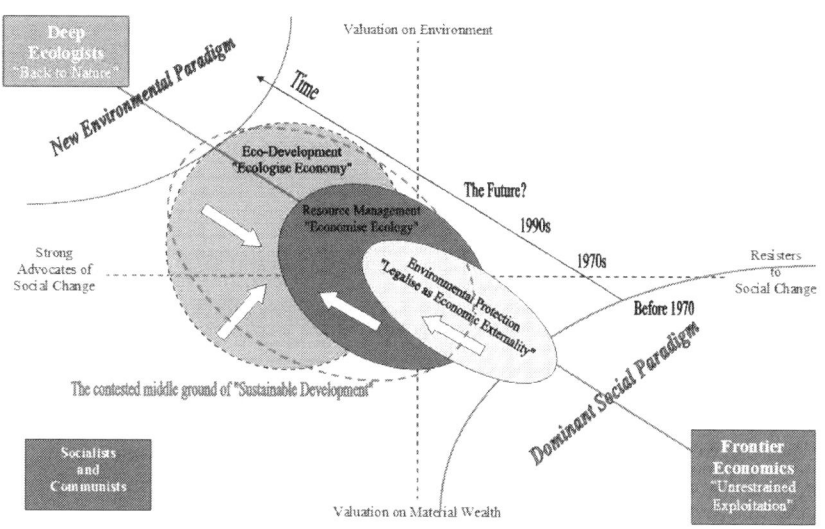

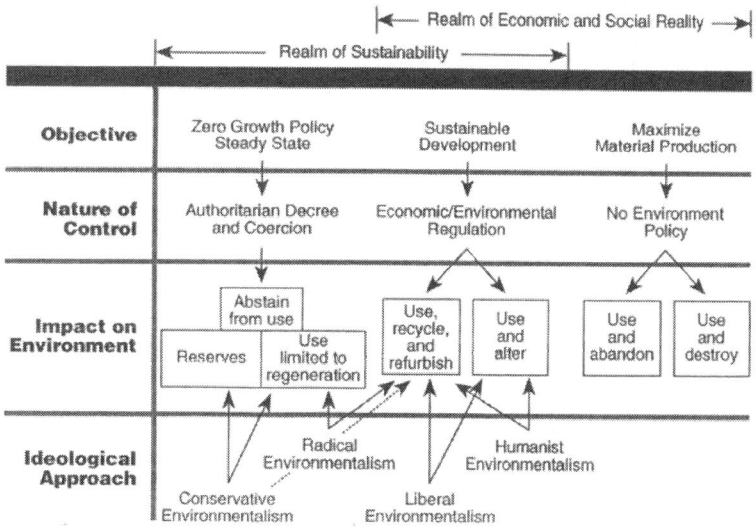

> If sustainability is considered ethics extended in space and time, what does this extension do to our models of ethical behaviour?

Unfortunately, once you get beyond obvious resource consumption, there's not a simple set of ethical rules for sustainability. Fortunately, we can get some of the way by considering ethics between people. Levinas argued that we are defined by our relationships with others. In sustainability terms, Fagan (2009) argues that:

> To live a particular lifestyle that, knowingly, impacts detrimentally on a neighbour – be that an individual living in the next house – or a country in the next Region, cannot, arguably, be tolerated. To know of poverty in the economically developing world and not use that knowledge to act to relieve it, could be considered unethical.

Bosselman widened the concept of the "other" to include the environment around us. The implication is that social justice ethics can be expanded into the environment. It is sometimes said that sustainability is ethics over time and space. **So let's expand ethics to the wider "other", and across time and space. The "Trolley problem", first described by Phillipa Foot (1967, in 1978) and explored by Thomson and Parent (1986) is a useful model (our expanded image shown):**

> A trolley is running out of control down a track. In its path are five people who have been tied to the track by a mad philosopher. Fortunately, you could flip a switch, which will lead the trolley down a different track to safety. Unfortunately, there is a single person tied to that track. Should you flip the switch or do nothing?

Clearly a utilitarian view would be to flip the switch, although this then involves you in the action (and perhaps a degree of culpability). There have been numerous variations on the Trolley problem. The "Fat man", for instance, describes pushing a (very) fat man in front of the trolley to stop it. Most people would find this less acceptable (yet most they can't explain why). Another variation describes a surgeon – would you harvest organs from an otherwise healthy person to save five others? usually even less acceptable. Other variations pose loops in the track; relatives on the track; railway workers versus children, and so on.

The point is that while there has been much exploration of such dilemmas in human morality, health etc (Foot originally posed the Trolley in a discussion on ethics of abortion), they have been little applied to sustainability:

- what if the 5 people live in Cambodia?
- what if it isn't a single trolley, but lots of little ones? (but with the same cumulative effect).
- what if instead of a single person, it is a forest (which the trolley will destroy), on which five people are completely dependent for survival? (what if that was 5000?)
- what if the 5 haven't been born yet? (not sure why, some freaky space-time trolley accident)
- what if the forest contains the last two remaining orangutan?
- what if the forest contains a the last of a really ugly mould, but one that locals believe has curative powers?

While these are hypothetical questions, we need to continue to explore the application of our unconscious moral grammar as applied to sustainability. We don't have good shorthand for this stuff. Peter Singer perhaps comes closest in *Famine, Affluence and Morality and The Life You Can Save (2009)*. In the latter, Singer poses a thought experiment involving a train, a child and an expensive car. The twist is that saving the car then selling it could save a great many children.

A Sustainable Lens would need to facilitate the expansion of ethics in space and time.

are there rules of sustainability?

> This node and relation diagram provides a way of seeing the complexity of global systems: change one thing and follow the links to explore the effects.

A necessary component of the *Sustainable Lens* is resource visualisation - we need to see the "smoke" representing the impact of our consumption - making the invisible visible. This though, is just the beginning. It is our contention that much of this work falls short of adequately recognising the complexity of sustainability – in oversimplifying the issues and the responses. Acting sustainably is not a (relatively) simple matter of changing ones driving habits or reducing home electricity consumption.

Sustainability is as complex as life itself. As in life we can use a macro lens and focus on a single aspect - a flower, or rescuing an individual penguin - but it is seeing the connections that defines sustainable seeing. Connected to that individual element are a myriad of other elements from a myriad of dimensions and perspectives. That penguin is affected by influences across physical, social, economic, cultural, and ethical spheres. Each of these influences will interact with each other and change over time and space.

One way of seeing sustainability is as the maintenance of a set of relationships between systems: "if mismanaged (eg exceeding certain tolerances) the ecological as well as social and economic systems may lose their ability for self-regulation and break down. Consequently, as a result of positive (ie destabilising) feedback mechanisms the other systems will also break down". Isaksson and Steimle (2008,9) explore these relationships between the main stakeholders - humanity and nature with a node-relation diagram (opposite).

Isaksson and Steimle's diagram shows "different important problems", including the five factors from *Limits to Growth* but with the addition of global heating. The factors are related by arrows with double dotted lines indicating "important reinforcing loops".

It is then possible to follow the influence of changes in one factor. Looking only at the elements in the lower right: increased wealth and consumerism drives increased industrial production (indeed this is a reinforcing loop). This industrialisation drives resource sarcity which drives conflicts which drives poverty. The industrialisation drives CO_2 and pollution which drives global heating, which combines with industrialisation to drive loss of biodiversity.

This image demonstrate a key element of a diagrammatic approach: it shows the relations between information in a way that can be experimented upon. The viewer can explore and ask questions: "what would be the things we have to change to reduce poverty?".

This diagram, though, lacks any precision. The circles are "important global factors" but are not consistently named ("biofuels" for example does not have an adverb). It is not clear why some factors have heavier lines. Nor does the diagram indicate the nature nor quantum of the relationships. This though, is not the point, as Isaksson and Steimle argue "the intention is to present approximate relations based on commonly known facts... There are probably important things missing and some of the relations could be disputed but still the relations show how humanity and nature could be affected by different activities". This is sufficient for their needs - in this case to help corporations retain a big picture view when describing their role in sustainable development.

A Sustainable Lens is interdisciplinary, systemic and holistic. Unfortunately this is not as simple as changing lens to a wide angle and seeing a bigger picture. Seeing sustainability is about seeing complexity. We need to see the connections.

need to see the complexity

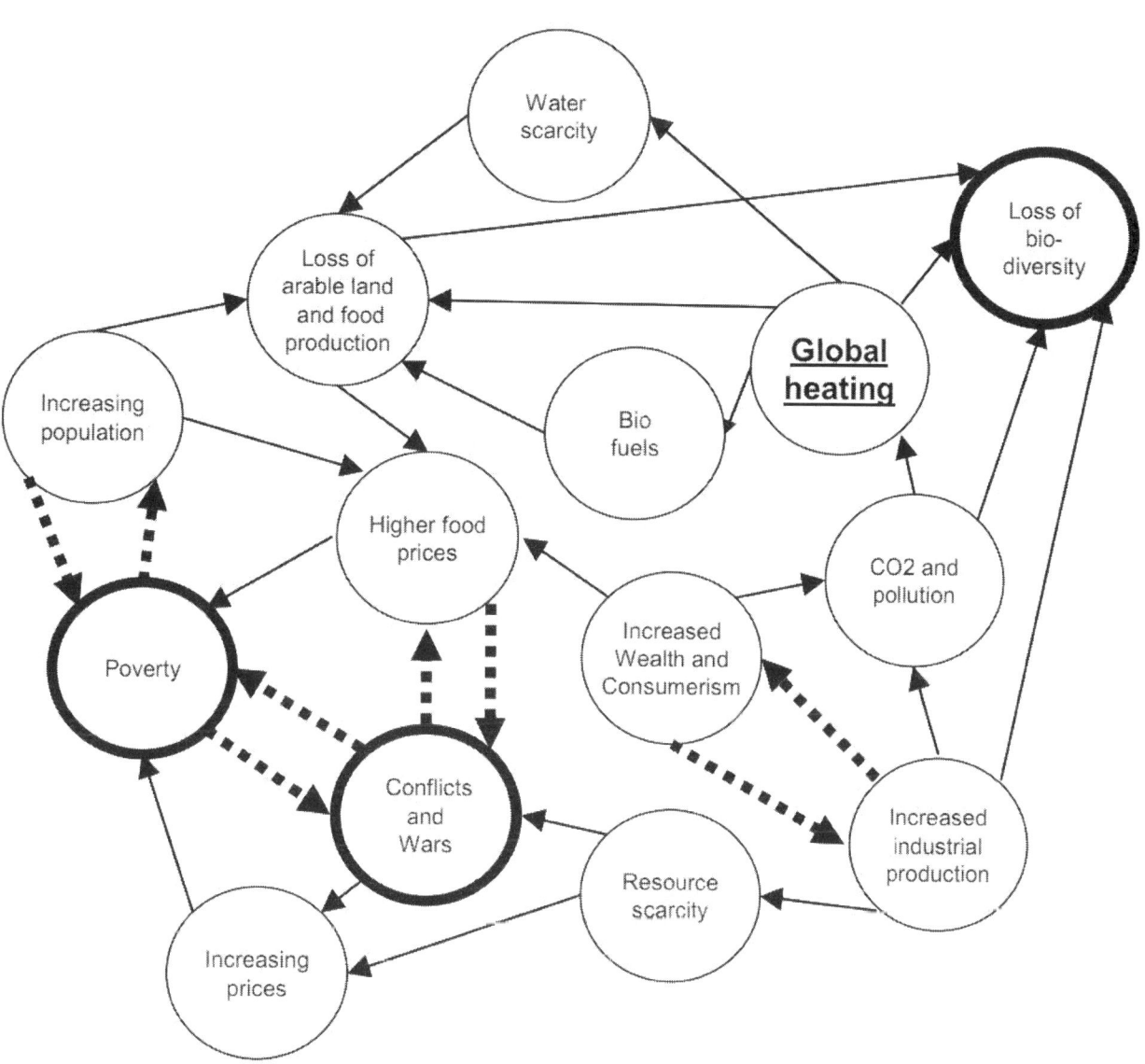

> The diagram opposite provides a pattern that can be used to explore sustainability (derived from a table in NRC 1999). **This sentence construction model can be used to produce your own version of sustainability based upon what is to be sustained; what is to be developed; the types of links that should hold between the entities to be sustained and the entities to be developed; and the extent of the future envisioned.**

Sustainability involves complexity, uncertainty, multiple stakeholders and perspectives, competing values, lack of end points and ambiguous terminology. It means dealing with a mess that is different from the problems for which our current tools and disciplines were designed - indeed it could be argued that they caused it. Unique decision situations that cannot be easily reversed, for which there are contradictory certitudes, without a clear set of alternative solutions These persistent and insoluble problems have redistributive implications for entrenched interests.

The sustainability journey is described as a "wicked problem" (Morris & Martin, 2009) and a "messy problem" (Wagner 1995). This has three implications:

1. the ambiguity of sustainability as a concept

2. the difficulty of specifying in detail sustainability problems.

3. the difficulty of specifying in detail sustainability solutions

Together these issues can form barriers for people whose paradigm is 'if you can't measure it you can't manage it'.

Sterling (2004) argued that sustainability, rather than a measurable outcome, is an emergent quality arising from sets of relationships in a system, whether viewed at the macro or micro scale. In this way it is rather like justice or health as Holmberg and Samuelsson (2006) argued. Despite all the attempts to make the concept more operational, "it is clear that it cannot be exactly defined".

> *Sustainability can be compared with the concept of health – as health cannot be defined in precise terms either, and yet, everyone has an idea about what health is and health is important for everyone. When we meet each other we often ask: how are you? Sustainable Development can be seen as the health of societies and the planet. If we are concerned about the present development and whether it is sustainable we instead ask each other: how are we?*

Lowes and Walker (1995) report that "natural resource managers are frequently faced with novel problems". However, Fedra and Reitsma (1990) pointed out that this is a class of problem that is not so unique that a one-shot effort would be justified, nor does it "occur frequently enough with sufficient similarity to subject themselves to rigid mathematical treatment".

In *The Timeless Way of Building and A pattern language: towns, buildings, construction* Christopher Alexander (and others, 1979) developed a pattern approach for architecture and urban form. Each pattern describes a problem and offers a solution. Together these patterns form a language with each pattern forming a word or thought of a true language rather than being a prescriptive way to design or solve a problem.

Somewhere between treating everything as a novel problem and treating everything with a stamped out solution, the *Sustainable Lens* needs patterns or frameworks to support the complexity of decision making required for a sustainable future.

but they're messy problems

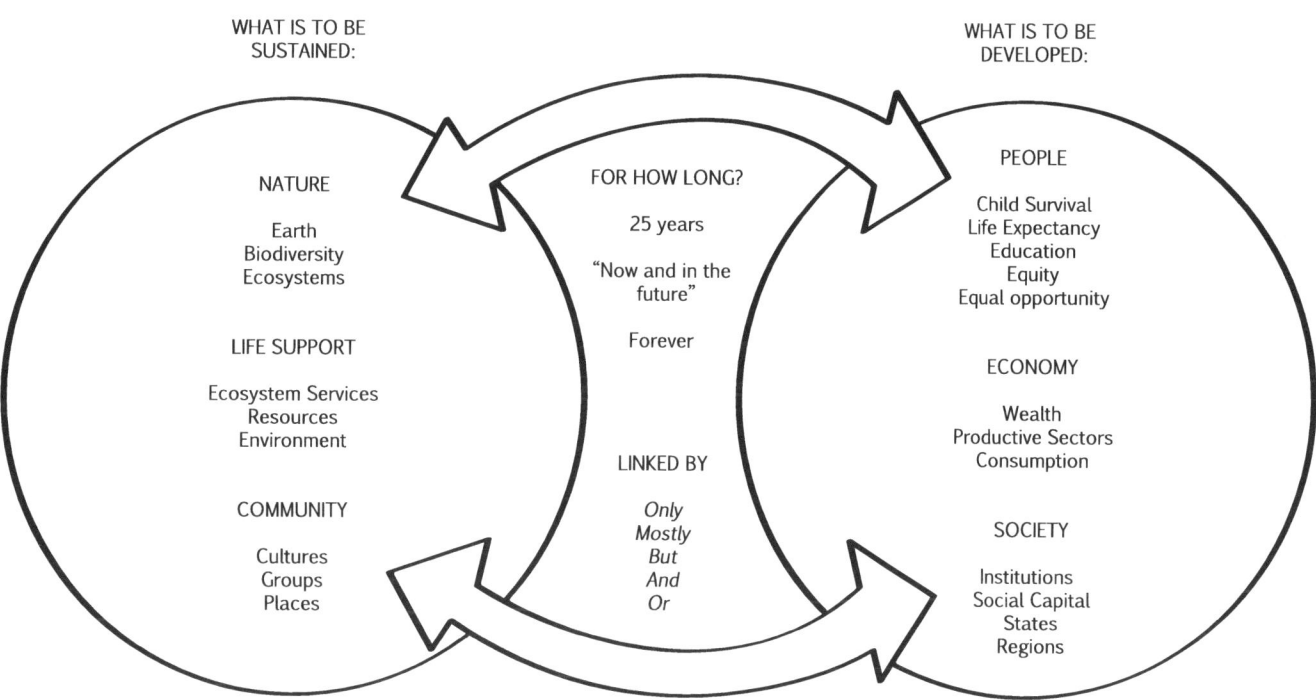

> Integral ecology provides a framework for integrating multiple approaches into a complex, multidimensional metadisciplinary approach to the natural world and our embeddedness within it.

Integral Ecology applies Wilber's integral theory to environmental thinking. Ken Wilber described a holon (1996). This is based on the dual nature of the entity or concept whereby a thing is a whole unto itself AND a part of some other whole. This duality leads to four quadrants based on the thing (x axis: whole, part of bigger) and the view of the thing (interior, exterior). Note that a holon is not a quadrant, nor does a quadrant contain a holon - the quadrants are perspectives shared by all holons.

Psychological or intentional quadrant (Upper Left): characterised by "I". The interior perspective of individual holons, which is the realm of individual mindsets, the self, consciousness, personal experiences, and values

Cultural quadrant (Lower Left) "We/you": the interior perspective of collective holons, which is the realm of shared values and visions, culture, worldview, and discourse.

Behavioral quadrant (Upper Right) "It/him/her": an exterior perspective on individual holons, revealing the structure and actions of organisms (e.g. humans)

Systems quadrant (Lower Right) "its/them": an exterior perspective on collective holons, revealing the shared structures and actions of groups and systems (e.g. technological, economic, institutional and ecological systems).

Wilber conceptualises an "All Quadrants All Levels" model of the holon (this version after Kira and van Eijnatten 2008) which carries several dimensions. The four quadrants form in the areas bounded by the axes of subjective/objective and relational/agentic identities. The distances on the diagonals relate to levels of development or functional capabilities, giving rise to a concentric circle pattern of "overall sustainability level". The line within the lower right quadrant, for example, relates to stage of social development: traditional (environment closely linked to people directly cared about); modern (technical, rational); post-modern (community partnerships); to integral (all truths partially right, aligned with deep motivations of each stakeholder, sum greater than parts).

The two right-hand quadrants provide the objective and interobjective perspectives. The objective is examined through composition and exterior behaviour, the interobjective through study of systemic structures and behaviours of collectives. This is considered useful, but lack the motivation for action. With just these two, the world becomes "flatland" where "industrialised objective approach "colonises and dominates the interiors" (Wilber). This right-hand is shown in the legend as "complexity in actions", while the left is "complexity in awareness".

Esbjörn-Hargens (2005) applied integral theory for the multidisciplinary interrogation of ecological problems. They argued that "anything less than a worldcentric capacity of holding multiple perspectives will cripple viable solutions to environmental degradation...the solutions to our environmental crisis are largely to be found in our increasing capacity to see through and beyond our ideological, class, cultural, racial, and gender differences".

> *Integral Ecology draws on the expertise of many disciplines and is able to offer extremely comprehensive, far-sighted, and flexible solutions, for the environment - solutions that can carry us into the right relationship, at multiple scales with the earth.*

Crucially, Integral Ecology is not a singular view, rather the focus is on the cultivation of mutual understanding between perspectives. This framework provides a *Sustainable Lens* an intelligent basis for discovering what questions need to be posed and how to formulate them most effectively.

integral ecology

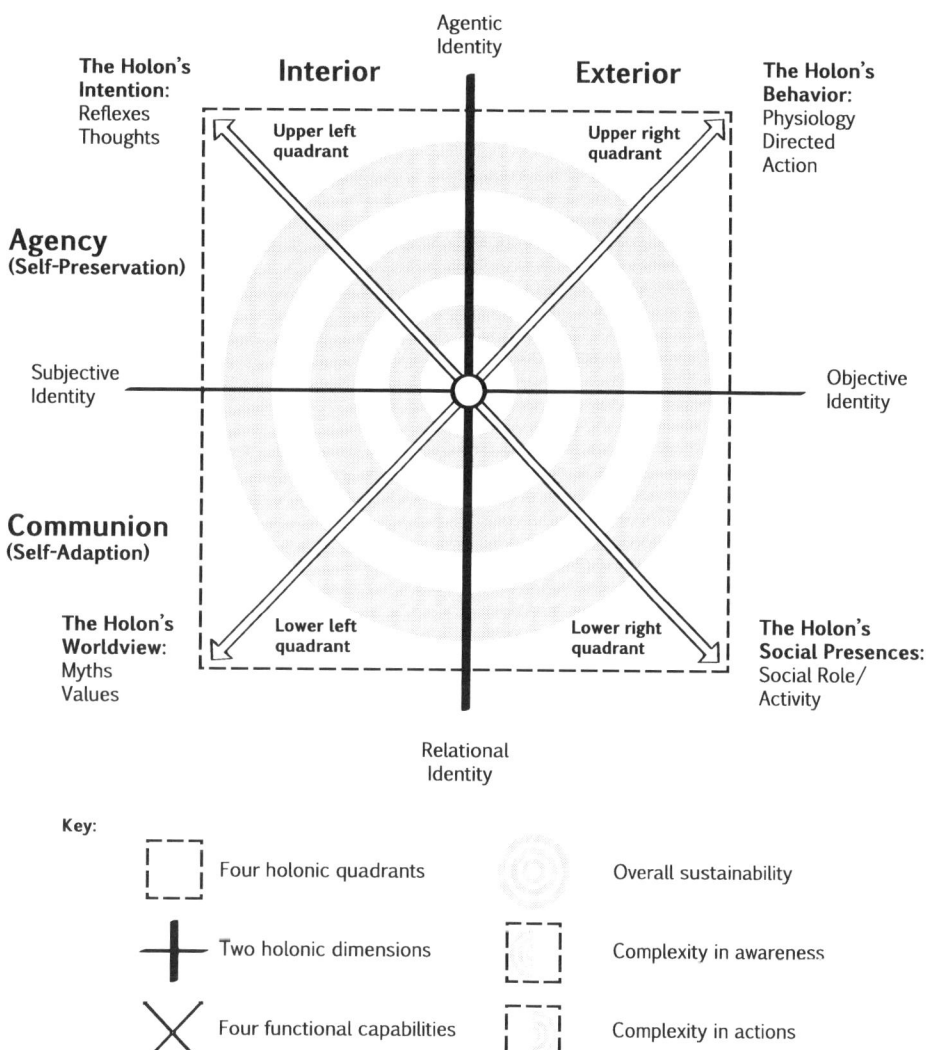

> Abstract models of sustainability operate in a dimensionless void. Sustainability though needs to explicitly consider the effects of drivers and impacts across multiple dimensions.

Herman Daly contrasts a standard (growth) economy with a steady state economy in the two upper images opposite. The growth diagram assumes the possibility of ever growing cycles of production and consumption without considering the role of the supporting ecosystem, thus establishing the belief that there are no biophysical limits to growth of the economy. By comparison, the Steady State Economy diagram (top right) represents stabilised population and consumption. Resource throughput and waste disposal remain roughly constant, the scale of economic activities fits within the capacity provided by ecosystems, there is fair distribution of wealth, and allocation of resources is efficient.

The steady state model would have to be seen to underpin a sustainable future. This, though, is not why we've put these models on this page. They are included because of what they don't show: any dimensions. In the top left image we can infer that the radius (and thus both x and y dimensions) represents the size of the economy - this increases in a production-consumption spiral. We can then translate the economic dimension to the right-hand image - the economy is bounded by the ecosystem and flows occur within this limit. This representation of the economy is unidimensional and highly abstract.

Sustainability, on the other hand is multidimensional. Sustainability can be thought of as ethics extended in time and space. We can consider impacts and drivers across scales and thresholds This means we need ways of thinking sustainably in multiple dimensions, and hence seeing these multiple dimensions.

Unfortunately, we are not very good at this multidimensional thought. The lower figure is from Edwin Abbot's 1884 book Flatland – "A romance in many directions". In the two dimensional world occupied by geometric figures who slide about, the society is based on rank according to the number of sides of a polygon (triangles, squares, hexagons, up to priestly circles; Women are straight line segments so are pointedly dangerous when coming towards you!).

The narrator – a square – dreams about visiting single dimensional Lineland. He is unable to convince the monarch – a point – of the possibility of the extra dimension. The square is then visited by a sphere – a three dimensional object like us, from Spaceland. The sphere is able to convince the square of the possibilities of the 3D space. Square gets excited by the possibilities of yet more dimensions but Sphere can't, and neither does anyone else when he returns to Flatland and he is thrown into gaol for his evangelical proclamation of the Gospel of Three Dimensions.

So, here's the question: What could we learn by thinking about the *Sustainable Lens* as seeing extra-dimensions? What would those extra dimensions be? And how might we see them? And how do we avoid being evangelical when those around us cannot comprehend those dimensions? First, what might be the extra dimensions?

sustainability is multidimensional

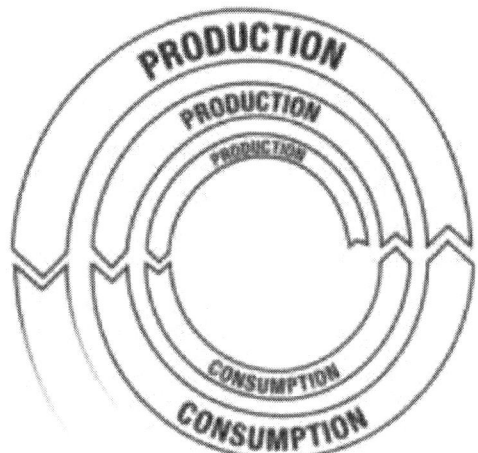

Standard (Growth) Economy diagram

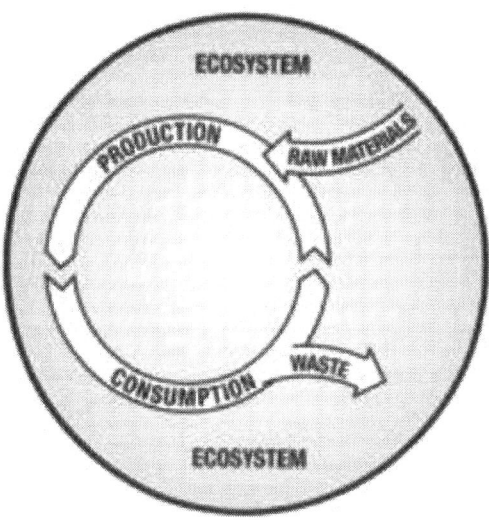

Steady State Economy diagram

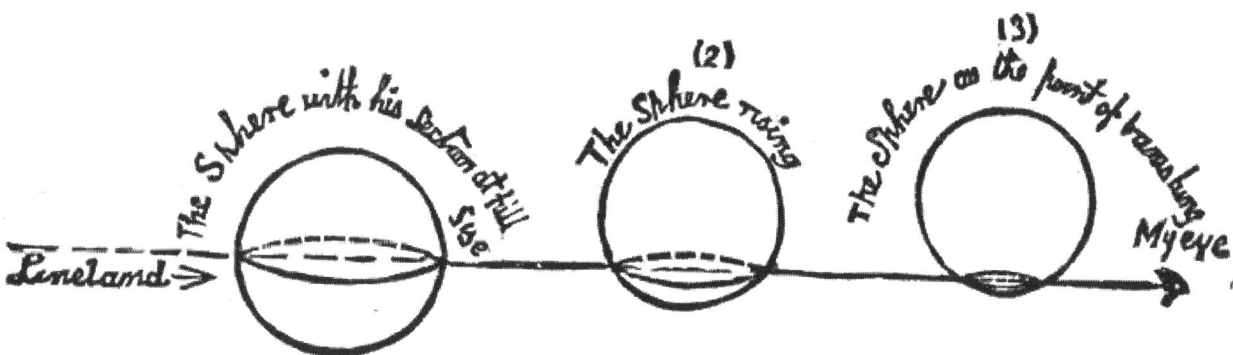

> The *Sustainable Lens* needs to see (and think) across scales and thresholds in time, space, systems, culture and information.

In the first season of the *Twilight Zone*, the narrator Rod Serling described the fifth dimension as imagination:

> *There is a fifth dimension beyond that which is known to man ... a dimension as vast as space and as timeless as infinity. It is the middle ground between light and shadow, between science and superstition, and it lies between the pit of man's fears and the summit of his knowledge. This is the dimension of imagination.*

His quote finishes with "It is an area which we call The Twilight Zone". Maybe it is also what we hope to see with a *Sustainable Lens*.

Space already forms our three dimensions. Seeing across scales though is perhaps something else. How do we see the cumulative impact of hundreds or thousands of decisions? How do we see the impact of our purchasing decisions on a village on the other side of the world? Here we discuss time, space, systems and uncertainty as dimensions for the *Sustainable Lens*.

Time is already considered the 4th dimension (as spacetime rather than something to travel in a time-travel way). We need the *Sustainable Lens* to represent past decisions, cumulative actions, alternative futures. This needs to happen at time scales more in line with the Long Now Foundation (which news stories from today will still matter in a year; ten years; 100 years; 10,000 years?). They also need to based in the present so I can actually do things.

Rather than just the surfaces, we need to see systems that make up the objects around us. This is not just an x-ray of hidden operations, we need to expose complete life-cycle and supply-chain impacts. Bonanni's open supply chain maps (2010) hint at the complexity of this dimension.

Rather than uncertainty being a matter of error of representation for the other dimensions, and Taking Vitek and Jackson's (2008) call for an ignorance based worldview I think that humility is a dimension itself.

For each of these dimensions, the primary instruction is to think bigger. **Meredith's (2000) exploration of approaches for assessing impact (four images on left) sees an evolution in environmental decision-making** whereby more time is considered (Cumulative impact assessment) more space (Regional impact assessment) or more systemic depth (Strategic Environmental Assessment). With each increase, the task (shown by the box) gets bigger. Sustainable development requires ongoing, integrated and systemically complex analyses, and the task is both large and complex.

Martens (2006) similarly argues that sustainability is larger scale in terms of time, space and areas of knowledge (right). He contrasts this with short-term goals and simple or cheap means of achieving them.

> *To facilitate decision making, sustainability scientists must assist in the task of making concrete both problems and solutions on all relevant temporal and spatial scales. This means that sustainability at the systemic level must be assessed, bringing to bear the following procedural elements: analysis of deeper-lying structures of the system, projection into the future, and assessment of sustainable and unsustainable trends. Evaluation of the effects of sustainable policy and the design of possible solutions through sustainable strategies also belong here.*

In short, the *Sustainable Lens* needs to see the bigger picture.

what are the dimensions?

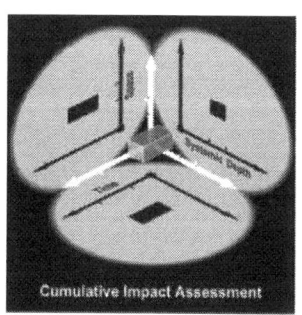
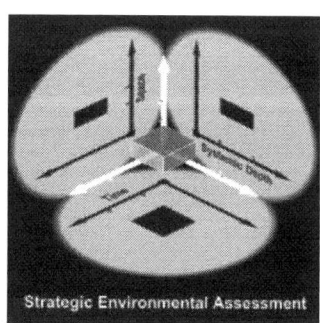
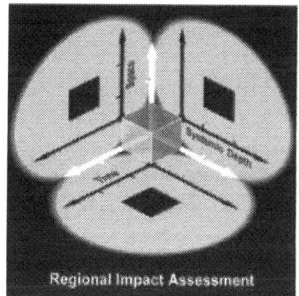
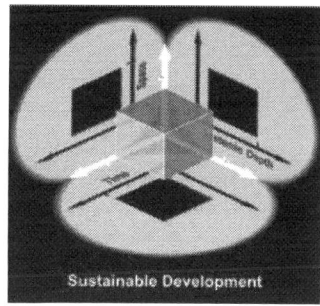
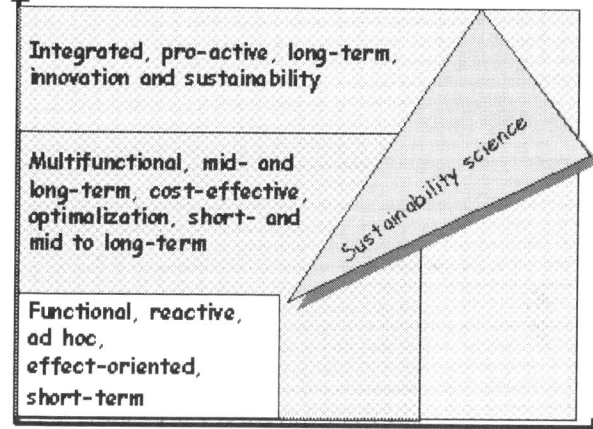

> What happens when you go up (or down) a scale? We get variations, thresholds, hierarchies and emergent properties.

The image opposite returns us to a pillars model of sustainability, but its purpose here is to introduce the interaction of the a systems approach with a spatial hierarchy. **The diagram from Vugteveen *et al.* (2006) represents river system health as an interaction of ecological, economic and social health systems, each with its own sub-systems and all in the context of an interaction with a larger scale (the surrounding landscape).**

Hutchinson (1965) described an 'ecological theatre', to which Wiens (1989) added that "to understand the drama we must view it at an appropriate scale". Choosing the appropriate scale may be difficult because as Hutchinson pointed out, the environment should be considered "a hypervolume in hyperspace". We need our *Sustainable Lens* to be able to see along hierarchical lines with a continuum of scales in time and space.

Sustainability can be considered at many scales: from analysis of points in a farmer's field to global change models. It may be thought, then, that technologies such as Geographic Information System would be well suited to the task of examining the patterns (and thus the processes) involved. With little effort a pattern can be examined at 1:5000 then zoomed out to examine the same features at 1:250,000. This may work well for facilities' management, as in examining the shape of a road or the distribution of electricity transformers, and can lead to interesting technical issues such as line generalisation (Jones and Abraham 1986), but may not be appropriate in environmental management. One approach to scaling in the ecological sciences is through application of hierarchy theory (O'Neill 1988; Rastetter *et al.* 1992, Naveh and Lieberman 1994) and it has at least two major consequences for us.

By considering complexity in terms of hierarchical systems, where subsystems are nested in time and space within larger systems, the overall situation can be made clearer (Bailey 1985). Hierarchy theory holds that below the scale of interest there is noise (or alternatively explanation) and above that threshold, the constraints within which the processes of interest operate. At each level, new processes emerge that were not present or evident previously. Hence, properties from one level are not the same at the next. Further, to predict the effects of management at one scale, then the processes in each of the larger and smaller scales should be examined. The main impact is that simply by zooming in and out, one will discern essentially the same information from further away, but this is not sufficient to meet the ecological criteria of scaling (Levin 1992).

Seeing bigger through a *Sustainable Lens* is not just a matter of standing further away, when scaling is introduced, it brings with it thresholds, hierarchies and properties that only emerge at different scales.

scaling effects

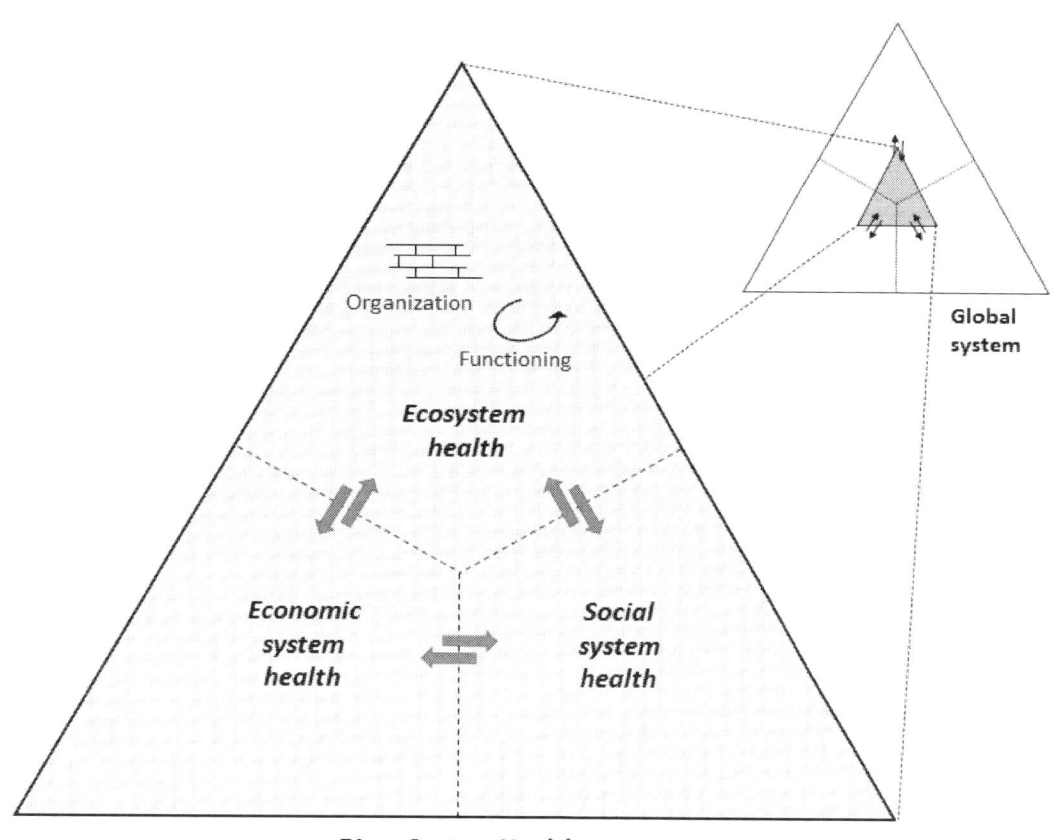

> Feibleman (1954) argued that "for an organization at any given level, its mechanism lies at the level below and its purpose at the level above" (in Bergandi 2000). In other words, to analyse a given level, a study of at least three levels of integration is required

An implication of hierarchy theory is that measurements at one level are usually difficult to apply to another and to do so requires some form of processing. Some measurements are relevant at different scales, which O'Neill (1988 p 38) called "interactive state variables", -- for example nutrient balance equations (Smaling and Fresco 1993) -- but most environmental parameters are not such variables.

Scaling in any dimension is more than a zoom function. As scale increases (larger area, longer time) we would expect the complexity of a system to increase. We would expect processes to be slower over large scales. While change at a large scale has a immediate impact on lower scales, it takes accumulation for effects to rise and then the emergent properties that happen over the larger scale are usually different from a simple additive effect of things on the smaller scale. These emergent properties are usually more significant than might be expected from a simple additive function.

We can borrow from Landscape Ecology which studies the interaction between spatial and temporal pattern and ecological process (Naveh 2000). Landscape Ecology has an emphasis on the relationship among pattern, process and scale and its focus on broad-scale ecological and environmental issues. Key to this coupling between biophysical and socioeconomic sciences is the concept of the hierarchy. A landscape might be considered to be made up of patches which at different levels might consist of drainage basins, local ecosystems, populations, communities, species and individual trees (which might be an entire ecosystem for smaller species). Crucially for us, the scale is not just looking from closer or further away, rather as the patch of interest gets bigger or longer, its characteristics change. A landscape has critical thresholds at which ecological processes will show dramatic changes, and these have effects across scales. The large scale patterns we see might be the result the integration of changes at many different scales.

Feibleman (1954) argued that "for an organization at any given level, its mechanism lies at the level below and its purpose at the level above" (in Bergandi 2000). In other words, to analyse a given level, a study of at least three levels of integration is required. If, for example, the subject is an ecological system such as a community, it is necessary to consider simultaneously not only the population level, but also the ecosystem level.

Gasto et al. (2009) described the core problem of sustainability as not respecting the highest hierarchical levels, of exceeding their limits of universal lawfulness (top). A good decision must be sound in each and all of the hierarchical levels. The should be a relationship between the dimensions of the problem and the human actions taken (bottom).

The implication for the *Sustainable Lens* is that it is necessary to consider all the levels simultaneously. And not just spatial scale. The same applies to temporal, systemic and so on.

emergence in space

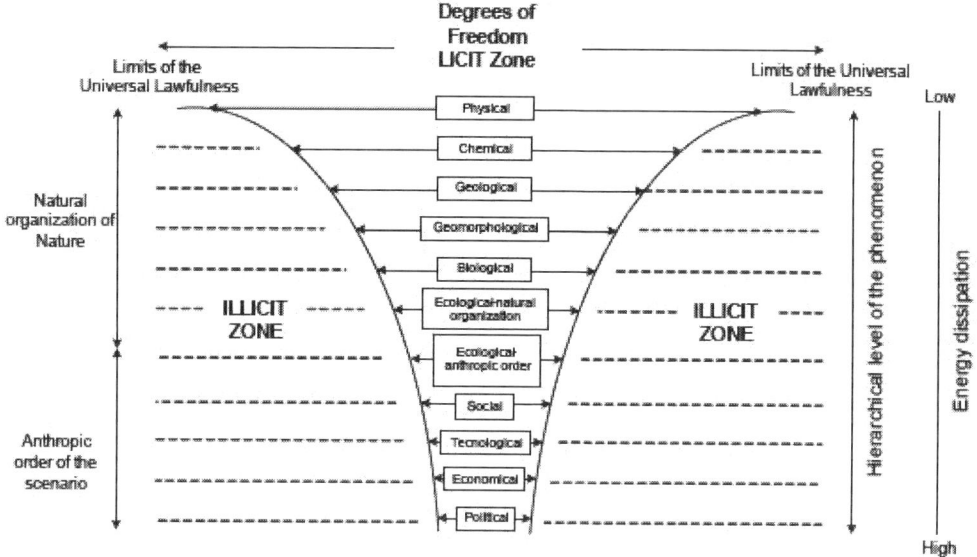

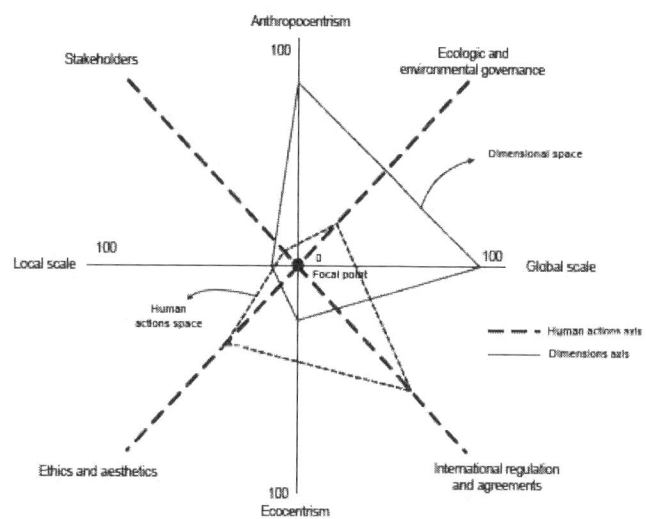

> Scaling over time raises two important issues: cumulative change and a requirement to consider variation in a timeframe.

Time is fundamental to sustainability. The Brundtland definition has sustainable development meeting the needs of the *present* without compromising the ability of *future* generations to meet their own needs.

Despite this, time is not explicitly considered in most considerations of sustainability. Until this chapter, time is missing from almost all the diagrams so far in this book (notable exceptions being Hubbert's peak oil, the output from the *Limits to Growth* model, and Marten's larger scale).

Seghezzo (2009) argues that the temporal dimension is neglected because of the inclusion of the economic in the pillars, they are: "rooted in the belief that nature and culture are a dichotomy that can only be reconciled by the economy". Using the economy as the integrating element brings a basis in visible and tangible assets - of which time does not fit. In my experience, it is to the environmental that people ascribe the temporal dimension as in "we're protecting the environment for future generations", but this is usually seen in opposition to the economics - see earlier discussion on balance.

Others have different interpretations of the various terms. Adomssent *et al.* (2007), for example see sustainable development from a holistic perspective, it can be understood simultaneously as a concept, a goal and as a process or strategy. The concept speaks to the reconciliation of social justice, ecological integrity, and the well-being of all living systems on the planet. The goal is to create an ecologically and socially just world within the means of nature without compromising future generations. Sustainability refers to the process or strategy of moving toward a sustainable future.

The role of time is well explored by Barbara Adam (1998). She proposed to pay more attention to 'timescapes', the temporal dimension of our environmental problems, in order to improve our understanding of their nature and impact.

The first challenge is that with cumulative change, the actions and consequences separated by time. Much environmental change stems from a multiplicity of small, independent decisions made by numerous individuals. Each decision may result in an increment of environmental change that is individually insignificant but, repeated over time and dispersed over space, may accumulate and lead to significant environmental change (Spaling and Smit 1993). Thus small effects at one level have to be considered for their impacts elsewhere.

Lee (1993 p 562) argued that strategies for alleviating the "mismatch between biological time and human time remain underdeveloped". Part of any visual representation should be of process operating at the appropriate 'speed'.

This raises the question of what is the appropriate speed for sustainability? Or in other words, how long does something have to be to be sustainable? The Long Now Foundation hopes to creatively foster responsibility in the framework of the next 10,000 years. To emphasise this horizon, the group writes years using five digits instead of four: 02011 instead of 2011.

The Life Diagram comes from the Jennifer Ranville's Human Life Project. Participants of all ages are encouraged to prepare a life diagram to explore the most significant days and events of their life. With whole families participating an awareness develops of different perspectives, especially the role of the family in mediating the transience yet permanence of events in time.

The *Sustainable Lens* then, is *about* time, and *of* time. In order for us to see sustainably, we need to see time.

sands of time

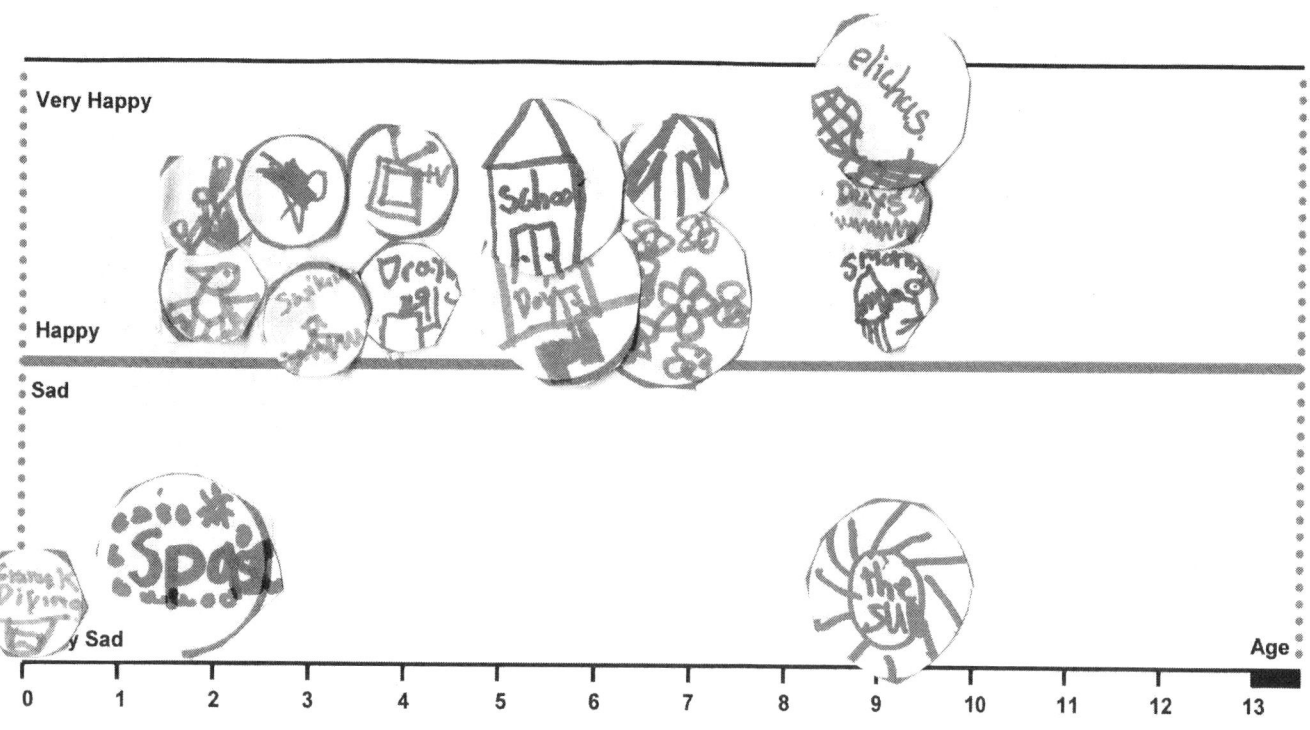

> Attempts to value the future result in a commodified time, that exists only as a means to profit from today.

The image opposite is from an Australian Treasury 2010 report on inter-generational challenges "Australia 2050". They argue that the country should aim to not just maintain the current level of wellbeing for future generations, but to improve the wellbeing of current and future generations. Both wellbeing and sustainability are considered as multi-dimensional concepts that go beyond material living standards - in this case the "prism of the stocks" of resources (essentially pillars).

The current state of each resource can be considered the stock - a multitude of interrelated tangible and intangible elements. The stock of resources inherited by a generation influences the set of capabilities available to them. The choices made by a generation will dictate the quantity and quality of the stock of resources available, or 'bequeathed', to future generations. In some instances, choices made by a generation that increase their wellbeing will necessarily expend a particular component of the stock of resources. For example, the consumption of non-renewable resources by one generation will reduce the quantity of non-renewable resources bequeathed to subsequent generations. In other instances, the choices made by a generation that result in an increase in their level of wellbeing may also result in an increase in the endowment of resources bequeathed to future generations. Human capital, such as education, is one example. Note that this is considered weak sustainability, a "strong sustainability" model does not allow transfer of natural capital to man-made capital in this way.

The sociologist Barbara Adam (1998, 2000, 2006) has written extensively on time:

> *Change rather than stability is the order of the day. In this dynamic world of mobility of everything, standing still means falling behind. This committed pursuit of novelty distinguishes the contemporary mode of being, so aspired across the world, from other socio-economic systems in which the creation of permanence and stability was and is the desired goal, where products were and are crafted to last*

The power to affect the future turned out to be far greater than the capacity to imagine and know it. Our economic, scientific and political structures lack the mechanisms to appropriately consider the future - except as a means of profiting from it in the present. Rather than being embedded and embodied, the future is emptied of content and divorced from context "the future is commodified". And once commodified, the abstract future can be exploited. And being empty and mixed with a quest for speed, a frontier spirit of exploitation takes hold. And as communication becomes instantaneous, "information loses its location: it is both nowhere and everywhere", the place becomes separated from space. Decisions are made with no thought to context or impact, we are "blindfolded at the controls". Unfortunately traditional ethics has not helped much:

> *Traditional ethics were consequently concentrated on actions of immediate reach and close proximity in time and space. The long-term future, in contrast, belonged to the non-human sphere of fate and chance, providence and destiny. It was out of human reach and thus beyond ethical concern.*

As we move beyond the city walls our influence is expanded not just to next of kin but to "unlimited realms of beings and organisms unborn and unknowable, thus taking it into virgin ethical territory". Attempts to value the future (eg by social discount rate) fail because different ethical standing is used for future generations "solely on the basis of their temporal location". And, she continues, "And yet, if there exists to date no socio-political structure to represent the unborn peoples of the future, what chance is there to represent other species, current and potential, and more difficult still, other forms of existence?".

accounting for time

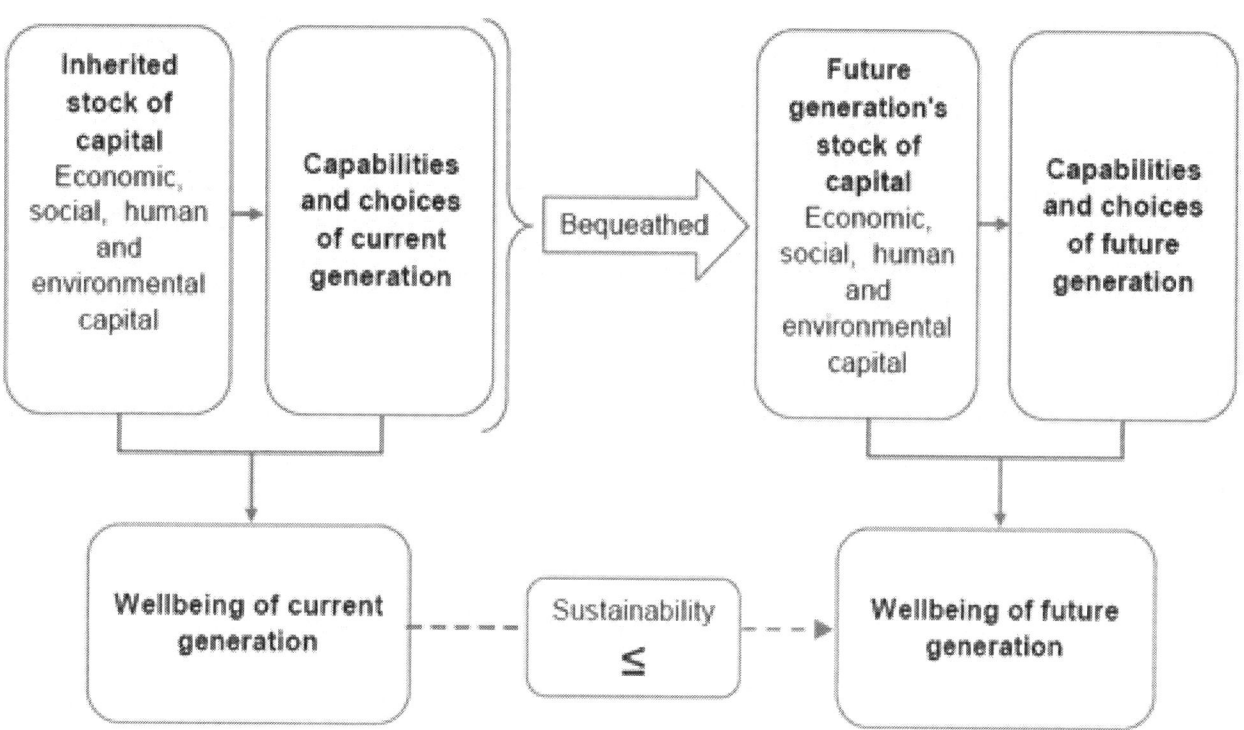

> Time rushes by at such a constant rate it is sometimes easy to ignore. On the other hand, if we see it as a basis for understanding, time can be used as an organising structure, allowing us to see sustainability as a process.

O'Neill (1988 p 40) argued that the aim should be to identify "the critical points in the behaviour of the biosphere, the points of bifurcation"; in other words, the thresholds of change. Managing for sustainability implies recognition of change over time, manifest in such theories such as catastrophe theory in rangeland dynamics (Lockwood and Lockwood 1993), disturbance concepts (Pickett et al. 1989; Sprugel 1991), and landscape dynamics (Baker 1989; Gilpin et al. 1992).

It is useful to acknowledge that processes are dynamic. Responses to change - defined in ecological terms such as 'stability', 'resilience' and 'thresholds' - are especially applicable (Marten 1988; Freidel 1991; Laycock 1991; Grimm, Schmidt et al. 1992). A *Sustainable Lens* needs to reflect the dynamic nature of the environment. Recognising resilience would be a good way of doing this. Resilience consists of the amount of disturbance that a system can absorb while still remaining within the same state or domain of attraction; the degree to which the system is capable of self-organization; and the degree to which the system can build and increase its capacity for learning and adaptation (Carpenter et al. 2001).

The Adaptive Cycle model describes the system dynamics in four fundamental phases: exploitation, maturation, liberation, and re-organization, which are arranged in two axes: accumulated capital, and connectivity (sometimes adding resilience for a third axis). This cycle reflects the magnitude of changes in accumulated capital such as nutrients, carbon, energy, and information, and the connections expressed as matter transportation, energy, and information, occurring in each change of state (Gunderson and Holling 2002).

A general model of the dynamics of complex systems proposed by Holling places an emphasis on the temporal dimension. Holling's argument is that an ecosystem never finds itself in a stable position; instead it goes through four different phases. Using a forest example, Phase 1 (r) consists of an area being colonised by different organisms and beginning to take it's form. Phase 2 (K) sees the trees begin to grow. This phase may take place over a long period of time and the thickening forest is often seen as fairly stable but the forest is highly sensitive to disturbances, sending the forest into phase 3 (Ω), the release phase. After the disturbance, in phase 4 (α) comes a reorganisation. The ecosystem consequently goes into phase 1 again, depending on the "ecological memory" this may be the same as before, or quite different. These cycles nest in space and time.

The Adaptive Cycle model can be applied to individual ecosystems or societies (eg Nkhata et al. 2008), or to the whole of sustainability as a panarchy:

> *The growth phase we're in may seem like a natural and permanent state of affairs-and our world's rising complexity, connectedness, efficiency, and regulation may seem relentless and unstoppable-but ultimately it isn't sustainable...I think rapidly rising connectivity within global systems-both economic and technological-increases the risk of deep collapse. That's a collapse that cascades across adaptive cycles-a kind of pancaking implosion of the entire system as higher-level adaptive cycles collapse, which causes progressive collapse at lower levels.* (Homer-Dixon 2009)

Nested complex adaptive systems are used to describe the transition of coal mining in Australia's Hunter Valley to a post-carbon society (Evans 2008). The smallest scale (lower right), comprises linked ecosystems and human communities - from pre-colonial indigenous society into the current capitalist agricultural and industrial society dominated by the coal industry. A potential transformation is shown. The global energy markets in a Post-Carbon Society is similarly shown (upper right)

By using time as an organising structure the *Sustainable Lens* can see sustainability as a process.

time as basis for understanding

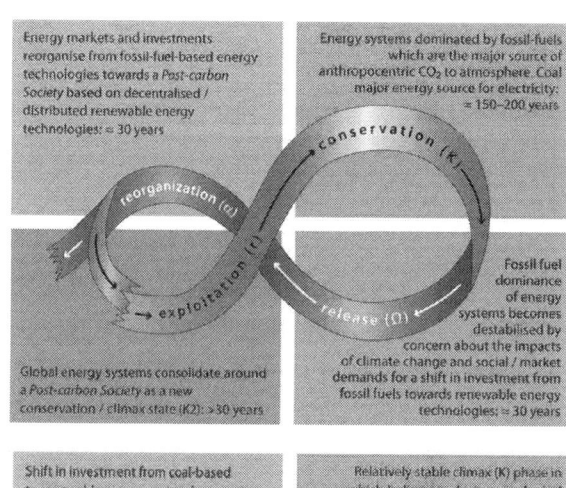

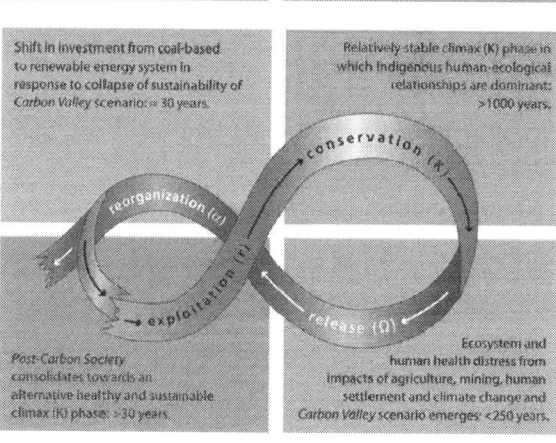

> Recognising what we know, don't know, can't know, and will never know, leads to an understanding that we can manage based on uncertainty. **In this United Nations Environment Programme diagram, issues are plotted according to management difficulty (ie uncertainty and reversibility (GEO4 2007).**

There's an old adage that you can't manage what you can't measure.

Measurement though, means problem definition. As Wilson (1994) pointed out, after strict problem definition the problem is limited to whatever the developer perceived as a problem, which results in a forced description of it. Wilson sees this as part of the "unrelenting pressure to translate vaguely stated socio-cultural [strategic] problems into clearly stated business [operational] ones". A second difficulty with strict definition is the inability of such systems to cope with unexpected developments. Grossman (1994) discusses how predictions of air-pollution completely failed as a result of the unification of Germany. They could not of course be expected to predict this, but had no mechanisms for dealing with this uncertainty. Burrough's (1986) statement that "carefully drawn boundaries and contour lines on maps are elegant misrepresentations of changes that are often gradual, vague, or fuzzy" is particularly applicable here.

Butler (1991) discussed how uncertainty is endemic to decision-making: "if there was no uncertainty as to the course of action to take, there would be no decision to make". Uncertainty in managing through a *Sustainable Lens* exists in the definition of goals such as the ambiguous 'sustainability', in variously defined measures such as 'biodiversity', in predicting the environment, in understanding, and in the error associated with statements about location. Lowes and Walker (1995) write of environmental data being "invariably partial and inadequate" yet decision-makers are faced with "overwhelming data of limited utility". Walters (1986) argued that all "key management decisions are essentially gambles", he suggested "embracing uncertainty" and using it to "stimulate imaginative thinking".

The *Sustainable Lens* needs methods for recognising and coping with uncertainty. In much of sustainability we can't measure, but we have to manage.

uncertainty in decision making

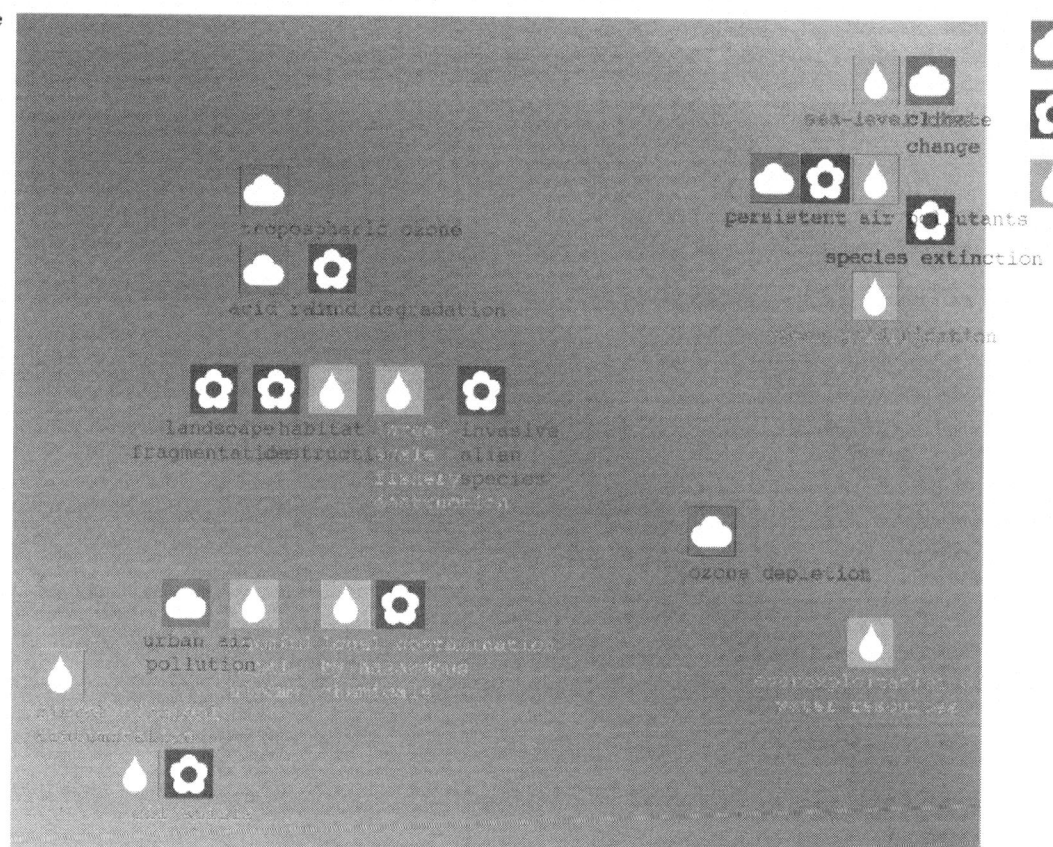

Source: Based on Chapters 2–5

> Habitat loss, over-exploitation, pollution, spread of invasive species and climate change can all be directly linked to human demands on the biosphere (Loh 2008). **Yet despite this "cause and effect" diagram, much is not known and degradation continues.**

In *The Virtues of Ignorance* Bill Vitek and Wes Jackson (with many contributors from a research camp) argue that a "knowledge-based worldview is both flawed and dangerous".

> Since we're billions of times more ignorant than knowledgeable, why not go with our long suit and have an ignorance-based worldview?

The upshot of this premise is a whole different way of looking at the world:

> What would human cultures look like, and how might we interact differently in the world, if we began every endeavor and conversation with the humbling assumption that human understanding is limited by an ignorance that no amount of additional information can mitigate? How would we educate our children differently or engage in scientific research? Might we be more cautious and more willing to listen to others-and not just other human beings, but the whole conversation going on all around us?

The knowledge-based worldview has led to three revolutions – scientific, political and economic. It has resulted in remarkable changes that have made possible individual freedom, economic growth, scientific progress, and the rejection of thermodynamic, material, and moral limits:

> Together these revolutions freed cultures to embark on pursuits that were heretofore forbidden or considered impossible: the control of nature; the creation of economies and technologies that went beyond subsistence; the freedom of individuals from governments, religious and family traditions, and the past; and a belief in human progress that is separate from evolution and unencumbered by moral and spiritual beliefs

So what's the problem? Twofold: first the resultant damage (injustices, ecological disasters etc), and second, the response to criticism or threat that the thinking mind will overcome all limits:

> Further, many of the solutions to these monumental challenges depend on the logic of plenty: finding more oil, increasing soil and seed productivity, promoting economic growth and material consumption, utilizing more land for human food production, and even increasing human population. Each calls forth a faith in the unbounded human spirit to rise to any occasion, to conquer any foe. The recipe for success is simple: unleash human ingenuity; utilize it to harness and commodify nature's immense and complex forces; enjoy the new and improved world that results; repeat.

> This means we have to "block the only myth that makes it bearable, namely, the belief that human knowledge is sufficient to get us out of the holes we've dug for ourselves and the world".

The complex adaptive systems surrounding us (and indeed that comprise us) mean that much of our basic knowledge turns out to be wrong. Vitek and Jackson argue that we need to acknowledge our vast ignorance – an ignorance-based world view:

> We call this view an ignorance-based worldview, and we predicate it on the assumption that human ignorance will always exceed and outpace human knowledge and, therefore, that before we make any decision or take any action, we must consider who and how many are involved, the level of cultural change that will be involved, and the chances of backing out if things go sour. In no way does such a view imply that we should not seek knowledge or that we are stupid or even wicked, but it does force us to remember things, cause us to hope for second chances, and provide an incentive to keep the scale small.

Seeing through a *Sustainable Lens* is an ignorance based perspective.

playing to our strengths

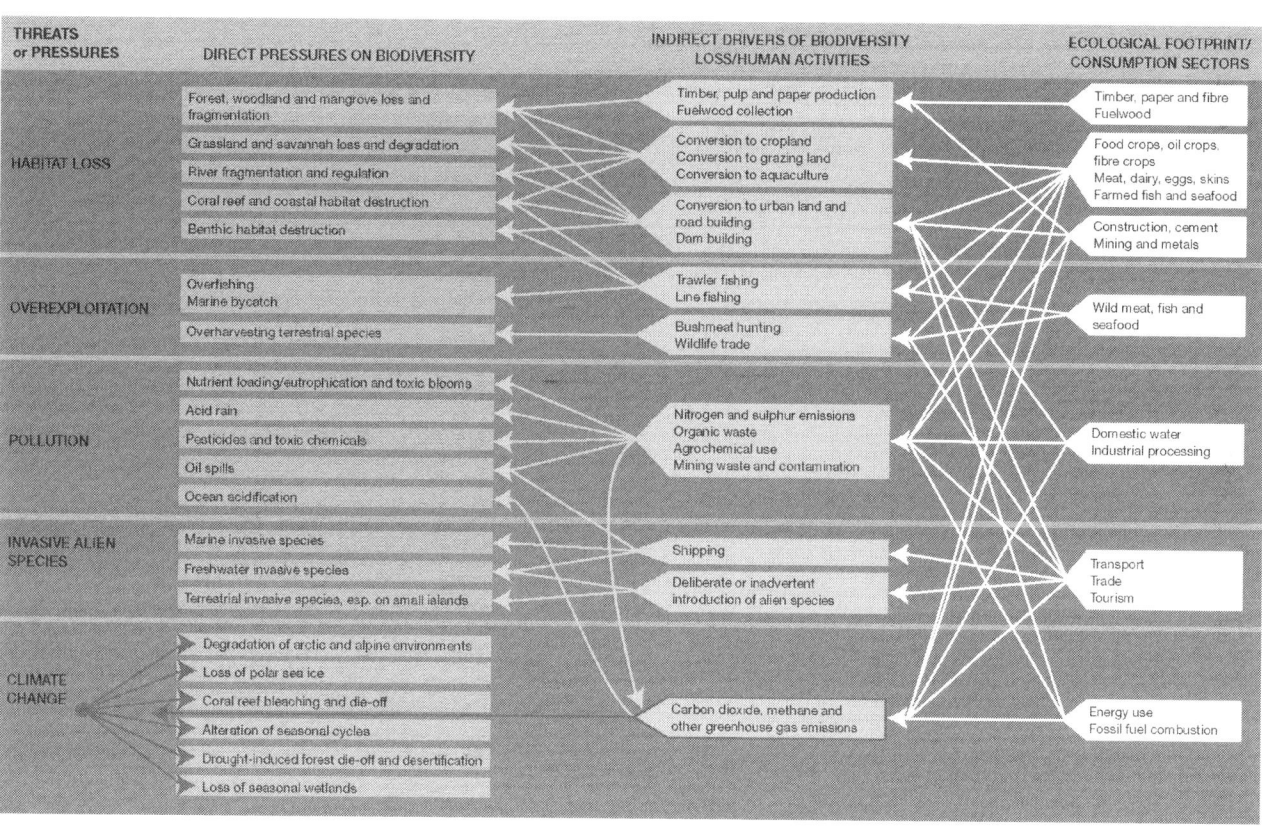

BIODIVERSITY LOSS, HUMAN PRESSURE AND THE ECOLOGICAL FOOTPRINT

> The knowledge of a relationship between a pressure indicator and a state or impact indicator can be used to manage the pressure (an environmental disturbance that might result in a change) in the interests of sustainability. **It is likely that there will be uncertainty in our knowledge of the relationship, and this uncertainty must be respected in management** (Tett *et al.* 2011).

Exploring the implications of the ignorance, or humility based world view, several authors have argued that the ignorance-based world view is not defeatist, and also celebrates knowledge. Paul Heltne (2008) has a simple take, arguing that there are at least two kinds of ignorance – differing such as to be considered opposing worldviews:

> *One ignorance world view is built on the belief that one knows or understands a situation or a subject rather thoroughly, perhaps even definitively or absolutely, when, in fact, one does not. This sort of ignorance-masquerading as- certain-knowledge often comes to us as whole systems of thought and work and with intellectual buffers that make its facts, claims, and practices beyond question. Its assumptions, often invisible or unstated, are thereby unassailable.*

The other, humble ignorance:

> *Acknowledging that one does not know is a humble kind of ignorance, one that is, in fact, filled often with the joy of discovery and wonder at what is discovered. This is the kind of ignorance-based worldview that can help us fathom the messes we are in, articulate assumptions and processes, entertain questions and be enriched by them, and imagine new ways and new knowledge.*

Robert Root-Bernstein (2008) argues that science is not a search for solutions but a search for answerable questions – it must become acceptable to say "I don't know".

> *Science is a way of asking more and more meaningful questions. The answers are important mainly in leading us to new questions. So try to learn some answers, because they are useful and interesting, but don't forget that it isn't answers that make a scientist, it's questions."*

Root-Bernstein challenges educators to train student to raise answerable questions that no one has ever asked (and we're not going to achieve that by always getting them to answer questions to which we already have answers).

Raymond Dean (2008) argues that as boundaries increase beyond our ability to comprehend, danger increases. He argues against a flat-earth (level playing field) model, instead suggesting we consider the world as a collection of interconnected leaky balloons. Dean suggests an approach of expanding and contracting physical and intellectual boundaries:

> *To solve a problem, expand or contract your thinking to find the critical region where it looks like there will be a few solutions- more than one but not a large number. Then, alternate between thinking "just within the box" and "just outside the box."*

A *Sustainable Lens* is based on curiosity and the search for meaningful questions.

managing with uncertainty

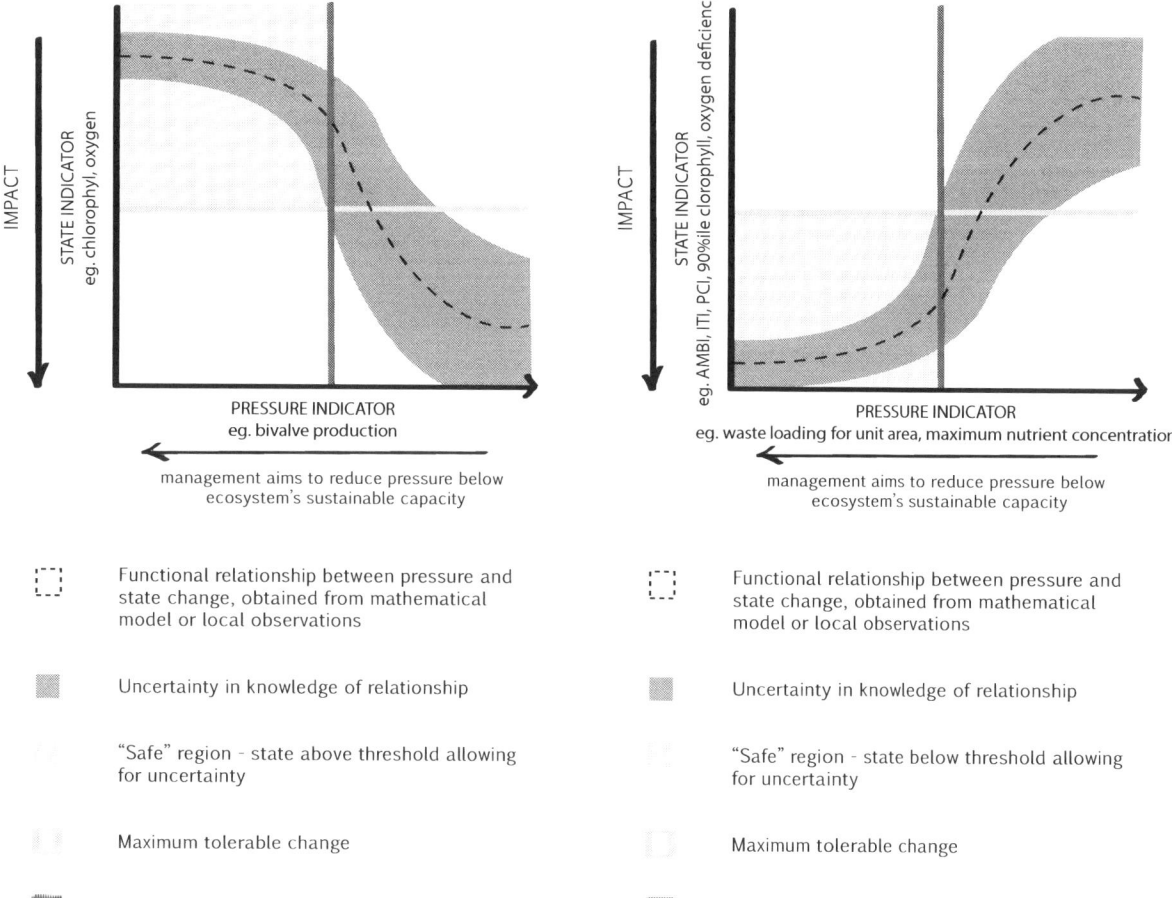

> Some questions are unanswerable.

One way of representing the puzzle of sustainability is to represent it as just that - a puzzle. Difficult yes, but tractable and engaging.

The **top image here is from the Center for a New American Dream (Affluenza.org) "New Dream Puzzle"**. They invite us to "Learn how the pieces of the puzzle all fit together...".

> the puzzle begins to demonstrate connections between various issues involved in a new American dream. Different people approach the consumption issue from different sides based on their personal experiences and interests but, as the puzzle demonstrates, all pieces must fit in place for true sustainability to be achieved.

Harry Fiddler describes a plan for a specific day on which a worldwide paradigm shift will occur (lower image).

> On this date, humanity will move in a whole new direction with respect to attitudes, laws, currencies, religion, science, material and energy use, etc. In other words, a sustainable civilization for the long term will be born. Initially, the infrastructure will appear the same, but humanity will enter a transition period away from our present collapsing unsustainable Western Civilization, and towards the new sustainable one.

The plan, according to Fiddler, involves a paradigm shift, a transition period, moving to renewable energy, and a transition to a DNA/Gene centered worldview. Much like a wooden version of the farmer crossing the river with a goose, fox and sack of grain, Fiddler presents the process as a puzzle.

Steve Talbott (2008) suggests a principle of caution but warns against absolute caution, which in accepting an ignorance worldview, would result in paralysis as " we are called to live between knowledge and ignorance, and it is as dangerous to make ignorance the excuse for radical inaction as it is to found action on the boast of perfect knowledge". Instead he suggests a conversation metaphor:

> We cannot predict or control the exact course of a conversation, nor do we feel any such need-not, at least, if we are looking for a good conversation. Revelations and surprises lend our exchanges much of their savor. We don't want predictability; we want respect, meaning, and coherence. A satisfying conversation is neither rigidly programmed nor chaotic; somewhere between perfect order and total surprise we look for a creative tension, a progressive and mutual deepening of insight, a sense that we are getting somewhere worthwhile.

The *Sustainable Lens* needs to empower us to engage, and to relish the challenge.

does my bum look big in this?

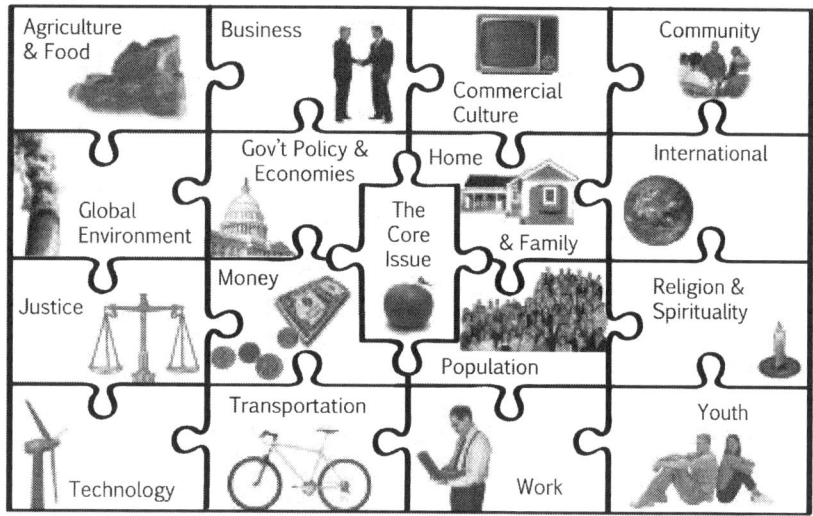

Puzzle Slide: Paradigm Shift (World View Shift)

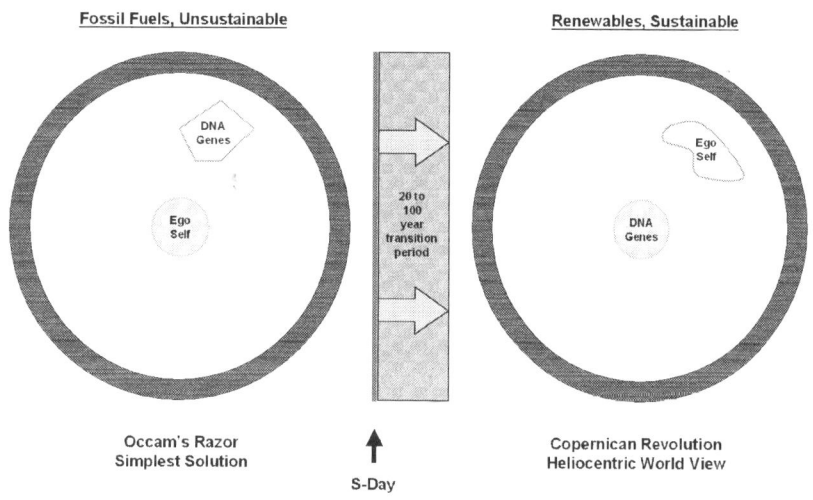

> We need multiple approaches that enable us to think simultaneously of drivers and impacts of our actions across scales and barriers of space, time, culture, species and disciplinary boundaries.

The Living Planet Report (WWF/ZSL/GFN et al. 2008) presents scenarios and strategies that could reduce the gap between human demand on nature and the availability of ecological capacity. Each of these strategies can be represented as a sustainability wedge that shifts the business-as-usual path towards one in which, when these wedges are combined, overshoot is eliminated. I think this gives some hope. This shows that what we do, individually and in groups can make a difference.

Breaking the entire overshoot into multiple wedges highlights the multiple approaches that will be needed in a Sustainable future (top). The Living Planet authors see each wedges as representing the three factors that determine footprint (population, consumption, intensity). Wedges can also be organised around consumption categories, a wedge might represent the food system, another shelter and so on. Here, I propose a third alternative, that the wedges could represent ways of thinking. For almost every authority on sustainability a different approach is proposed. We need them all, and we need them to work together.

AtKisson (2008) bases his optimistic approach on the "remarkable progress" humanity has already on many global scale problems, "to the point of already preventing global-scale catastrophes". Catastrophe is not inevitable.

David Orr talks of a type of post-modernism where we keep what is best of science and technology but use it for ethical ecologically enhancing ends. He wants us to reject modernism's apparent intent to render the whole earth into resources for the consumption machine (2004).

Stagl (2007) groups three learning theories and their roles in overcoming barriers to social learning for pro-environmental behaviour. In rationalist theories or information deficit models of public understanding and action the hindrance is seen to be a lack of knowledge so the solution is more knowledge. Social Structure focussed theories see the main hindrances to as being social obstacles. The recognition and enabling of multiple legitimate perspectives in decision making is key. Third, Stagl identifies evolutionary or complex systems-based theories. Here the very complexity of the sustainability issues and the resulting uncertainty is the main hindrance to pro-environmental behaviour. In this school of thought, learners need to develop ways to perceive complex problems and to address uncertainty. The consequence of this is a need for adaptive processes, and an acknowledgement that all actors are continuously learning.

Morris and Martin (2009) suggests that the answer may lie in the difference between a difficulty and a mess. Difficulties are problems which usually have a well-defined and clear boundary, involving few participants, short time-scales and clear priorities, with limited wider implications. Messes are typified by more human-oriented issues where values, beliefs, power structures and habit play a major part. There is no well-defined problem or solution, time-scales may be long and at best we can only seek to improve the situation. It may be a mistake to strive for clear, unambiguous problems with perfect solution. Thinking about sustainability involves questions about what aspects of our existence we want to sustain, how much are we prepared to compromise with others' needs and what unexpected results might arise from our actions.

This continuum of interest from Hemant Puthli (2010) recognises a plurality of approaches on four continua.

The *Sustainable Lens* is pluralistic.

multiple choice

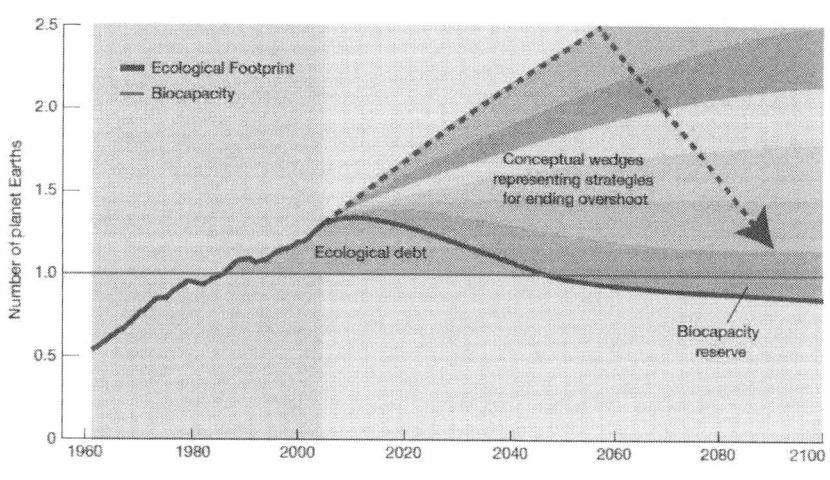

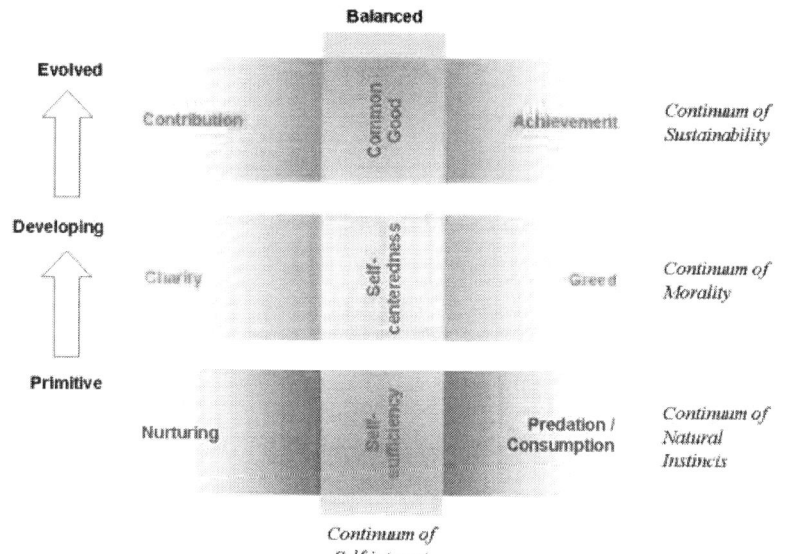

> A *Sustainable Lens* provides a framework for transferring principles across scales of all forms, and across areas of interest.

We need to be able to operate on multiple scales of time and space simultaneously. We need to be able to explicitly account for both our ancestors and future generations (along with "beings and organisms unborn and unknowable"). The temporal dimension has a third construct, that of change as a process. A *Sustainable Lens* needs to help us apply these understandings to whatever it is we are doing. This lens approach can be seen in the application of intergenerational equity. This is a cornerstone of sustainable development (*Our Common Future*, Brundtland):

> *Sustainable development is development that meets the needs of the present without compromising the ability of future generations to meet their own needs*

This definition of sustainability has both current and future generations at its core. These are described as intragenerational equity and intergenerational equity. The combination of the intra - the "needs of the present" - with inter-generational "without compromising the ability of future generations" is very deep-seated. It is the basis of much legal, religious and cultural tradition. It underpins the United Nations Charter and the Universal Declaration of Human Rights. (Note some have argued that the definition would benefit from an addition of the implied "all", as in "needs of *all* of the present", "*all* of future generations").

Intergenerational equity is usually applied to our relationship with natural resources – you can't despoil land – even if you own it – without reference to some consenting process that considers the wider picture. The concept was first systematically explored by John Rawls' concept of "just savings" and developed by economist Robert Solow in 1973 "an obligation to conduct ourselves so that we leave to the future the option or the capacity to be as well off as we are". We can use exhaustible resources but only to invest in productive capacity (strong sustainability later rejected this substitutability argument – but the core concern remains). In 1974 economist James Tobin applied the concept to endowed funds:

> *The trustees of endowed institutions are the guardians of the future against the claims of the present. Their task in managing the endowment is to preserve equity among generations*

Crucial here is the phrase "guardians of the future against the claims of the present". Intergenerational equity is about protecting the future from the claims of the present. It means not running down resources – be it fishing stocks, river quality, or, indeed money. In financial terms the proceeds of an endowed fund should not be spent a rate that exceeds the after inflation return on its investments. This ensures that the proceeds are spent equally on current and future constituents of the endowed assets.

The opposite of Intergenerational Equity is running down resources, this means reducing options, quality and access. This reduces the choices available to future generations. To do so is borrowing against the future. Some argue that intergenerational equity means future generations must pay their own way - thus justifying municipal debt - the exact opposite of the true meaning. However, while we're not paying our own way in not fully funding investment, deferred maintenance, and we're running down resources, it is morally repugnant to selectivity argue that future generations must pay their way

A *Sustainable Lens* provides a framework for transferring principles across scales of all forms, and across areas of interest. **Moffatt and Kohler (2008) provide a model for spatial scales, aggregation and specific effects. They then apply this to cultural, natural and material realms over spatial and temporal scales. In Suzuki *et al*. (2010) Moffatt expands the temporal dimension with "time rings". These are combined by Moffatt (pers comm) to create an integrated diagram.**

all systems, and across systems

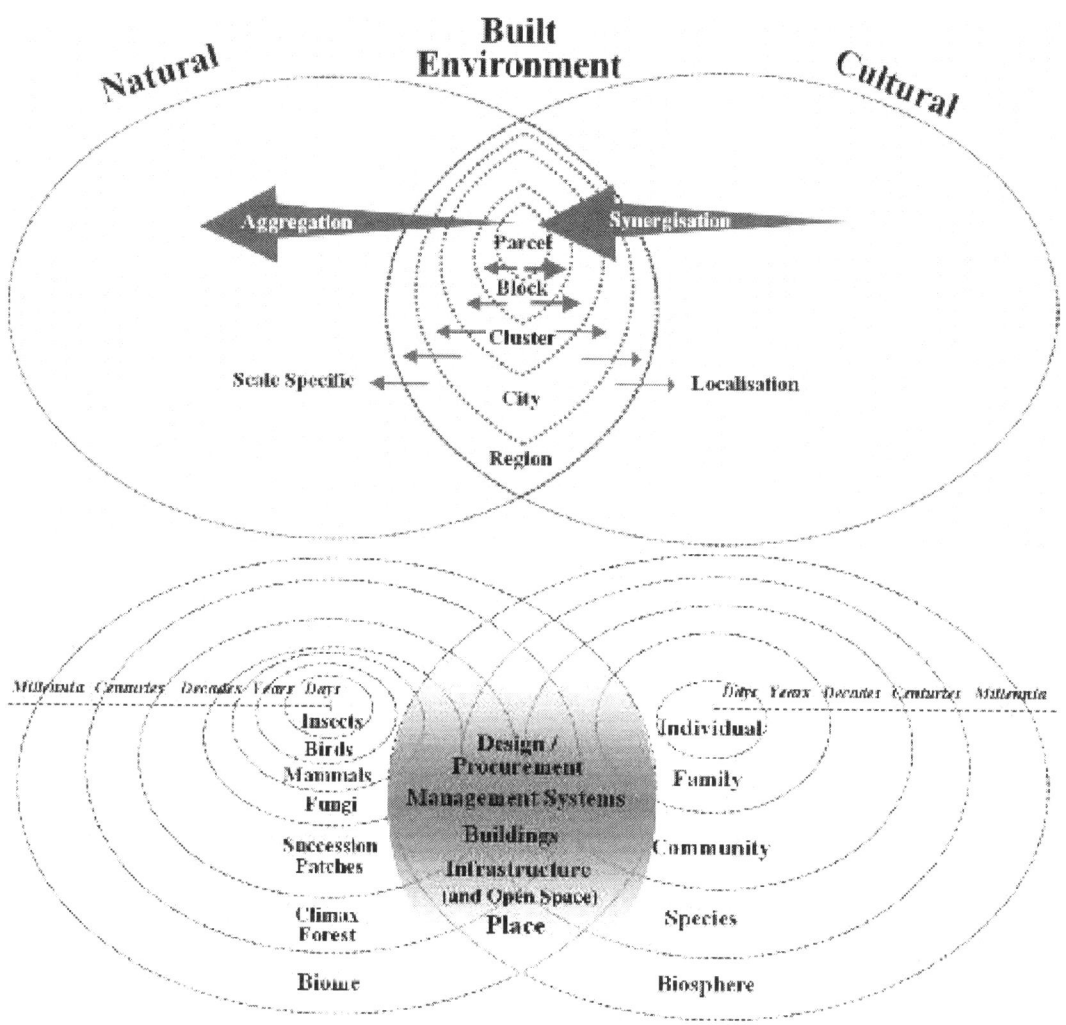

> While in the previous chapters we focussed on scientific dimensions of the *Sustainable Lens*, here I address the humanistic aspects. We go from science to ways of thinking. We get there via uncertainty.

There is not going to be a singular event that definitively signals 'peak oil is happening now'. Climate Change is the same. With gradual and insidious change (though with increasing occurrence of catastrophic events in both scenarios) decisions made now need to made in the context of the knowledge of those scenarios.

One of the biggest barriers to a sustainable future is the paralysis that comes from an uncertain future. This can be seen in arguments that "we can't do this until the science is in", or "we'll take this seriously when we see evidence of climate change", or "we'll do this when you come up with a definition of sustainability". Other barriers include paralysis by pretend action (see discussion on Journey metaphor).

The complexity of the sustainability challenge means that the science will never be "sorted".

Hunter and Goodchild (1995) distinguish between error and uncertainty. The former implies that some degree of knowledge has been attained about the differences between the results (or observations) and the 'truth'. Uncertainty refers to the lack of such knowledge that is responsible for doubt in accepting the results. Many environmental problems are "wicked" (McNamee, Bunnell *et al.* 1986 p 395), being particularly intransigent in terms of understanding". Holling (1978) concluded that our knowledge of environmental systems will never be enough to predict the future behaviour of those systems and, therefore, managers cannot be given the firm grounds for making choices between policies.

In principle, therefore, there is an inherent unknowability, as well as unpredictability, concerning evolving managed ecosystems and the societies with which they are linked.

This is a shift in thinking, we are all learning how to act and think as sustainable practitioners. This overcomes one of the strongest barriers towards integrating sustainability. It empowers us to say "I don't know the answers here – nobody does, that's the challenge".

In education terms, within the context of the discipline, the educator becomes a facilitator and enabler of change rather than a disseminator of knowledge (Polistina 2009). Freire and Freire (2000) said that an education that was all about imparting answers is inadequate. Howard Gardner (of multiple intelligences fame, 1993) says it is important to educate people so that they can ask new and interesting questions. Seeing through a *Sustainable Lens* brings identical challenges.

There are two positive approaches to the uncertainty (there are others such as ignoring it). The first is to adopt a scientific change management approach. The second is a more humble and humanistic approach. **The two approaches may at first seem contradictory, but, they are both ways of thinking - about risk, uncertainty, ambiguity and ignorance - and have much to offer each other. Alden Dow's Way of Life Cycle (opposite, in Maddex 2007) is one such approach to integration.** It starts with "individualism," and proceeds through "thinking and doing," "creativity," "facts and feelings," "honesty, humility, enthusiasm," "new expressions," "appreciation" and finally "finer standards".

seeing risk, uncertainty, ambiguity and ignorance

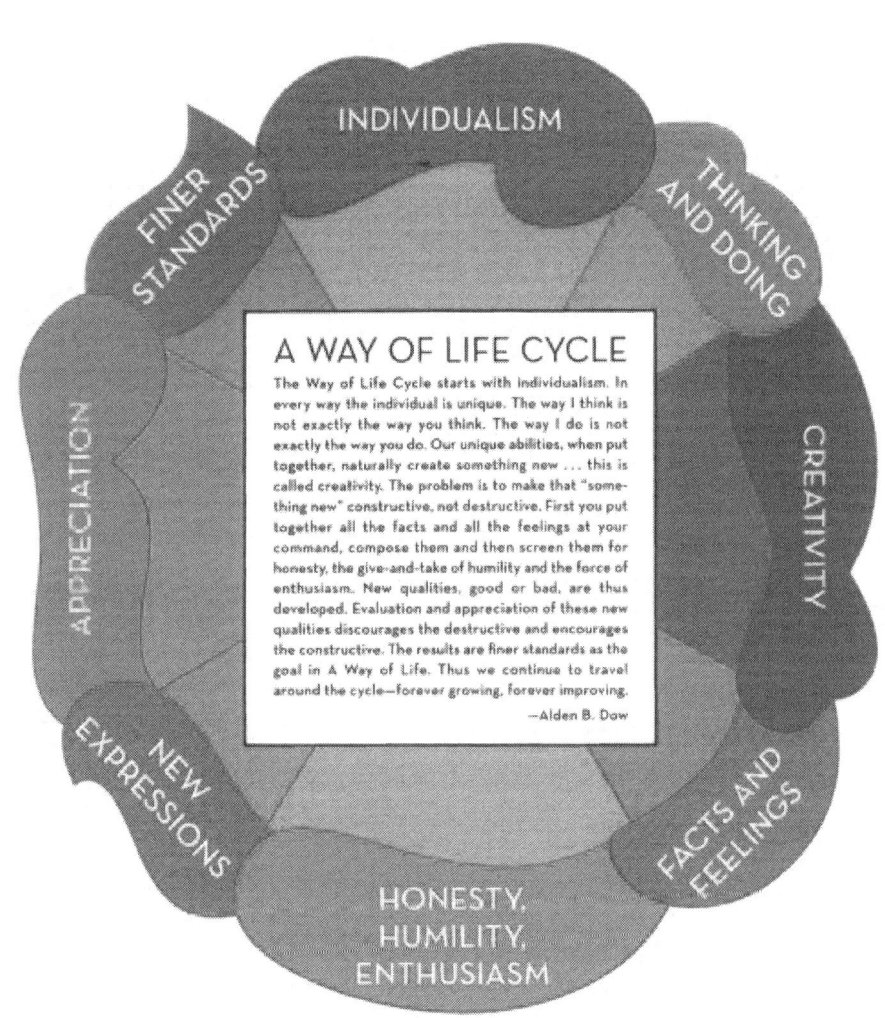

> **This diagram from International Network for Acid Prevention (nd), emphasises the fact that sustainability is not absolute.** Using a variation of Nijkamp's ternary plot, they argue that the point of equilibrium can come only from only through an "integrated consultative process involving all stakeholders".

I recently had to organise session on professionalism in computing for a national conference. Talking about this a function at work the conversation turned to ethics in the workplace – how much home photocopying is acceptable? is pocketing individual fractions of cents that would otherwise disappear acceptable if there is demonstrably no harm? How come our local hospital board systems (and auditors) overlooked a $17M fraud in the IT department? and so on.

I went home and re-read *Environmental Education, Ethics and Action* (Jickling *et al.* 2006). Bob Jickling and colleagues have pulled together some really nice examples that are intended for teaching, but also are really good messages for anyone. They lift ethics above the financial and legal aspects we talked about at work:

> *People around the world want better relationships between themselves, within communities, between communities, and between nations. And they know that this includes relationships between humans and the more-than-human world, or, for others, between humans and the rest of Creation. In using the term 'more-than-human world' we suggest that exploring new relationships with Earth not only benefits human beings and their needs (although we recognise how important these are), but also the needs and well-being of forests, fields, rivers, animals, creatures in the sea, and the atmosphere.*

This is one of our favourite quotes:

> *Exercising our ethical abilities is part of being human. It is an ability that should be built into our lives such that it becomes 'simply normal behaviour'. Ethics should not be an exotic activity performed by heroes, saints, and experts that reside elsewhere—it is a matter for everyone. It is the stuff of everyday activity.*

The definitions here are more inspiring than a Hippocratic non-maleficence "do no harm". Instead the focus is on what makes us noble. It is clear that sustainability cannot be defined without reflection on values and principles. Thus, any discourse about sustainability is essentially an ethical discourse (Bosselmann 2008).

So is sustainability just ethics rebranded? AtKisson (2008) argues that sustainable thinking involves much more than understanding simple physical chains of cause and effect. One must also understand the decisions that are taken either to change those causes or to respond to their effects.

In discussions with colleagues I have taken opposite views on whether sustainability is the super-set of ethics, or the other way around. Perhaps as soon as you can even entertain such a debate, then the very question is pointless – depending on your perspective both are true. That ethics both encompasses and contributes to sustainability is now an accepted stance. In other words, ethics and sustainability are fellow travellers heading in the same direction.

But most of us would like to think we already see through an ethical lens. So, what is new? Is sustainability different? Amidst the complexities of ethical literature, I like this simple observation from Koehler and Som (2005) in a discussion of pervasive computing: "*sustainability is ethics extended in space and time*".

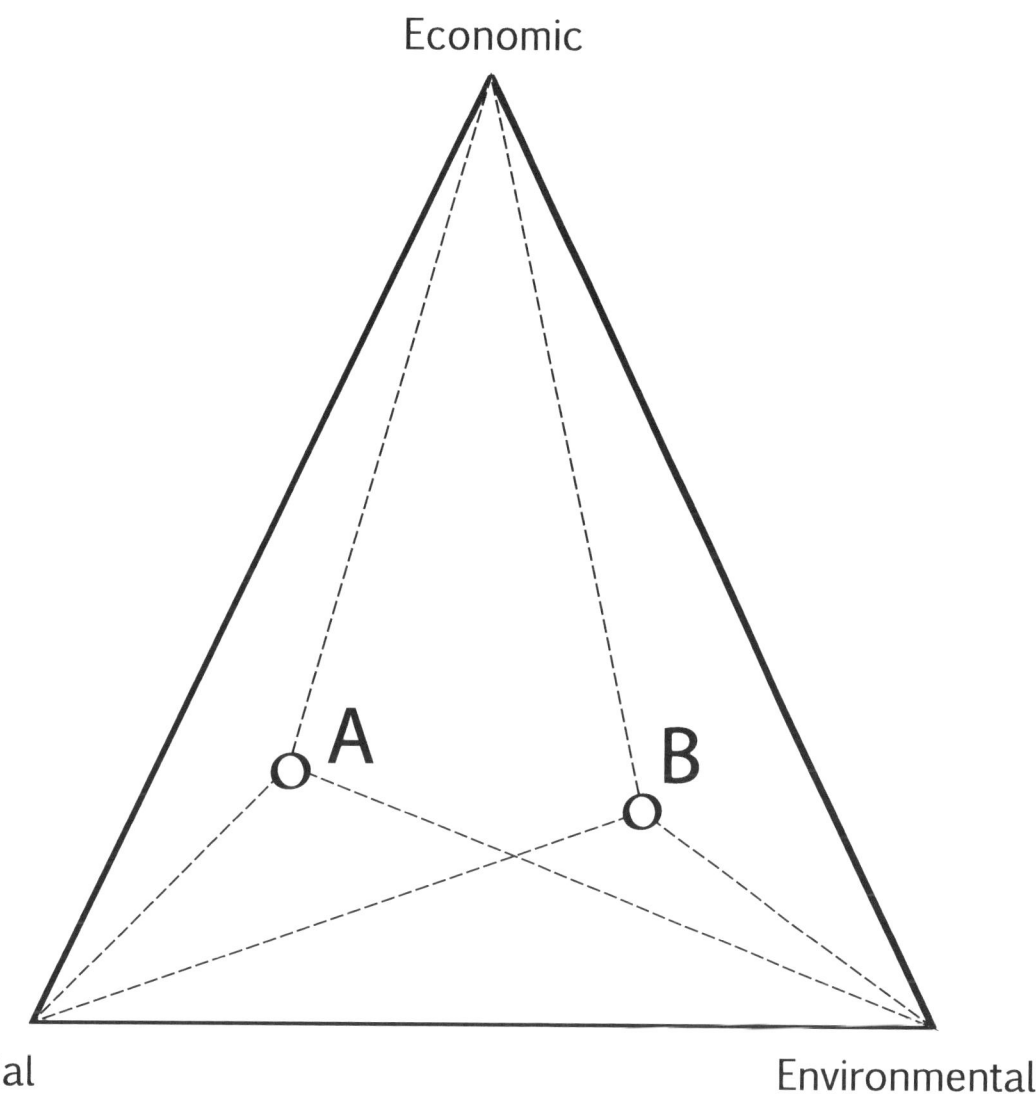

> Thinking bigger applies to everything we do.

The upper image is from van Mansvelt and van der Lubbe's (1999) checklist for sustainable landscape management. On the horizontal axis it contrasts a conservative perspective with a progressive perspective. Here "conservative" is taken to mean forces opting for what they perceive as care and respect for the established values. The vertical axis, meanwhile contrasts a narrow (reductionism) with a broad (holistic) perspective. The diagonals form the interaction of these forces. van Mansvelt and van der Lubbe describe how the polarisation of these forces leads to conflict but that appreciation for both sides an dialogue is needed.

In the lower left quadrant "derailed conservatism" blocks development with focus on individual sites or species. On the lower right ruthless exploitation of irreplaceable values and resources of nature and culture, in favour of some larger or smaller industrial interest groups, can be seen as the ego-centred bias of derailed progress. Clearly van Mansvelt and van der Lubbe prefer a holistic approach as they describe these more positively share the awareness of any object, part or moment in its spatial and temporal context. So when combined with conservative, we get:

> *A conservative respect for the world, in all its known and unknown beauty and wisdom created by evolution and history and perceived as requiring a most careful and retained handling, can be fully appreciated.*

This holistic conservative they describe as important for awareness of disturbing, unforeseen and unwanted side effects of technologies. On the top right the holistic and progressive is described as "a progressive and courageous dedication to discover the entire world as yet unknown secrets, releasing all its potential benefits for mankind as yet untouched or unused to the detriment of people's happiness, can also be very well appreciated".

The creative creation of shared meaning between groups that comprise the polar extremes of van Mansvelt and van der Lubbe's world brings together holistic and reductive thinking, conservative and progressive thinking. The same could be said for the IDEO product lifecycle (lower image). **IDEO challenges us to think more holistically about the process - to think bigger - but not in such a way that we neglect the details.**

thinking bigger in all dimensions

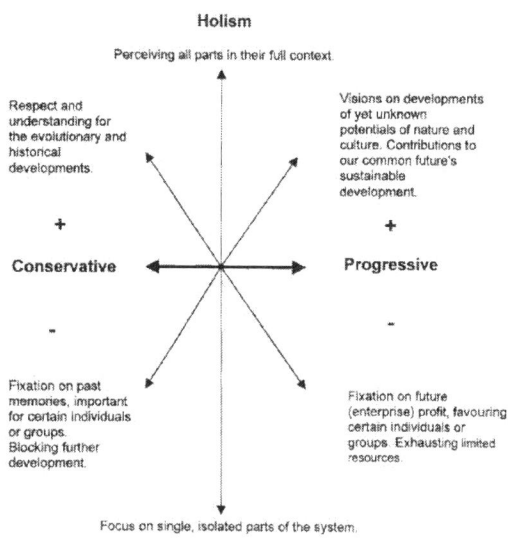

PRODUCT LIFE CYCLE

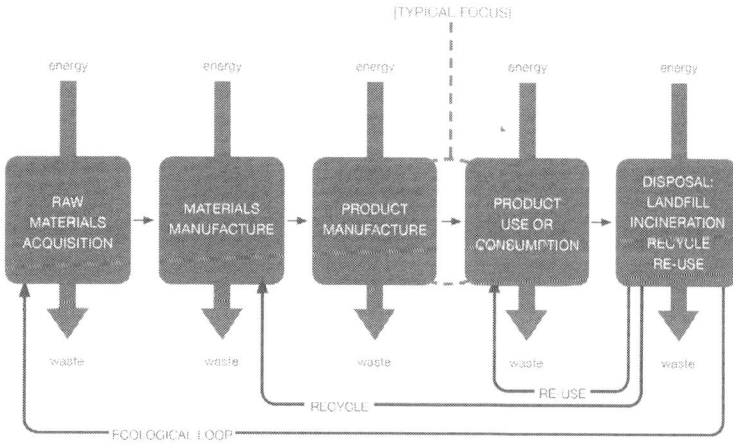

> "If global warming was being investigated as a murder, the fingerprints of business would be found all over the crime scene. Business would be the prime suspect; everyone else is a mere accomplice" (Schendler 2009). Make no mistake, however, a sustainable future is a business future. Sustainability can not be just an indulgence we do at home.

Healey (2009) finds a "mere 12% of the 419 business technology professionals we surveyed...report say they'd be willing to pay more for a greener product". Healey questions whether "our vaunted green IT initiatives really just returns-on-investment-based business decisions wrapped in environmentally friendly packaging?". Healey attempts to go beyond the decisions that have clear monetary return on investment but there's not much there. This is not because of a lack of personal understanding of environmental issues, nor a lack of personal commitment. A total of 92% agreed that they seek environmentally friendly alternatives in their personal life yet few are doing much at work. 40% say that they "drive their personal behaviour to green alternatives, even if it means paying more".

Why is green information technology (IT) such a "non starter?". Some is because it's difficult, a lack of tools in determining relative impact of options. Some is because of inconsistent policy and direction. Some stems from a lack of standards. Some from self-serving green IT messages (i.e. from vendors). Mostly though, it is because being sustainable is not highly rated in the business environment (except perhaps as a marketing tool). And sometimes it is because we have deluded ourselves. Healy:

> We'll call it out now: Virtualization isn't about being green, and we all know it. Sure, the green effect is a great side benefit, but it's not the driver. Most poll respondents list green as a minor factor in the decision process, with 76% saying it was a minor or non-factor in the decision to virtualize.

Although Healey clearly sees the impact of Green IT as going beyond power consumption/virtualisation and advises "Think Broad", he still stays safely with IT's own footprint - advising a wider focus on things like paper supply.

Others have reported similar findings to Healey. IBM and the NZBCSD (2008) survey of New Zealand businesses reported that 94% of people recycle at home "for environmental reasons". At work, however, only 11% of the same people recycle. The same applies in environmental transport decisions – at home: 40%; at work only 6%.

At home, it seems we are starting to care. An encouraging 72% of us report environmental considerations affecting purchasing decisions. Yet, at work only 28% report any environmental consideration in purchasing at their workplace.

We seem to have gotten to a position where caring for the earth is something that is acceptable, even expected before school, the evenings and weekends, but is not something we do from nine to five. Why is this? Presumably people know that any hope we have to make the world a better place to live and work depends on making changes at home and at work.

And these changes at work will have so very much more impact that those we can do at home. While I applaud people who recycle their compost at home it starts to pale into insignificance if they spend their days driving 1000s of kilometres primarily focussed on selling more cheese than a competitor (who is doing exactly the same). There has to be a better way.

Even if people try to make an artificial distinction between living in the world and working in the world, the *Sustainable Lens* must address business. **As every discipline practices within business, this means sustainability must apply to every trade, every profession (this image comparing traditional accounting with sustainability accounting is from David Bent, Forum for the Future).**

nine to five

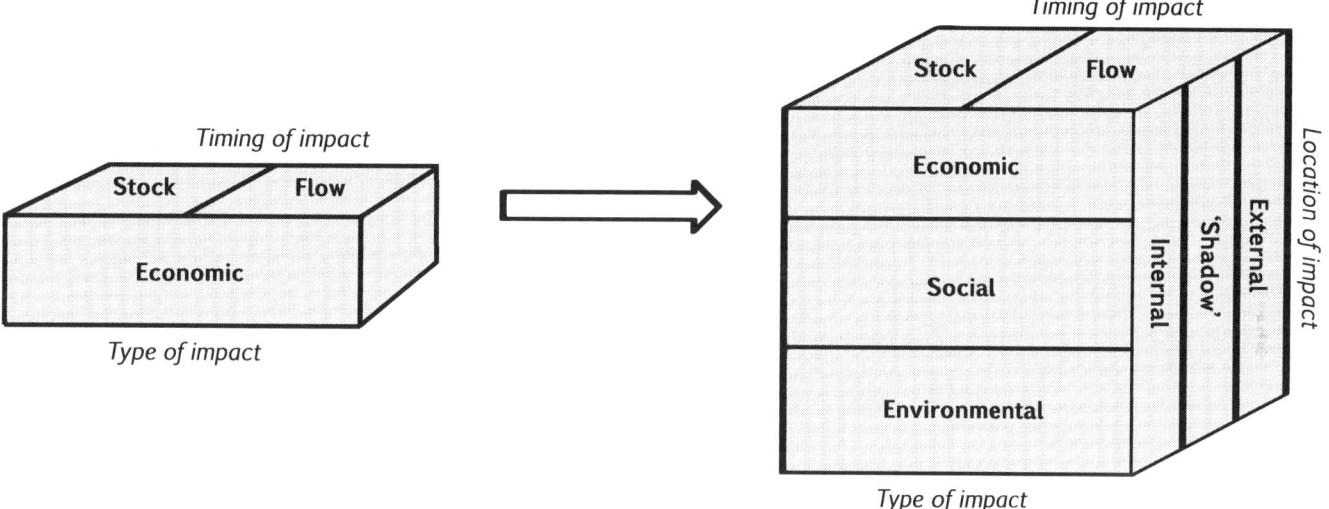

> Whole systems approaches form the new business as normal.

What is the business case for sustainability? There are several interrelated responses to this question.

First - and please excuse the frustration - do we insist on a business case for truth, or for democracy? What was the business case for ending slavery?

The second response is to demonstrate a business case over the short term – usually involving savings through efficiencies. For example, the Global Action Plan (2007):

> The link between increased energy consumption of ICT and man-made climate change is clear, as is the link between increased energy consumption and increased cost. Putting aside the important issues of global warming and energy security, tackling the carbon footprint of ICT is simply good business practice. Being green will help organisations stay out of the red.

Schendler (2009) urges caution on this approach. He argues, convincingly but perhaps counter-intuitively "don't treat business in purely economic terms"

> You can't be a leader in the green business field without a moral mandate. Why? Because in the real world, most management teams will adopt a green approach only if it promises profits. And not every environmental action is profitable. To repeat: If sustainability were cheap and easy, businesses would have achieved it by now. The problem is that it's fundamentally difficult and often expensive.

The third approach is to highlight the reliance of business on the environment. This is the approach taken by the *Millennium Ecosystems Assessment* (2005) which catalogues both the state of the environment and the effect of this on effect on society, cultures and commerce:

> People everywhere rely on ecosystems and the services they provide. So do businesses. Demand for these services is increasing. However, many of the world's ecosystems are in serious decline, and the continuing supply of critical ecosystem services is now in jeopardy.

The fourth approach – business *for* sustainability – is described by sustainability maturity inventories (Willard 2005, Markevich 2009).

> Many opportunities exist for businesses in emerging markets to benefit from actions which advance sustainable development. Matrix of measures of business success and dimensions of sustainable performance to create a sustainable business value model. Crowe (2002)

This trajectory of environmentally responsible design (Reed nd, 2007, left) illustrates a continuum of design (business) practices. The horizontal axis shows the energy required for the business practice. The vertical axis is shows a trend position for the system (not defined but a total human ecosystem is implied). Business approaches are arranged on the right. The lower two "fall below the bar of sustainability" as a they are still degenerating ecosystems and human health. Sustainability is set here at the neutral impact by Reed. Restorative design - which takes into account the whole system - and regenerative design - encompassing a full understanding of living systems (including humans) - are above the "bar of sustainability". We would question the neither good nor bad interpretation of sustainability, in our conception the regenerative aspects are strongly a part of sustainability. **In this alternative version (right), the entire diagram is surrounded by a circle, indicating, according to Reed (pers comm), that "all levels are necessary. One does not abandon level one and go to another".** Reed also rotates the diagram, making the previous diagonal the horizontal.

We need seeing through a *Sustainable Lens* to become 'business as normal', but recognise that it is a new normal.

business case for gravity?

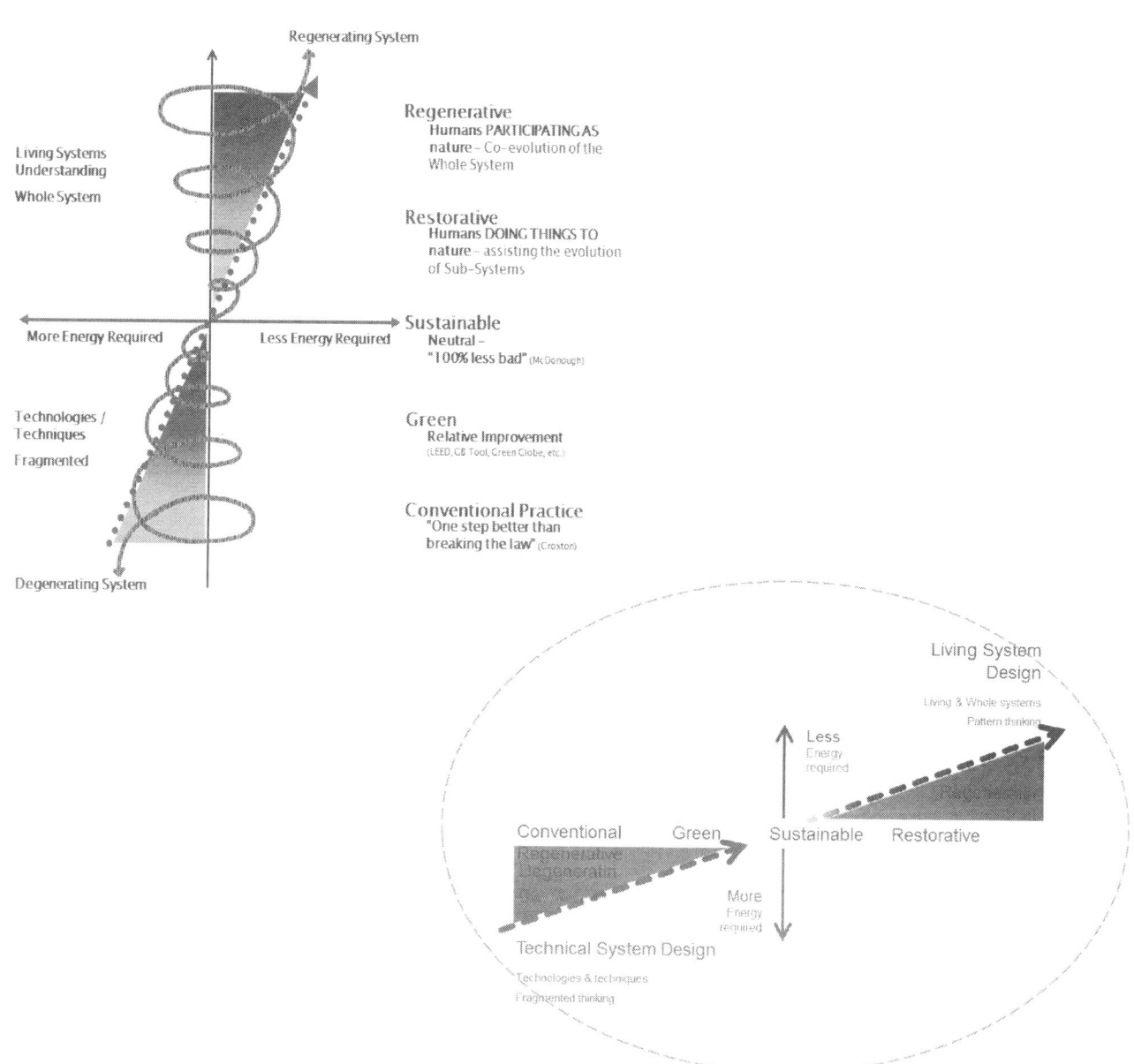

> Moving from compliance and efficiencies, a sustainability

How long is a piece of string? Willard (2005), McEwan and Schmidt (2007) provide inventories of stages of business maturity for sustainability. These go from a position of regulatory compliance through to mission transformation. They describe points on a business continuum.

Markevich offers 6 perspectives. Where do you fit, where would you like to be?

1. Regulatory compliance and trying to pre-adapt before practices are legislated against, reactionary.

2. Incremental mitigation 'But such efforts are typically add-ons to what remain essentially unsustainable business operations.

3. Value alignment to match those of employees. 'Translating employee interest in sustainability into competitive advantage requires creating real opportunities for employees to apply their creativity and initiative to progress towards sustainability.

4. Whole system design 'we need a new approach to technical design, one that optimises whole system for both efficiency and sustainability.' Green builders 'they design each part of the building to serve multiple purposes.' "Such design is best pursued in parallel with the integration of sustainability as a true organizational value.'

5. Business model innovation. Such innovation involves the redefinition of business scope, the redesign of internal processes and the modification of relevant customer and supplier processes in order to achieve economic and environmental benefits for stakeholders.

6 Mission transformation: Does the business and its products and services truly serve the development of development, human welfare, dignity and authenticity – instead of just contributing to the expansion of an economic system that treats material consumption as the ultimate goal of human existence.

A complementary perspective comes from Willard's (2005) scale of organisational sustainability maturity.

Pre-Compliance: ignoring sustainability and opposing related regulations

Compliance: obeying laws and regulations on labour, environment, health and safety. The business manages its liabilities by obeying the law and all labour, environmental, health, and safety regulations. It reactively does what it legally has to do and does it well. Emerging environmental and philanthropic social actions are treated as costs, projects are end-of-pipe retrofits, and CSR is given lip service.

Beyond Compliance: recognizing the opportunity to cut costs mainly through higher resource efficiencies and reduction of waste, leading to both financial and ecological gains. Sustainability is still separated from core business development.

Integrated Strategy: Sustainability is integrated in the company's vision and informs key business strategies to be more successful than competitors through innovation, design, and improved financial risk

Purpose and Passion: This is actually not a next stage of development for most companies but rather a special type of companies, being originally designed to 'help saving the world'.

A *Sustainable Lens* will see different things depending on where you sit on the maturity ladder. Wherever your rung, the *Sustainable Lens* should provide motivation to progress towards the transformed and purposeful top rung.

growing up business

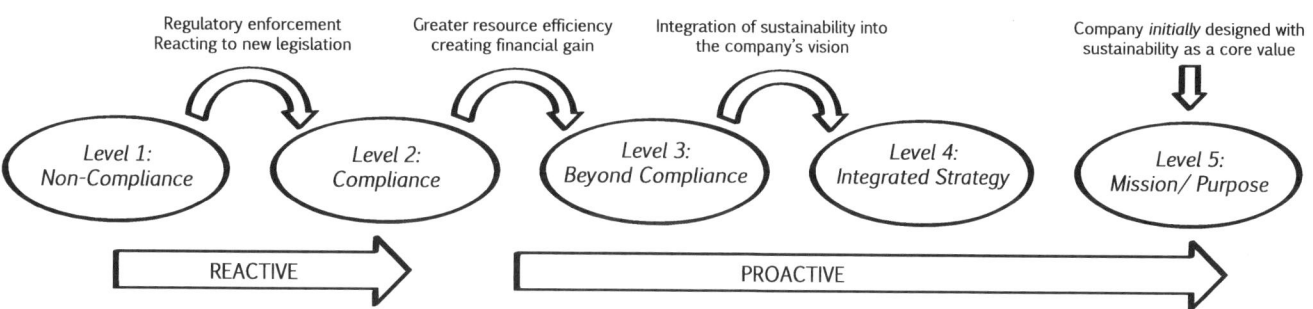

> This **Sustainability Entrepreneurship model (Young and Tilley 2006) embeds sustainability as the core of the business.** This is preferable to a marketing driven surface greening.

Bell's (2008) report titled "Green is the new sex – in a marketing sense" demonstrates an entry point for some companies, but also how far we have to go to reach level demanded by the *Sustainable Lens*. Doing something because there is a marketing benefit rather than because it is "the right thing to do" is not something I would encourage. It leads to a box ticking approach:

> *Every vendor is ticking the boxes" for energy-saving, acceptance of recycled equipment and other environmentally sensitive measures (John King in Bell).*

The trouble with a marketing driven "box ticking" approach is that the boxes are unpredictable and keep changing. What we need is a holistic approach, a realisation that actions will have impacts, positive and negative, intended and unintended, across scales: temporal; spatial; social and cultural.

Bell then goes on to report on how much money can be saved by decreasing power consumption. Bell reports Hamish McNee:

> *Yet many ICT users, individual or corporate, are still resistant to such ideas, even when it is clear they save money.*

This is the danger of danger of assuming that lean=green. Just because this year's green IT solution happens to save money, doesn't mean this will always be true. If we get a mindset that we can be green only because it saves money it's going to make for difficult arguments when we hit something that requires more cash.

After this shaky start though, Rod Oram hits the jackpot:

> *ICT is a tool to reduce consumption as well as a target. "You can use your IT stuff to help you measure and manage it"*

We're starting to get traction on the idea that the bigger impact of computing is going to be from our ability to affect other areas:

> *…collaboration online to reduce travel. Rather than prohibiting the more business-oriented "social networking" services such as Facebook in the office, companies should be giving "unfettered access" to them, says Oram.*

We have made significant progress with recent focus on data consolidation and virtualization. But, while every bit counts, it is small compared to the potential impacts of applying IT. Also, we've been fortunate that being green has happened to align with cheap. Next year's challenges may not provide such easy options – lean doesn't necessarily equal green, and green isn't necessarily lean. Are we prepared to support a technician who points out that a supplier doesn't have good labour relations in the 3rd world? What would happen, say, if someone showed that avoiding child labour meant a 50% increase in costs? Do we actually read the green blurb that is attached to most RFP responses? Could we make decisions on the basis of it? Do we support an accounting system that really supports a triple bottom line approach?

A *Sustainable Lens* perspective sees beyond opportunities to market green business, instead it asks questions that might truly transform a business.

green is the new sex

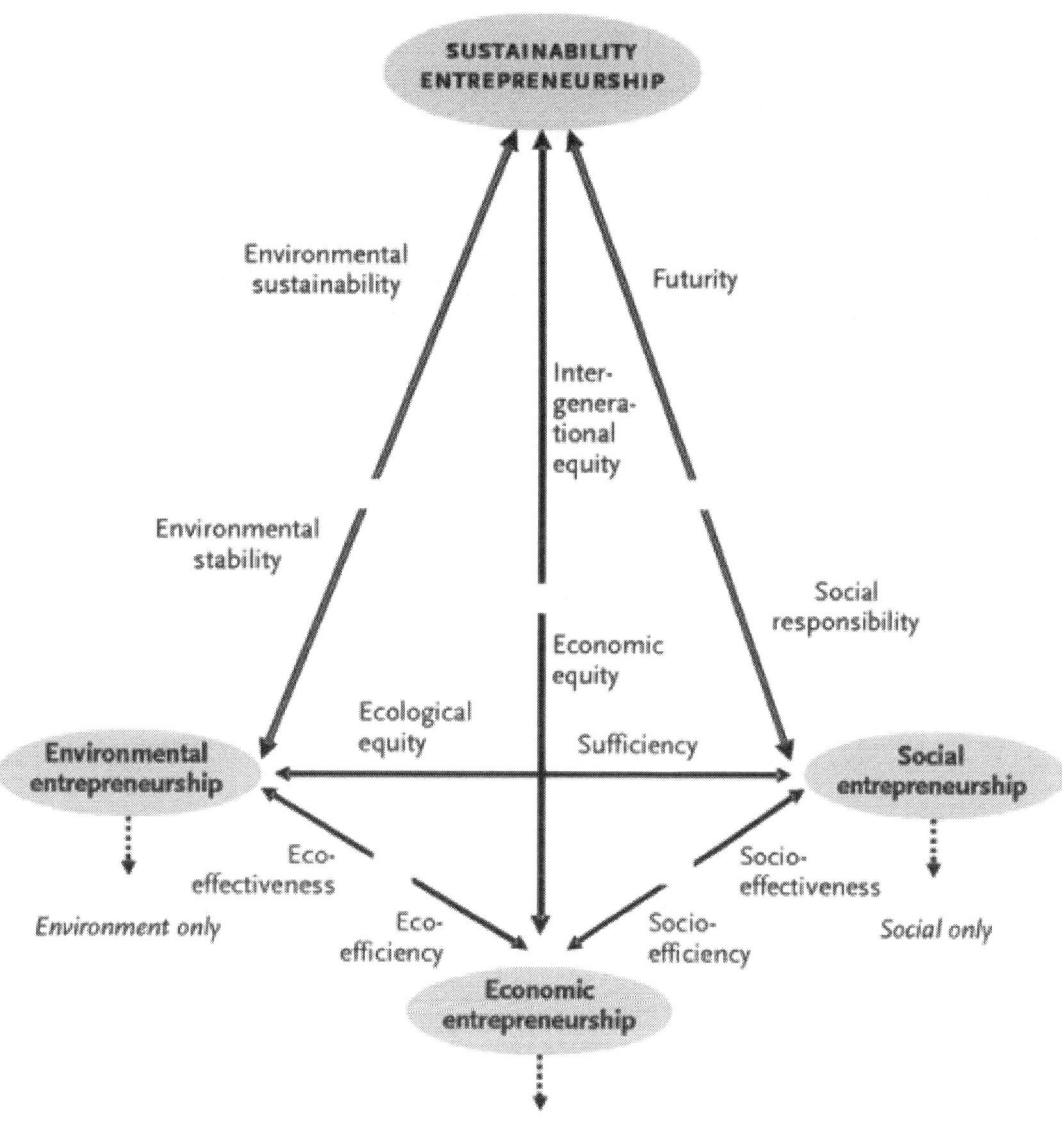

> The *Sustainable Lens* should challenge, but do so in the right language.

Sustainability is about doing. We need everyone to see through the *Sustainable Lens*. This thought, however, is not universal. The adoption of sustainability by certain industry and sectors considered by many to be inherently unsustainable. In *Hijacking Sustainability*, Parr (2009) describes sustainability as a camouflage:

> *The more the power of sustainability culture is appropriated by the mechanisms of State and corporate culture, the more it camouflages the darker underbelly of both—militarism and capitalism.*

On capitalism:

> *Any brand—whether it is an ecobrand or not is irrelevant—is premised upon the idea that the landscape (understood not just as a geographic area but a territory defined by relations formed between social, economic, political, ecological, and cultural life) is passive, meaning it is there as a medium for consumption.*

On the military:

> *Clearly, the proposition to transform the culture of the military to be more environmentally friendly and focused on advancing and using principles of sustainability is a cynical exercise… it is used to conceal the fact that the effects of military power are fundamentally unsustainable… that the policy to green the military is insincere at best because it conceals the fact that the military's function is to conduct war.*

Environmental degradation, poverty, war and inequality all stem from the complex. The perversity of an 'environmentally friendly' killing machine does not go unnoticed. Nor should we making sustainability a responsibility of the military: the issues are global and not "a selective problem of security, exclusive to any one particular nation".

While I agree with much of Parr's sentiment, I am also pragmatic. We need mining, we need roads. Arguing that capitalism as whole is doomed won't get us anywhere. We probably will always need a military. People working in these areas have a far bigger impact on sustainability than someone working in an organic food market. For sustainability to get traction within sectors, we need to aim for models of sustainability that best align with the models of the sector. This is not to say that these shouldn't challenge the sector - the whole point is to engender change - but rather to use perceptual models that are familiar.

Augnebroe and Pearce (1998) describe a required paradigm shift for the construction industry. They do this, though in the context of a familiar model - the project or management triangle. The value of the triangle is to highlight the interaction between the constraints of cost, time and quality. While often reduced to the maxim "cost, quality, time: pick any two", there are, of course an infinite number of positions within the triangle. Augnebroe and Pearce make use of this image to argue for a broader look in both time (full life cycle assessments), space (the object in its wider system settings) and costs (greener cost metrics than pure monetary). They then operationalise the wider perspective through a set of sustainability indicators.

The triangle suffers from the same limitations we saw with earlier triangles - namely that it assumes a zero-sum: human satisfaction is in opposition to environmental impact and energy.

We cannot afford (in sustainability terms) to be alienating the people whom we need to make the biggest changes. The concept of the *Sustainable Lens* is most important for areas we might think inherently unsustainable.

even bad business?

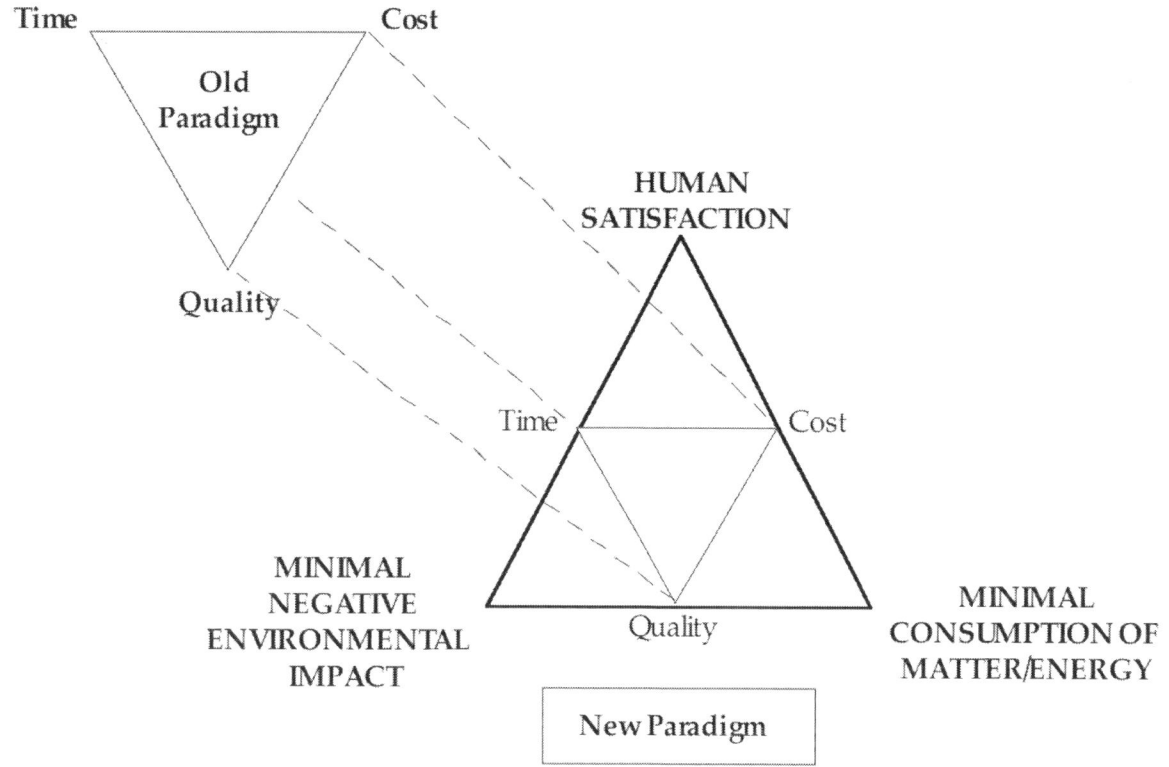

> Going beyond the products themselves, different organisations are examining the whole business model in terms of sustainable systems.

Describing the role of a sustainable practitioner at an conceptual level is quite easy, I've done this with several groups: Find an 'Introduction to x (Accounting, Medical Sciences etc)' textbook. In the first few pages, there will almost certainly be a section describing why anyone would chose such a career – beyond the technical details, what are the characteristics of the discipline. I would be very surprised if that description does not align with statements about sustainability. It is not far from here to write statements about that discipline's contribution to sustainable futures.

On a more practical level, it is also relatively easy to describe what the members of a discipline can do to begin a journey towards sustainability. What are the things that move towards that sustainable future? Thinking of both the footprint (negative impacts) and footprint (positive impacts) makes this much easier. It also helps to think of up and down the supply chain, and of the impacts and drivers at different scales of time, space and species.

The work being done within the design field is a good example. Rather than a singular concern for their own impact – the source of paints (say), they have taken seriously the wider role of their discipline. Here's the opening line from the Queensland Design Strategy 2020 (QG 2009): "Good design is sustainable design". This definition comes from the British Design Council's *Good Design Plan* (2008). Sir Michael Bichard introduces the British document by saying that the establishment of design stems from problems:

> Now in the 21st century the UK, alongside all other nations, faces even more thorny challenges. Solutions frequently seem elusive or at odds with each other. For example, addressing the business challenges of intensified global competition must be reconciled with pressure on natural resources and the threat of climate change. Equally, the universal provision of essential services, such as healthcare, must take account of an ageing population, rising levels of chronic disease and limited resources.

Bichard recognises that design is more than products, "but in helping us conceive the systems behind them". The Good Design document goes on to present five objectives for the national strategy. Crucially, they see sustainability as vital to the success of the design industry and Britain as a whole. Sustainability is not seen as an isolated factor such as climate change, but seen holistically, and integrated with teamwork, adapting to change and community.

These diagrams represent the "typical company of the 20th Century" (left) and the "prototypical company of the 21st century" (right) from Ray Anderson of Interface (2003). At the start the "contemporary corporation — its vision, its processes, its ways of doing business — simply does not include sustainability". Through two intermediate stages (not shown) the company undergoes a transformation by eliminating damaging linkages and introducing sustainable linkages. Interface arrived at this prototype model by considering a natural metaphor.

> There was no blueprint for this kind of organization in business. But there was in nature. If nature designed an industrial process, what might it look like? How could we translate the operations of nature into a model for a business?

> Nature has some fundamental operating principles: it runs on sunlight and other renewable energy sources, it fits form to function, it recycles everything and it is extremely efficient — never creating excess or wasting — and, finally, it rewards cooperation.

Interface thus used biomimicry as a means to transform their business. The *Sustainable Lens* can enable a view of the whole business as a sustainable system.

buisness as sustainability systems

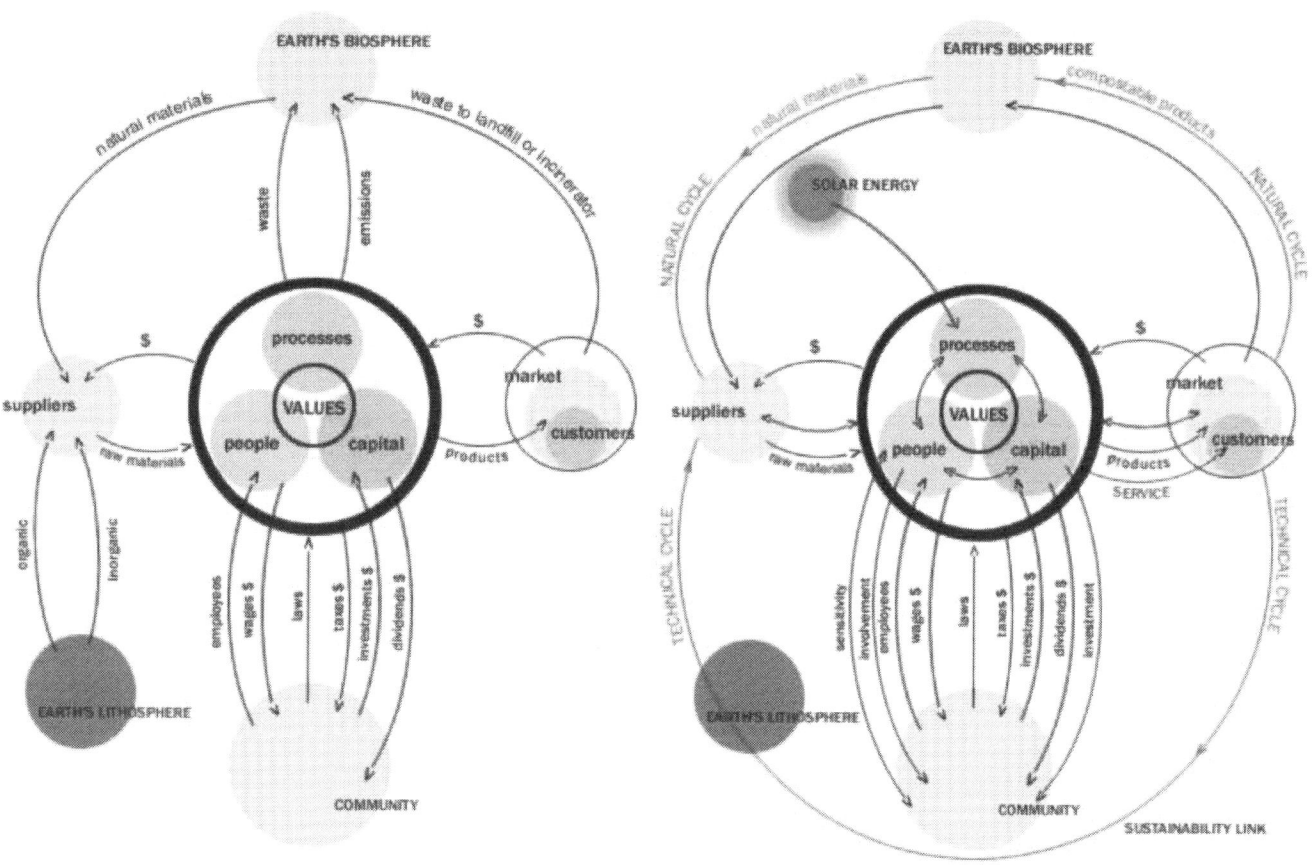

Each rung in Arnstein's ladder represents a grade in citizen power in influencing planning and policies. The bottom rungs describe "non participation", where engagement takes the form of manipulation or therapy (she was writing from a perspective of public health). The middle rungs platforms adopted by planning authorities in attempting to fulfil their participation responsibilities while still maintaining the dominant power structure. The top rungs represent a model where participants are able to establish a partnership with the state planners and have the power to share decision making responsibilities. In addition, they are able to influence and control outcomes.

Core to many sustainability frameworks is the notion of multiple legitimate perspectives.

> Meeting essential needs requires not only a new era of economic growth for nations in which the majority are poor, but an assurance that those poor get their fair share of the resources required to sustain that growth. Such equity would be aided by political systems that secure effective citizen participation in decision making and by greater democracy in international decision making.
> World Commission on Environment and Development (WCED, 1987)

There is an implicit assumption in most public policy writings and practice that participation is a good thing. **Further, there is a common notion that the more participation, the better. These notions can be traced to Sherry Arnstein's (1969) "ladder of participation" (on the arrow on the centre of the diagram).**

At the top rung of Arnstein's ladder: citizen control, the "have-nots" handle the entire job of planning, policy making and managing a programme e.g. neighbourhood corporation with no intermediaries between it and the source of funds.

This diagram from Regional Planning (Manitoba; right) shows the relationship between the Manfred Max-Neef's Human Needs Scale, Arnstein's Ladder of Citizen Participation (1969) and different types of development plans.

Tritter and MacCallum (2008) propose more nuanced model (also in health). They see that the Arnstein ladder uncritically endorses citizen control as pinnacle of involvement and question whether protagonists (the "somebodies" and "nobodies") should be conceptualised as opponents. Tritter and MacCallum see missing rungs, snakes and multiple ladders. The missing rungs are missing aspects of involvement in particular that Arnstein conflates means and ends - implying that user empowerment is the sole aim with a failure to consider the essential role of users in framing the problems, not just designing solutions. The ladder comes with adverse effects of application of the mode: snakes. Lastly the single dimension of power with a hierarchical model of user involvement. It fails to capture the dynamic and evolutionary nature of user involvement - multiple ladders might be better. Tritter and MacCallum suggest a different model: a tile mosaic - where tiles of different colours without systemic integration reveals only chaos.

A *Sustainable Lens* promotes participation but does so from a platform of empowerment and equality.

a ladder of participation

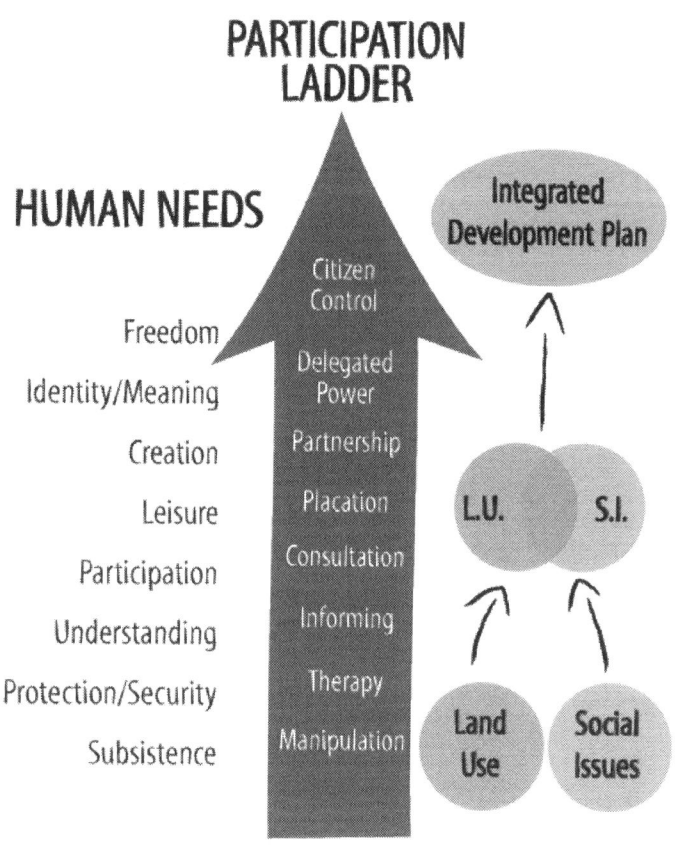

> A participatory community requires true involvement and engagement that results in real change. The nature of sustainability requires that initiatives must be both 'top-down' and 'bottom-up'. It relies on a well-informed, sensitive leadership and on community-wide support.

Development without the participatory element can result in "big brother sustainability" (as Wals and Jickling, 2002 apply to Education for Sustainability: left). Writing in Education for Sustainability terms but more widely applicable, Jensen and Schnack (1997) describe:

> *Education for democracy, or political liberal education, is, in itself, a fundamental educational task. We do not believe in educational efforts in relation to the environment, health and peace which are divorced from this fundamental perspective...democracy is participation. In a democracy, the members are not spectators, but participants; not equally active participants in everything all the time, naturally, but always potential participants who decide for themselves in what and when they will be involved.*

This puts the choice to be involved in the hands of the people. An important role of the government - or indeed the change agent at any level - is to provide opportunities for real engagement. This real engagement means cooperation as equals which might require education and capability building. In this regard Lyons *et al.* (2001) describe three forms of empowerment and the related focus of development for each. A focus on the unit and mechanism of empowerment reflects a realisation of rights through improving negotiations with external agents. Such goals are addressed through building communities or organisations. A focus on the purpose of empowerment is aimed to realise the rights to enable greater control over livelihood resources. Here the focus of development is on structures to manage resources and on capacity building to do that (ie education of participants). Lastly a goal of development of individuals where economic and social constraints act as prime barriers, focusing primarily on 'human capital' is addressed through building social structures to enable participation by overcoming these "psychological barriers.

The last barrier of Lyon's reflects a common issue with initiatives that attempt to increase public involvement but without addressing underlying issues of political and economic systems. Kraft (2004), for example, describes the greatest obstacle to increased public involvement is technical and complex nature of sustainability issues - but without addressing a need for transformation of systems. Seemingly agnostic terms as "public interest" and "public good" are "problematic in a deeply stratified society for they tend to reflect the worldview of the dominant group in seemingly apolitical terms" (Geczi 2007).

MacGregor (2000, right) developed an analytical model for assessing community sustainability based around the three pillars - environment, society and economy, but arranged according to participation. The vertical axis is a measure of strength of community, which when combined with the pillar dimensions (MacGregor describes as three, but is represented in x,y) gives a triangular image that aims to convey the impression of a community that is disparate, diffuse and lethargic at the bottom as opposed to one that is sustainable, highly united, integrated and committed at the top. The vertical hierarchy is divided into five levels - from bottom to top: basic needs; information; attitudes; activity; and, completion. At the apex of the model is the sustainability 'vision'. MacGregor sees an alignment between the meeting of needs of the community and the structure of the community - basic needs must be satisfied before the level of information becomes important. Although they are arranged sequentially, and hence suggesting dependence, this is not seen as absolute.

A *Sustainable Lens* perspective is based on informed participation. This results in better decisions but is not an easy road.

participation goes both ways

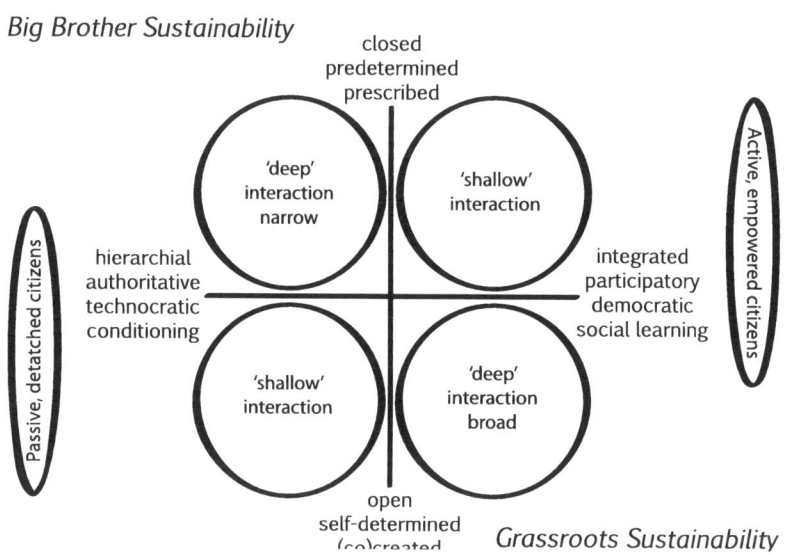

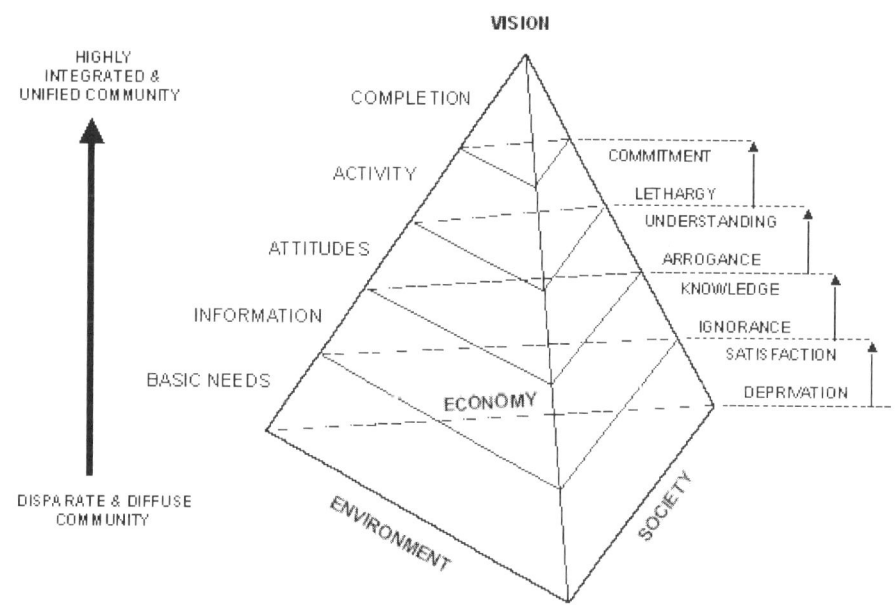

> Sustainability here is constructed from space, time, and human dimensions.

This model by Iribarnegaray and Seghezzo (2011) has a Venn diagram in common with the Barbier Venn diagram. Like the Barbier Venn it has overlapping circles, each of different elements, and like, the Barbier diagram it only has sustainability in the middle - the intersection. However, unlike the Barbier diagram, the pillars are dimensions rather than topic areas.

Iribarnegaray and Seghezzo outline what they see as shortcomings in the Brundtland definition of sustainability - a definition which as we've seen is described, albeit imperfectly by the Barbier Venn diagram.

Iribarnegaray and Seghezzo argue that the "essential anthropocentrism of the (Brundtland) definition makes it a weak conceptual framework to discuss issues of development". He asserts that the definition overestimates the explanatory power of economic reasoning and does not pay enough attention to other, fundamental aspects of development. Seghezzo rejects the notion that nature and culture are a dichotomy that can only be reconciled by the economy. The economy, he argues, is incompatible with the long term thinking required to attain intergenerational justice - tools such as cost-benefit analysis and discounting are at best perverse in the favouring of current generations.

Iribarnegaray and Seghezzo propose an alternative model that instead seems to be an abstraction of the learnings from Traditional Ecological Knowledge with temporal and spatial dimensions explicit, and recognition of values and wellbeing.

A triangle is formed by dimensions of 'Place', 'Permanence', and 'Persons:

(a) Place, the three-dimensional physical and geographical, but also culturally constructed space where we live and interact. This includes an embodied nature.

(b) Persons, the fourth dimension, a symbol of people as individual human beings and not as undifferentiated members of society. Seghezzo sees individual needs involving feelings - love, safety, identity, esteem and self-fulfilment - as distinct from social aggregations.

From this base of "real, objective and concrete things" a dimension of "ideal, abstract and subjective" is projected.

(c) Permanence, the fifth temporal dimension, provides for intergenerational equity - our intertemporal moral relations (this notion is co-opted from Adam 1998). This dimension is not a maintenance of present conditions, it includes change and improvements.

The triangle is overlain with a Venn diagram, with sets formed by the vertices of the triangle: Intergenerational Justice, Intergenerational Justice, and Identity/Happiness.

Iribarnegaray and Seghezzo argue that this new conceptual framework could augment or complement previous paradigms, instead of replacing them.

A *Sustainable Lens* using dimensions constructed from space, time, and human aspects can then place reources and decisions in a plane of sustainability.

people, time and space

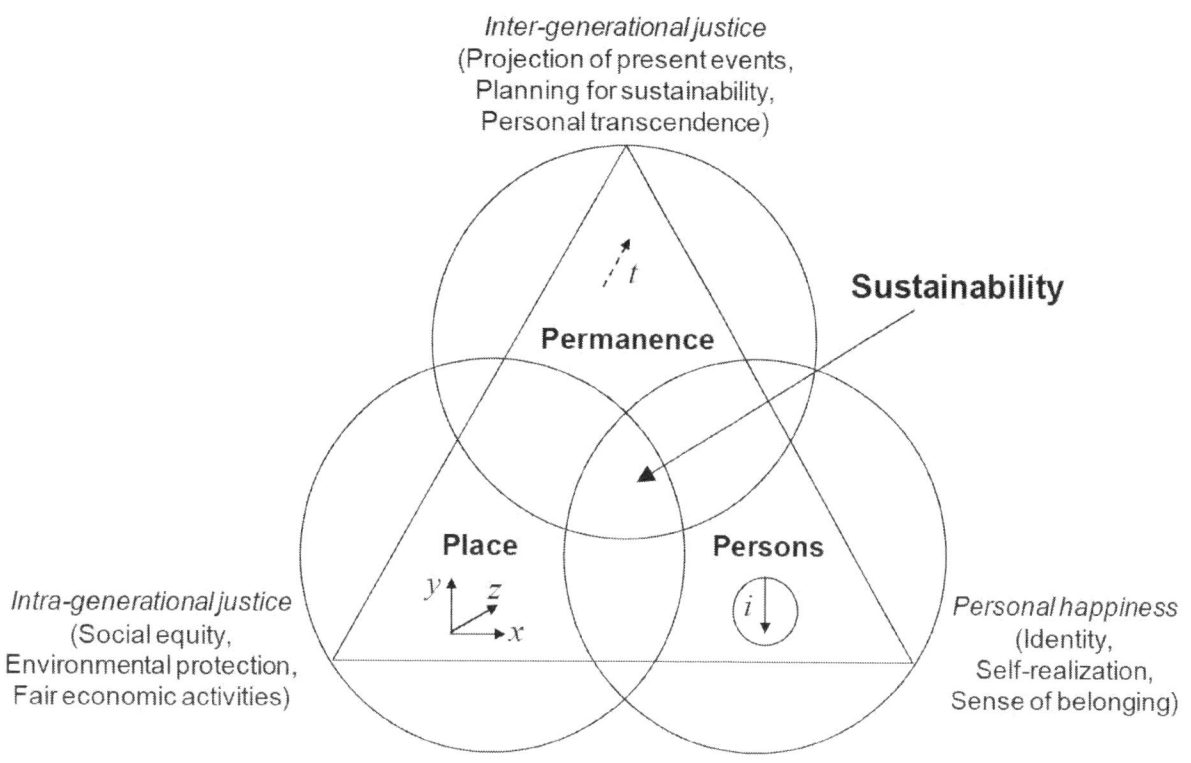

> Perhaps the most significant development in sustainability in recent years is a recognition of the need for action. While this has long been the case on the individual and small scale, it is now increasingly realised that actions speak louder than words. It is critical then, we use our *Sustainable Lens*es to see potential change and structures to be able to make things happen – or in other words that we are change agents (AtKisson 2009, Robinson 2009, or "change champions" Darnton *et al.* 2005).

Schendler (2009) describes the scale of the problem as being "so great that to many people it is incomprehensible". He describes how individual actions – using canvas bags at the supermarket – are necessary but inadequate: "we can't afford the delusion that such individual action is enough". Instead, he argues that we need to define meaningful actions, and then "get those jobs done". Thus, he says, we should indeed change our light bulbs, but more important is the task of figuring out "how can you help ensure that everyone on the planet changes their light bulbs?". These are people "dedicated to promoting sustainability ideas and innovations – are needed in every field, in ever increasing numbers", they are, AtKisson says, the "sales force":

> *Change agents help the innovators translate their ideas to the mainstream. They learn how to 'work the system', so that new ideas can begin beneficially infiltrating the cultures, institutions and organizations where they are sorely needed.*

On a similar vein Schendler (2009) argues that we all need to be change agents. This is more than making changes for oneself. Schendler maintains that our challenges will not be solved merely by motivated individuals addressing their own footprint. While necessary, these actions are also insufficient, even if "every single one maxes out their opportunities". Even more important than one's own footprint is "what matters more is ensuring that everyone on the planet is also doing what you do".

Schendler sees the bigger picture – becoming a change agent – as the primary focus.

Schendler argues:

> *"To lessen the charges of hypocrisy that could be brought against any of us, it seems obvious that the best thing to do would be to implement even more sustainable practices— the real ones, things that really matter and drive real change. To do that you need to be clear-eyed about how you can make a real difference: you need to find your biggest lever and use it".*

For Schendler, a manager in the Aspen ski business, his lever was leadership through brand recognition, for Walmart, he argues, it is supply chain influence ("what really matters is what's on the shelves"). For educators, for example, our biggest lever is our ability to positively influence the skills, values and behaviours of our graduates. This leverage extends beyond sustainability. It is, of course, why we have an education system at all. **For computing professionals, for another example, it is in the potential impact of the system improvements we enable** (Forum for the Future's Connected: *ICT and sustainable development*, Madden and Weißbrod 2008).

Schendler argues that "our job is to find out how we can have a vastly disproportionate impact". James Samuel of Waiheke Island leads a movement for a sustainable future. He says that he aims to spend no more than 20% of his time talking about what needs to change, and instead focuses on demonstrating a more vibrant future.

A *Sustainable Lens* will ensure that people have addressed their own footprint and then move onto to creating a better society - not through coercion, but by demonstration and true leadership as change agents.

levers of change

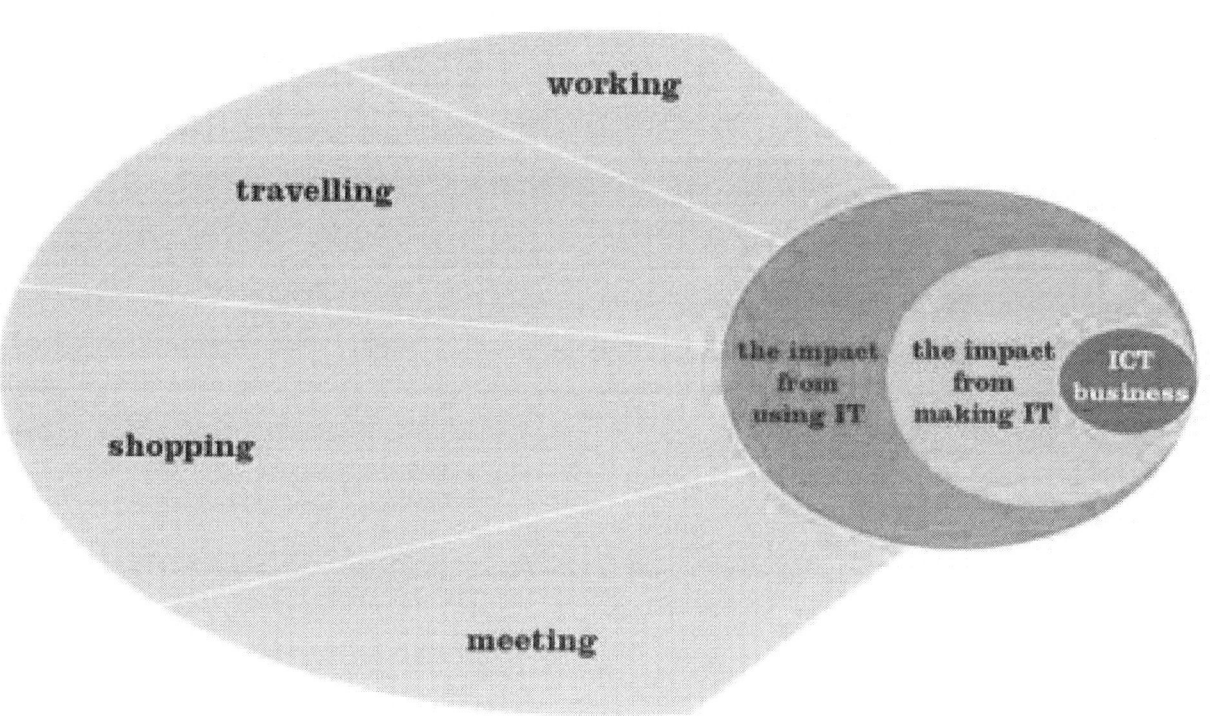

> Ethics is about doing the right thing (or doing good, or navigating between two extremes) and a sustainability paradigm gives us a framework for doing good, for recognising that coexisting on a crowded planet with limited resources means our actions can adversely affect others. These ethical underpinnings of sustainability can be found following numerous pathways through philosophy and theology.

Our Common Future described sustainability as an issue of ethics. Brundtland "tried to show how human survival and well-being could depend on success in elevating sustainable development to a global ethic" (WCED).   The binding between the "goal of development" and the "proviso of sustainability" is clearly rooted in ethics. For Fagan (2009), the ethical imperative is the basis of sustainability:

> "To live a particular lifestyle that, knowingly, impacts detrimentally on a neighbour – be that an individual living in the next house – or a country in the next region, cannot, arguably, be tolerated. To know of poverty in the economically developing world and not use that knowledge to act to relieve it, could be considered unethical. This position holds profound implications for politicians, schools and universities".

Immanuel Kant's ethical stance was the categorical imperative: act as though your behaviour could become a general rule i.e. could everyone else do the same? Can your behaviour become the norm?   Jean-Paul Satre's first ethic was about the individual realizing the potential of their own freedom and not making excuses. Satre's second ethic is that, if we are free we should then work towards the freedom of others.

Emmanuel Lévinas also emphasised the importance of the existence of the other (other persons) the interaction with whom plays a crucial role in the creation of ourselves. If we only had ourselves to bounce off, life would be meaningless. Helping others and having a responsibility for them (even if it's simply exchanging pleasantries heartfelt or perfunctory) allows us the chance to move beyond ego.   For Lévinas, responsibility is threefold; having enough knowledge to be able to respond appropriately, the ability to choose the good response, and an obligation to care for the other person. In *The Heart of Justice: Care Ethics and Political Theory*, Daniel Engster (2008) places caring at the centre of a moral and political theory:

> *Our moral obligations to care for others thus generates collective responsibility to organise our political, economic, international and cultural institutions at least in part to support caring practices and care for individuals in need.*

Developed to "make ethical reasoning explicit" in health fields, this diagram is David Seedhouse's (2009) Ethical Grid. The grid consists of 20 viewpoints or issues, arranged in four concentric rings practicalities, outcomes and priorities ("the good"), moral duties ("the ought") and basic purpose. Brooks and Atkinson (2008) describe Seedhouse's grid as "a landscape of moral reasoning" and apply to wider socio-technical decisions (eg computing).

A *Sustainable Lens* should help provide a framework - or a context for living - where decisions are not black and white.

responsibility for the other...

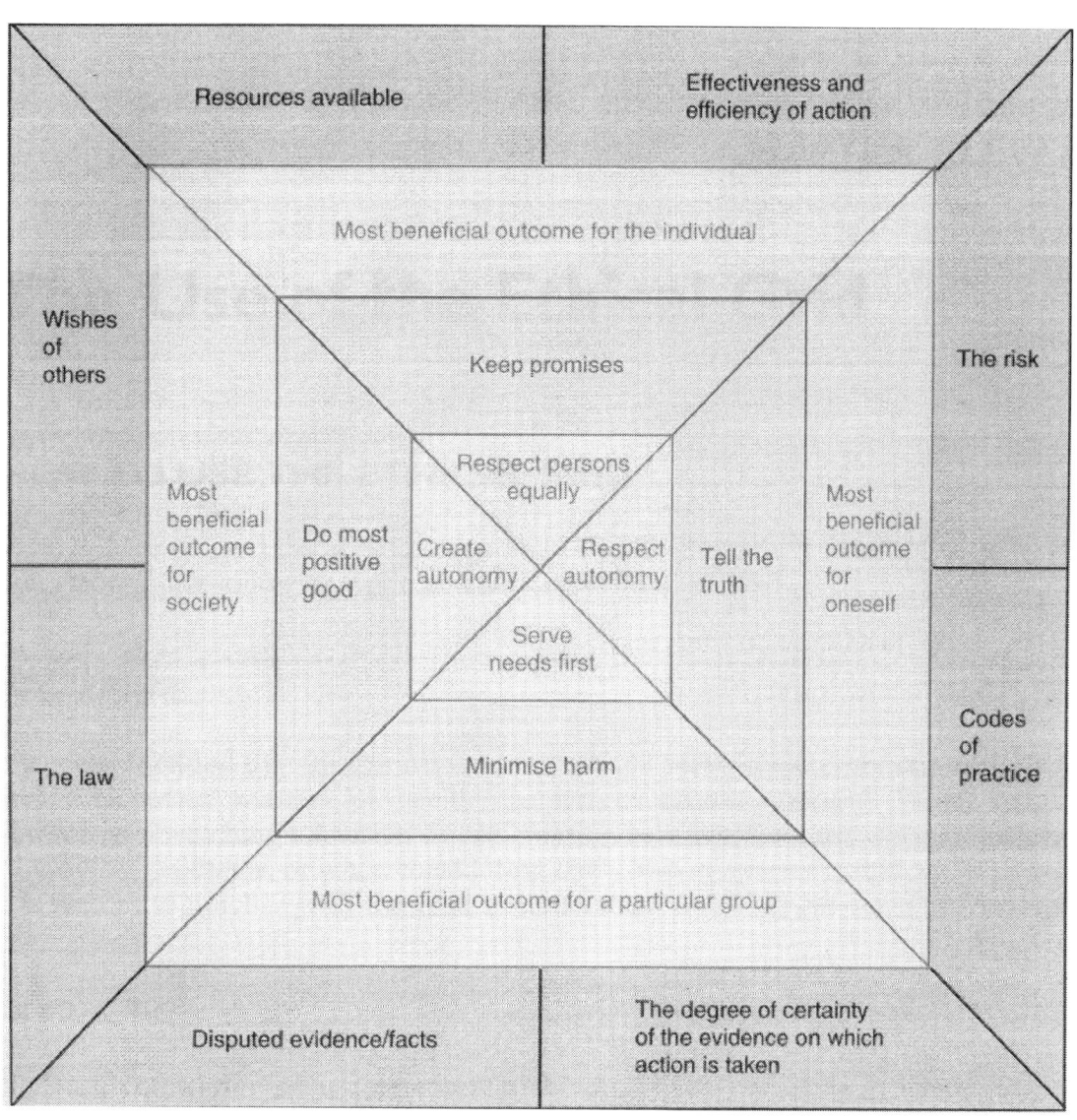

> Responsibility is deep, and stretches time and space.

Engster (2008) saw dependency as the basis for human rights:

> 'All human beings depend upon other human beings to survive, develop and function, we all make claims on other human beings for care. Our universal dependency on other human beings for care thus gives rise to a universal framework of human rights.'

We are dependent on others and so there is a reasonable (and reasoned) expectation that they can depend on us. This is expressed in the Child rights ecology model (UN Convention Rights of the Child: left) That human rights both encompasses and contributes to sustainability is now an accepted stance:

> Agreement among human communities on a set of basic needs has led to the - still evolving - concept of human rights. The first generation of human rights was civil and political in nature and was based on the cardinal value of freedom. The second generation are economic and social human rights, based on the cardinal value of social justice. At this stage a third generation of rights is needed consisting of inclusive ecological rights and based on solidarity with future generations and with non-humans.
> Lautensach (2004)

Noel Preston (2008) pulls these arguments together in an ethic of response which for him, combines the trinity of ethical approaches (utilitarian = create the most happiness and the least suffering, Kantian = act in a way that your actions could become a universal rule, virtue ethics= take the golden mean between two extremes) and enables us to apply them in the real world. The relevance here is simply because Lévinas said we have a responsibility to the other. Can his philosophy be applied to sustainability that talks about inter- and intra generational equity, caring for the Earth's resources for our descendents and for other people living now (and their descendents). Can the other also be extended to non-human individuals.

Preston argues that an ethic of response takes seriously a basic human experience of men and women as being in dialogue or conversation with themselves, with their god, with nature, with each other: man/woman 'the answerer or responder' is the key image. In that dialogue we inquire, to assess the situation: What exactly are you responding to? What are the facts? Who are the stakeholders? What will be the consequences?

Peter Singer (2010) the Australian Utilitarian philosopher has a drowning thought experiment. You're in a nice suit and you walk past a small shallow pond where a child is drowning. Without hesitation you wade in and rescue the child. The only sacrifice you've made is some shoes and a dry-cleaning bill. Everyone agrees that they would wade in so then Singer says that if you're willing to do that then you should be able to give a sizable amount of money to trustworthy charities to help people in poorer countries. A small amount can save a life.

The twist brought to this by a *Sustainable Lens*, are the geographical and temporal dimensions of sustainable development - we need to practice these ethics across space and time (Langhelle 1999: right).

...the river is wide, deep, and long

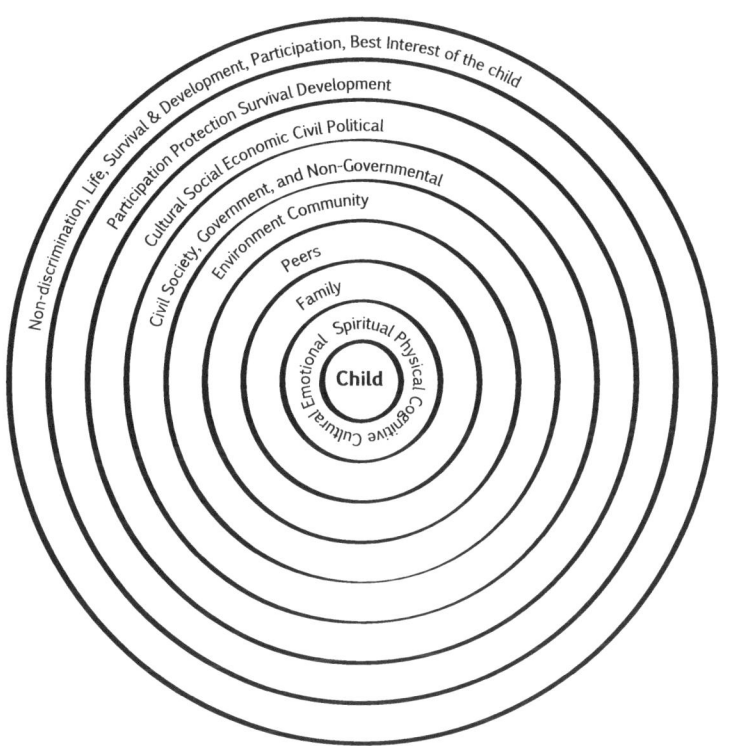

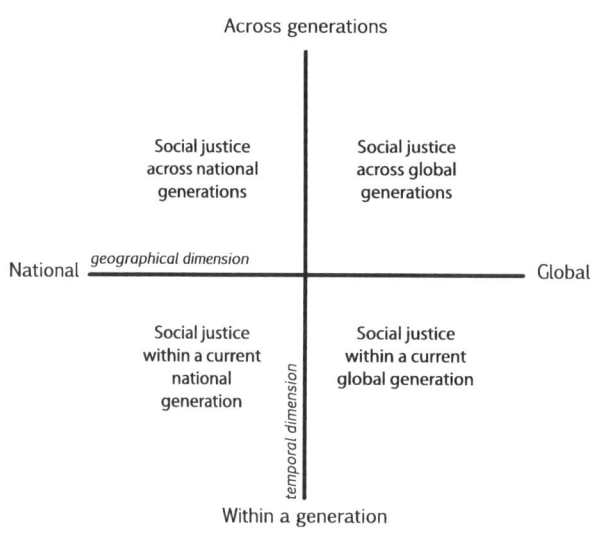

Marshall and Toffel (2005:left) apply Maslow's needs hierarchy to human and natural environment (essentially combining the top layers - self actualisation etc, which they see as devaluing sustainability) focussing on survival aspects.

Ethics is about doing the right thing (or doing good, or navigating between two extremes) and a sustainability paradigm gives us a framework for doing good, for recognising that coexisting on a crowded planet with limited resources

Bosselmann (2008) argues that a third element needs to be added to Brundtland's concern for present and future generations of human beings: "concern for the non-human natural world" (interspecies justice or equality).   Going the other way: social justice has been an important concern of ethics. Now we are called to extend our notions of justice, embracing the sacredness of all forms of life and granting rights to other species, ecosystems and the Earth as whole. As Thomas Berry remarked (2000, 2009), our moral concerns should include biocide and ecocide as well as homicide and genocide. This wider ethics calls for solidarity with the entire Earth, ecological sustainability, lifestyles of sufficiency, and a more participatory politics.

> Perhaps we are beginning to move towards a new global ethic
> which transcends all other systems of allegiance and belief,
> which is rooted in a consciousness of the interrelatedness and
> the sanctity of life. Would such a common ethic have the power
> to motivate us to modify our current dangerous course? There
> is no ready answer except to say that without a moral and
> ethical foundation sustainability is unlikely to become a reality.
> UNESCO (1997)

The implication for the *Sustainable Lens* is that we need to see in a way that forms an interpretive dialogue. Our *Sustainable Lens* has to act to facilitate a two way communication with shareholders (which might be giant land snails). We need to elicit a wide range of sources and interpret this information *"within a framework of social solidarity and life's interconnectedness, after consideration of appropriate values, principles and the character disposition of the moral agent".* Preston suggests respect for life, justice and trust as three guiding values in the decisions that form part of the dialogue.

This image from the Spangenburg (2005: right) has an institutional imperative of strengthening participation . The image is of a triangular pyramid with the vertices as pillars (plus institution), and elements on the six edges. The participation vertex extends the usual interaction between the pillars to include justice, care and democracy.   As with all triangular representations there is an unsighted point of sustainability, and a perhaps unintended message that sustainability requires a trade-off between these factors.

...and inclusive

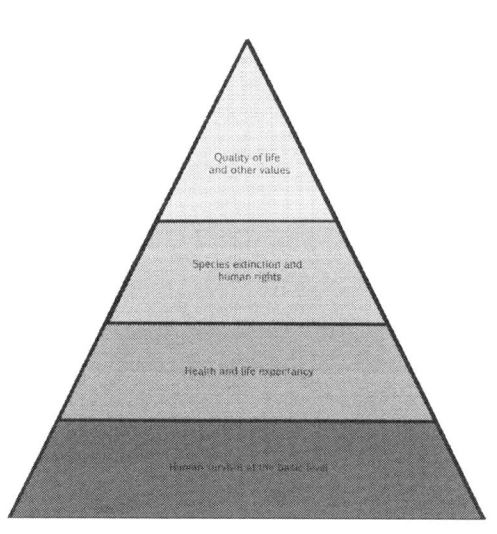

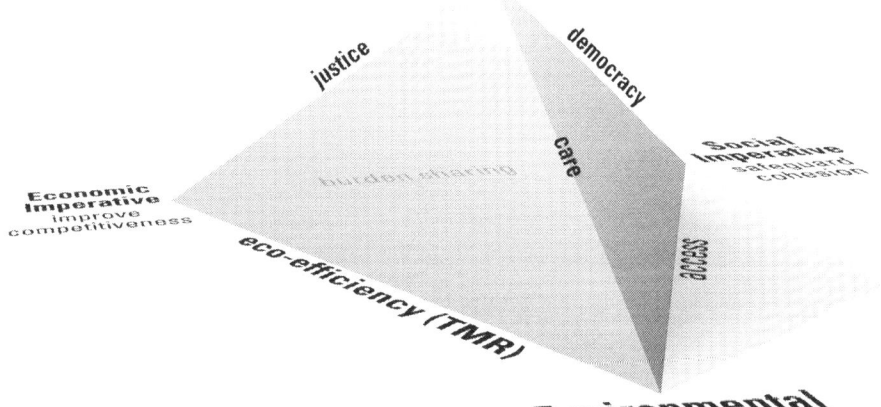

> "Learning to be" is an holistic concept that includes values.

The Age of Enlightenment refers to the time beginning the in 17th Century when reason was advocated as the primary source of human authority. This is the basis of much of our culture, science and philosophy, and eventually the new industrial world order. There is a reluctance (in Western dialogue at least) to discuss things at an ethical, moral or even religious level. The result of this aversion is that everything is now determined on a "rational" and "economic" and "scientific" level, while many of us still think in other terms. Unfortunately, the Enlightenment is not value free. As part of this transformation human beings were placed in a "privileged position, apart from the natural world, above it, and empowered to exploit nature in any way that served their immediate interests. Hossay (2006) argues that from this "enlightened" perspective, the "environmental damage done was no tragedy; quite the reverse, it was in keeping with the natural order".

In 1972 Edgar Faure's *Learning to Be: the world of education today and tomorrow* saw education as "reaching out to embrace the whole of society and the entire lifespan of the individual". In 2005 this lifelong learning was used as the basis for UNEVOC "learning to do" values framework (Quisumbing and de Leo 2005).

The argument of "Learning to Be" is that within vocational and technical education, there needs to be a on formation of values, attitudes, modes of behaviour and ways of life that may lead to a culture of peace and sustainability.

> A sustainable knowledge based society must be values-centred, anchored on the respect for human life, human dignity, the plurality and diversity of societies, human labour and work as source of self fulfilment, as well as the power that fuels all economic and social development.

Values are defined here as the "ideals that give significance to our lives; that are reflected through the priorities we choose; and that we act on consistently and repeatedly. UNEVOC's role is vocational education, so generic values such as sense of self worth, self esteem and dignity, are joined by an ability to work with integrity and honour, honesty, and punctuality.

They start, though, with dimensions of a person as an individual as a member of society: physical, intellectual, moral-ethical, aesthetic, socio-cultural, economic, political and spiritual. This society scales from family to world (top left).

These principles become core values (top right) when a direction is added to each dimension. Thus "intellectual" becomes "truth and wisdom", physical becomes "health and harmony with nature". These then form eight core values: holistic health and harmony with nature; truth and wisdom; love and compassion; creativity and appreciation of beauty; peace and justice; sustainable human development; national unity and global solidarity, and global spirituality. **These core values then expand out to form personal and work values, (lower image).** (note the same values are repeated, it is not clear why they are slightly rearranged). Self worth and dignity of labour are central "powerful overarching values".

The logic on the lower image is slightly circular. The outer ring describes "culture of peace for a sustainable quality of life for all", yet both peace and sustainable development are stated as values. Sustainable development is defined as development consisting of social and economic benefits, equitably shared, security and self sufficiency within the family and community, and a general sense of well being about oneself and others. It is sustainable when it is continuing and independent, and provides for the welfare of present and future generations. Within this core, there are future orientations, just stewardship for resources (caring attitude, wise use and equitable sharing), work ethic and responsibility.

valuing values

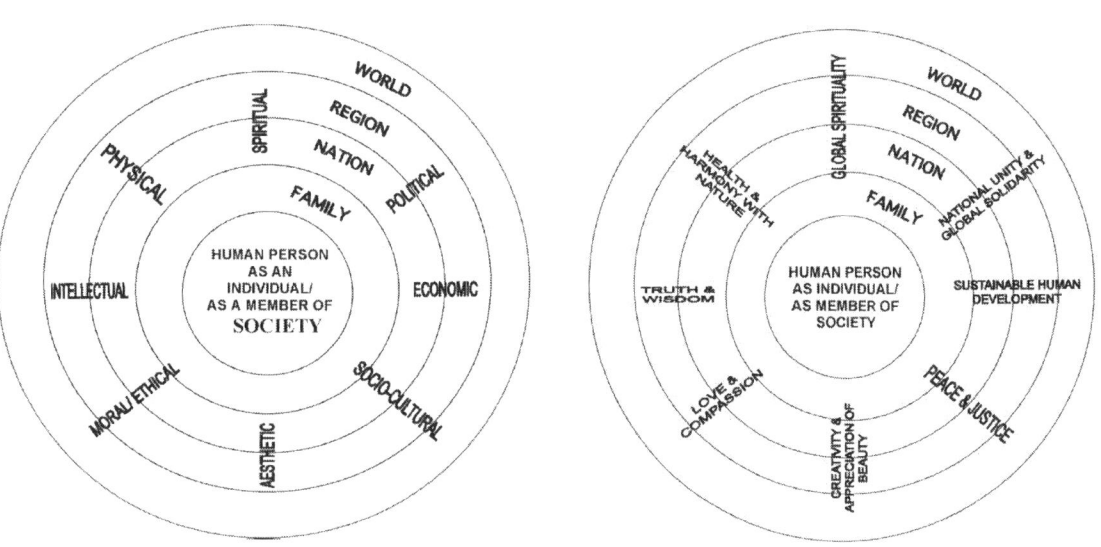

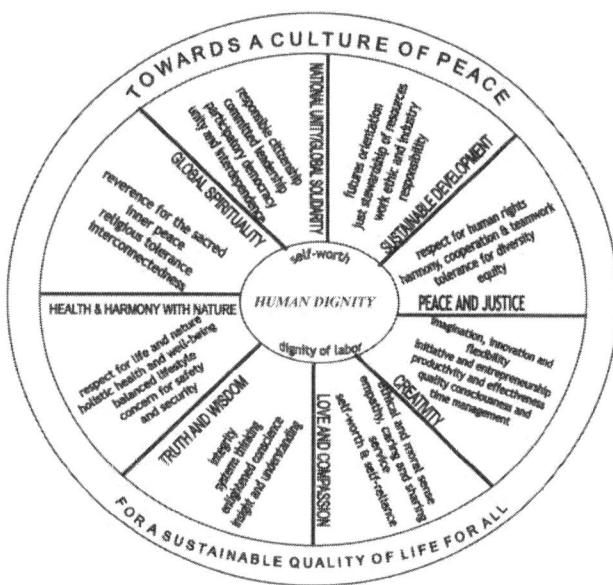

> It was good.

In 1967 Lynn White (1967) argued that Christian beliefs were critical to why science and technology turned against nature. In "The Historical Roots of Our Environmental Crisis" White argued that Christianity inherited from Judaism the Genesis story of the creation, wherein God established all of nature for the benefit of people. Being created in his own image these people were both separate from and have dominion over all of creation. Genesis, White argued, set modern Western people, through science and technology, on a collision course with nature. He concluded:

> *Both our present science and our present technology are so tinctured with orthodox Christian arrogance toward nature that no solution to the ecological crisis can be expected from them alone.*

As might be expected, White's essay prompted a huge response, and continues to do so. While theological philosophers describe a more positive Christianity/Nature relationship, the tensions remain sufficiently stressed for Norgaard (2002) to ask "in an atmosphere of rising tensions on key fronts between religion and science, especially biology, is there any hope of joining forces to save nature?".

This image of the Five Earths of the Bible comes from The Lamb and Lion Ministries. The first earth was created in the beginning. It was perfect (Genesis 1:31). It is the formation of the earth and what God said to Adam that causes accusations of arrogance towards nature - or, depending on your standpoint - stewardship.

> *And God said, Let us make man in our image, after our likeness: and let them have dominion over the fish of the sea, and over the fowl of the air, and over the cattle, and over all the earth, and over every creeping thing that creepeth upon the earth.*

But because of Man's sin, God placed a curse upon the earth (Genesis 3: 17-19) and makes an enemy of the land: "cursed is the ground because of you; in pain you shall eat of it all the days of your life... thorns and thistles it shall bring forth for you; and you shall eat the plants of the field". After the Flood "God blessed Noah and his sons and said to them, "Be fruitful and multiply and fill the earth" (Genesis 9:1). He also reaffirmed the controlling role over animals and plants "Into your hand they are delivered" (G9:2) - indeed mankind was now allowed to eat meat.

The third earth is where we are now. Beyond the Genesis account of Creation, the Bible - both the Old and New Testaments are peppered with messages that could be interpreted to indicate sustainability: Before Moses led the wandering Nation of Israel, he spent 40 years as a shepherd caring for a flock; Deuteronomy, even in a siege, don't destroy orchards (20:19-20); Job's does the hawk fly by your wisdom? (39:26); Psalm 104 describes the majesty of the ongoing creation - sentiments repeated in *Morning has Broken*; while Ecclesiastes (3:19) "For everything there is a season... a time to love, and a time to hate, a time for war, and a time for peace" (aka Peter Seeger's *Turn Turn Turn*). There are a multitude of quotes from Jesus on caring for others, from the Sermon on the Mount (Matthew 5-7), to selling what you have and giving to the poor (Matthew 19:21), to the Parable of the Good Samaritan (Luke 10:25-37) where Jesus commands to love your neighbour as yourself.

The fourth Earth will come seven years after rapture (accompanied by earthquakes). The "wolf and the lamb shall graze together" indicates very different relationships (Isaiah 65:25); mankind will be freed from the curse and once again be able to live in harmony with nature. After 1000 years Satan will leave the earth polluted and devastated (Revelation 20:7-9). God will take the Redeemed off the earth, place them in the New Jerusalem, and then cleanse the earth with fire (Peter 3:10-13).

Wider notions of caring are paramount in many belief frameworks. The beliefs represented in the Buddhist Bhavacakra (Wheel of Life), for example, represents Samsara, the process of coming into existence as a differentiated moral creature. Buddhism includes an an ecological vision and principle of interdependence that integrates all aspects of the ecosphere. There is a rejection of hierarchical dominance of humans over humans, and humans over nature. There is concern for the total living environment, extending loving kindness and compassion beyond people and animals to include plants and the earth itself.

A *Sustainable Lens* can make use of people's existing beliefs and value frameworks.

belief frameworks

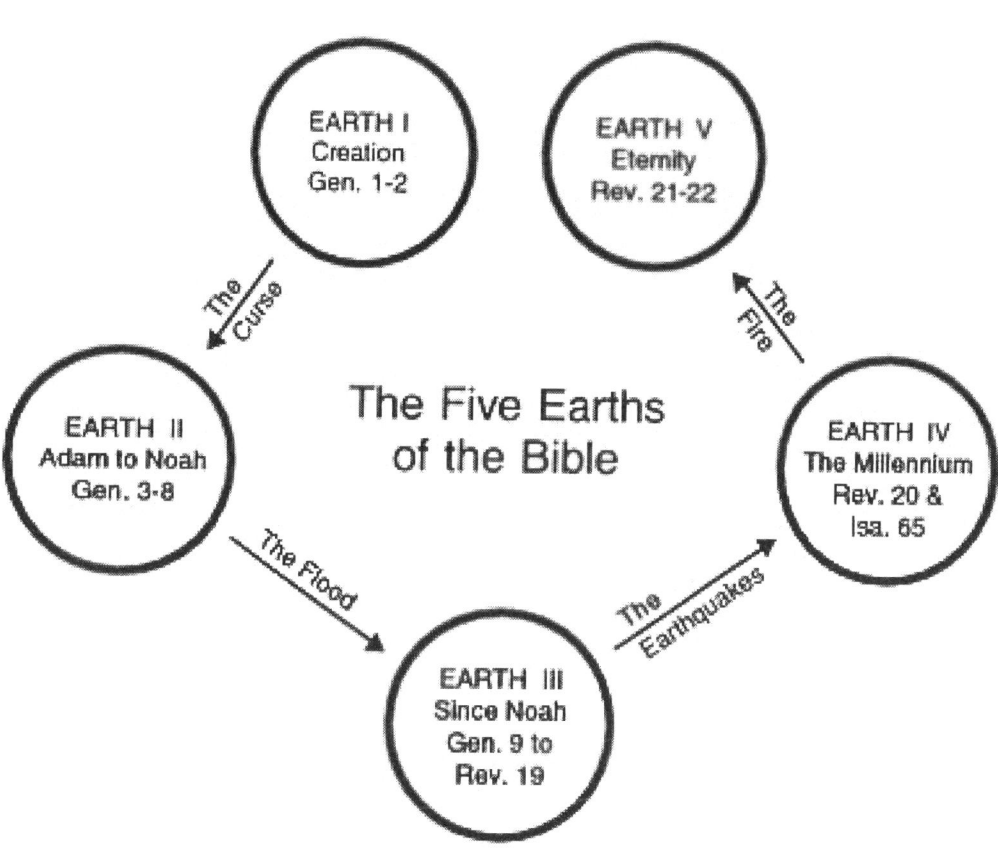

> The *Sustainable Lens* needs to recognise narratives of place.

David Orr (1992) described the role of an ecologically literate population. Such people, he argued are "able to distinguish health from its opposite and to live accordingly".

Glenn Albrecht (2010) questions the paucity of words and concepts in the English language that relate psychological states to the state of the environment. The Hopi have such a term - *koaanisqatsi* - meaning that human life is disintegrating and out of balance with the world. Albrecht aims to rectify this shortage by coining some words:

A *Pyschoterratic* illness arises from a negative relationship to our home environment, be it at local, regional or global scales. This makes explicit the connection between the Earth (terra) and mental state (psyche). The negative relationship may involve a loss of identity, loss of an endemic sense of place and a decline in well-being. It may be accompanied by a somaterratic (bodily) illness.

Solastalgia is the place based distress from the lived experience within the home environment (again, at any scale) of unwelcome environmental change. Solastalgia is derived from nostalgia which is the feeling of loss from dislocation from home environment in either time or space.

This image reflects the "invisible losses" felt by First Nations communities in Western Canada and the United States (described by Turner *et al.* **2008).** These eight losses are overlapping and cumulative: cultural/lifestyle losses, loss of identity, health losses, loss of self-determination and influence, emotional and psychological losses, loss of order in the world, knowledge losses, and indirect economic losses and lost opportunities. Turner describe how these losses are often place based and can be both dramatic (eg prohibition of access) or cumulative such as a general decline in the productivity of traditional food species because of habitat change from fire suppression over several decades. Turner argues that these factors should count in decision making, and suggest ways in which they can be made more visible such that decision making processes can be made more transparent (upwards arrows).

The term topophilia was coined by W.H. Auden in the introduction to John Betjeman's (1947) *Slick but not Streamlined* to refer to the love of a place. It was resurrected by Yi-Fu Tuan (1974) *Topophilia: a study of environmental perception, attitudes, and values.* Tuan defines topophilia as the affective bond with one's environment--a person's mental, emotional, and cognitive ties to a place. While this is often little more than a mild experience, it can become powerful where human emotions or cultural values are carried by the environment.

By adding an action motivation, Glenn Albrecht extends topophilia in a way that approaches sustainability:

> *Soliphilia is the love of the totality of our place relationship and a willingness to accept the political responsibility and solidarity needed between human to maintain then at all scales of existence.*

A goal of the *Sustainable Lens* must be to "equip a person to live well in a place".

sense of place

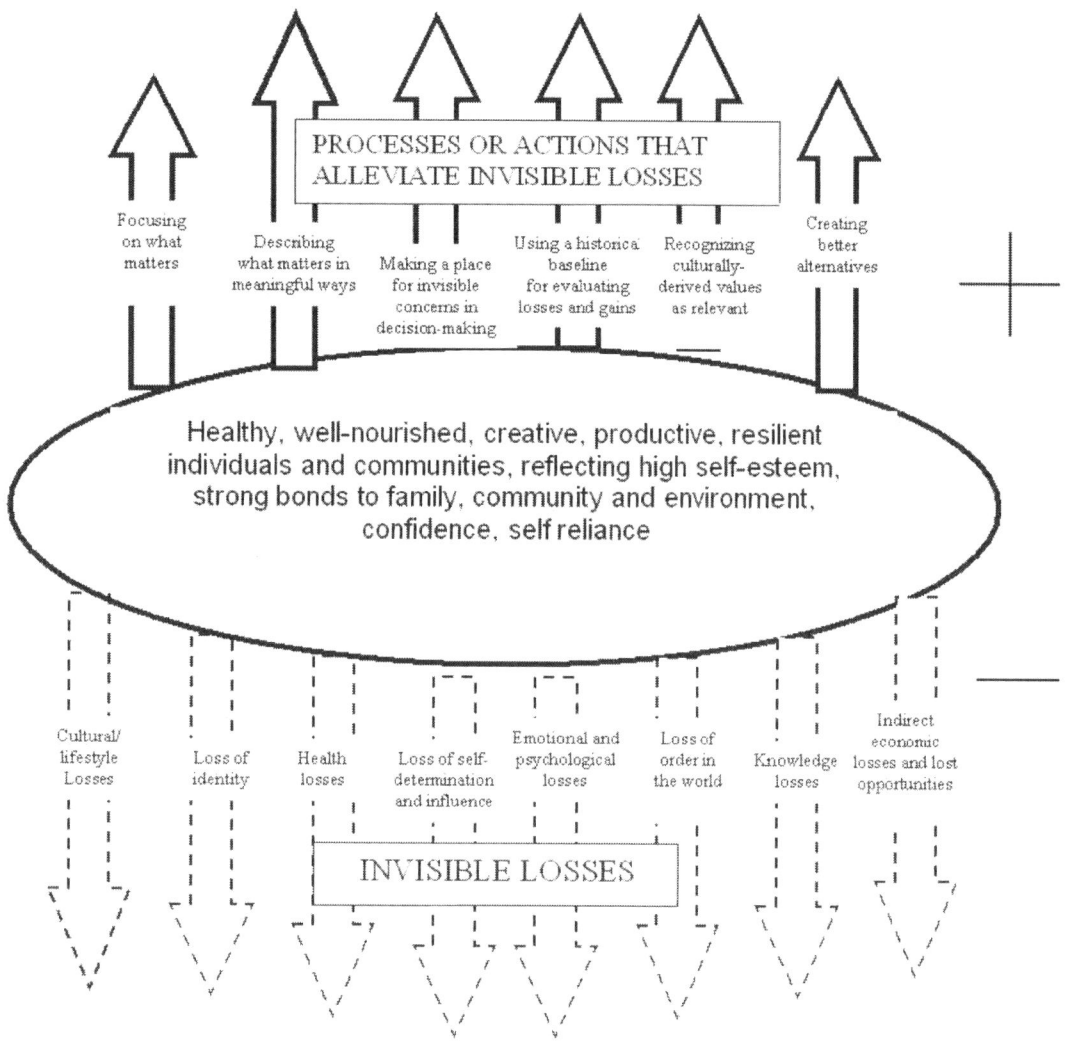

> Deep ecology seeks a more holistic view of the world we live in and seeks to apply to life the understanding that separate parts of the ecosystem (including humans) function as a whole. "The equal right to live and blossom is an intuitively clear and obvious value axiom".

Arne Næss (1973) described the "Deep Ecology Movement". Næss argued that ecology should not be concerned with man's place in nature but rather with every part of nature on an equal basis because the natural order has intrinsic value that transcends human values. Thus we should "not only protect the planet for the sake of humans, but also, for the sake of the planet itself, to keep ecosystems healthy for their own sake". The "Deep" comes from the deeper and holistic engagement the approach entails - asking why?

This "Deep Ecology" Næss contrasted with "Shallow Ecology movement" that has a focus on a "fight against pollution and resource depletion" and has the central objective of "the health and affluence of people in the developed countries".

Deep Ecology has eight principles (three general and five derived, Davell and Sessions 1985, see also Doak 1994). The eight principles are:

1. The well-being and flourishing of human and nonhuman life have value in themselves (synonyms: intrinsic value, inherent worth). These values are independent of the usefulness of the nonhuman world for human purposes.

2. Richness and diversity of life forms contribute to the realization of these values and are also values in themselves.

3. Humans have no right to reduce this richness and diversity except to satisfy vital needs.

4. The flourishing of human life and cultures is compatible with a substantially small human population. The flourishing of nonhuman life requires a smaller human population.

5. Present human interference with the nonhuman world is excessive, and the situation is rapidly worsening.

6. Policies must therefore be changed. These policies affect basic economic, technological, and ideological structures. The resulting state of affairs will be deeply different from the present.

7. The ideological change will be mainly that of appreciating life quality (dwelling in situations of inherent value) rather than adhering to an increasingly higher standard of living. There will be a profound awareness of the difference between bigness and greatness.

8. Those who subscribe to the foregoing points have an obligation directly or indirectly to try to implement the necessary changes.

Deep ecology's core principle is the claim that, like humanity, the living environment as a whole has the same right to live and flourish. Thus, humans do not exist independently in the environment, rather we connect with a much larger sense of self by extending our sense of identification to wider sphere of relationships. This relational thinking provides a wider concept of Self ego (beyond the ego self), allowing a viewpoint to understand our complicated systems such as ecosystem, social systems.

Næss's "Apron Diagram" (2005) used to demonstrate the complementary logical relationships between Deep Ecology and other philosophies and diverse practices that together form the total view.

This integrated view of Deep Ecology provides a platform for the *Sustainable Lens*.

deep ecology

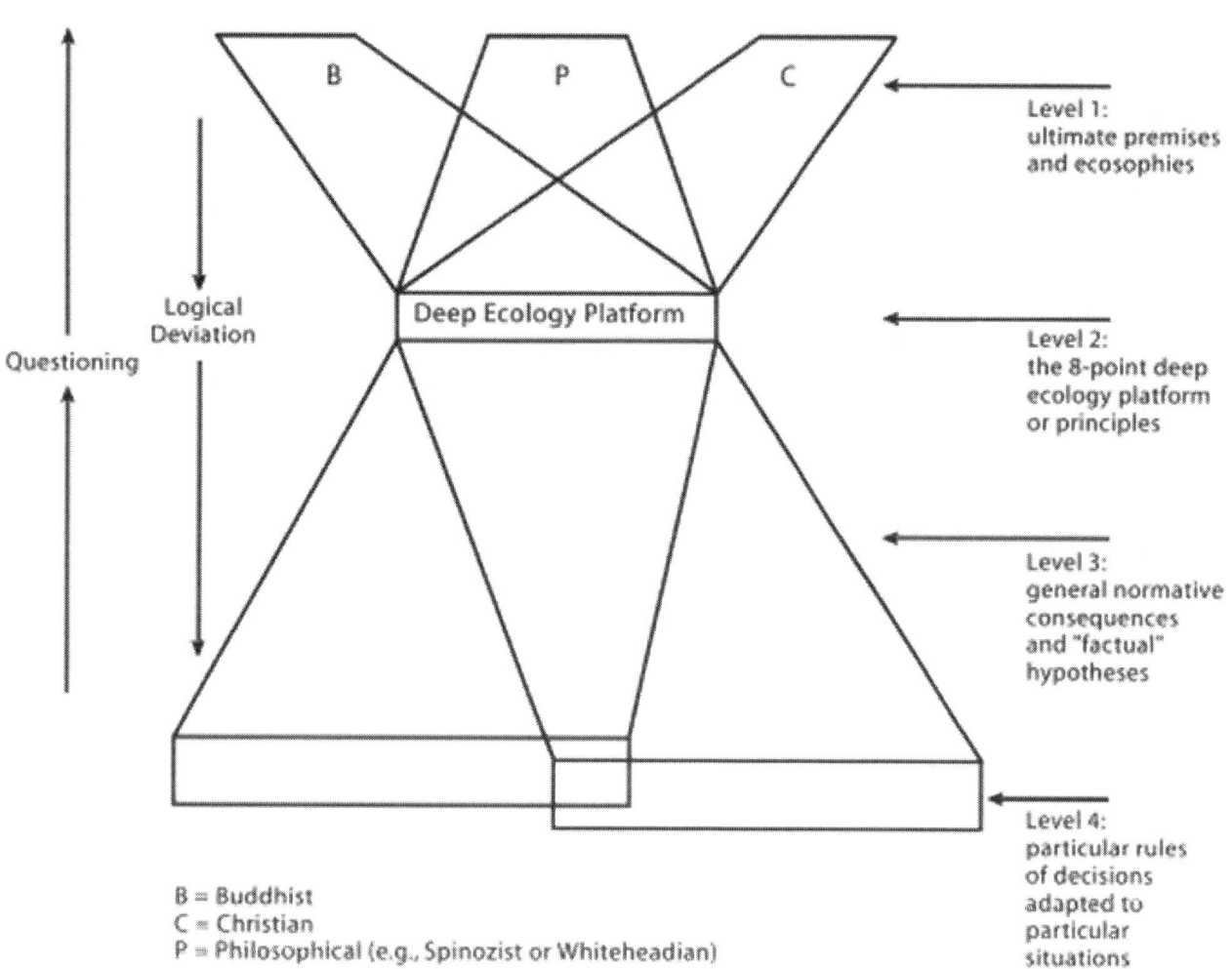

> Recognising that 100 percent sustainability is a perfect state that is practically unattainable by anybody or any system is an empowering position. It accepts that no matter what their behaviour, everyone can be seen as on a journey towards sustainability. We then have to decide how to behave on that journey.

Fagan (2009) holds that "sustainable literacy…holds within it the axiom that simply 'to know or to know about' is not sufficient. The purpose of knowing is to act: to live the new knowledge". **Onwueme and Borsari (2007) argued that everyone carries a sustainability deficit. Their sustainability asymptogram shows that perfect sustainability is not possible.** The relationship between the sustainability index (x axis) and the % sustainability (y) is asymptotic, meaning that it approaches near but reaches perfect sustainability.

An implication of this is that if everybody carries a sustainability deficit (everyone is somewhere short of 100 percent sustainability) then, there is need for more humility and sensitivity in conveying the sustainability message to others.

> *A holier-than-thou attitude towards people with a lower sustainability index is likely to stigmatize the listener and harden resistance to the message. Such sanctimonious superciliousness only invites resistance from those we are trying to inform and educate. An alternative position could be the one that recognizes the shared frailty or culpability of speaker and listener, in that each one carries a sustainability deficit, large or small.*

100 percent sustainability is a perfect state that is practically unattainable by anybody or any system. No matter how good a person or system is, there is always a sustainability deficit that cannot be overcome, as entropy affects living systems and their physical habitats without exceptions. This means that there is always room for improvement. Different persons or systems are located at different levels on the curve, with larger or smaller sustainability deficits, but with deficits all the same.

In describing Ecological Literacy, David Orr (2004) stated that in order to avoid the "curricular outbuilding to the big house of formal schooling where the really important things go on", the goal must be "not just mastery of subject matter but making connections between head, hand, heart, and cultivation of the capacity to discern systems". These competencies are described in terms of a "global citizen" by Oxfam (in Parker *et al.* 2004). Oxfam identified a global citizen as someone who:

- is aware of the wider world and has a sense of his or her own role as a world citizen;
- respects and values diversity;
- has an understanding of how the world works economically, politically, socially, culturally, technologically and environmentally;
- is outraged by social injustice;
- participates in and contributes to the community at a range of levels, from the local to the global;
- is willing to act to make the world a more equitable and sustainable place;
- takes responsibility for his or her actions.

In using "outraged", Oxfam takes value-based and action-focussed further than other sustainability statements. This is, of course a value statement in itself, their "citizens" are not passive but can be described as having a "sense of identity and self esteem…a belief that people can make a difference". They back these attitudinal statements with skills in critical thinking; an ability to argue effectively; an ability to challenge injustice and inequalities; and cooperation and conflict resolution.

A *Sustainable Lens* provides a humbling vision - none of us are perfect. All of us are both empowered and have a responsibility to act.

from deficit to global citizen

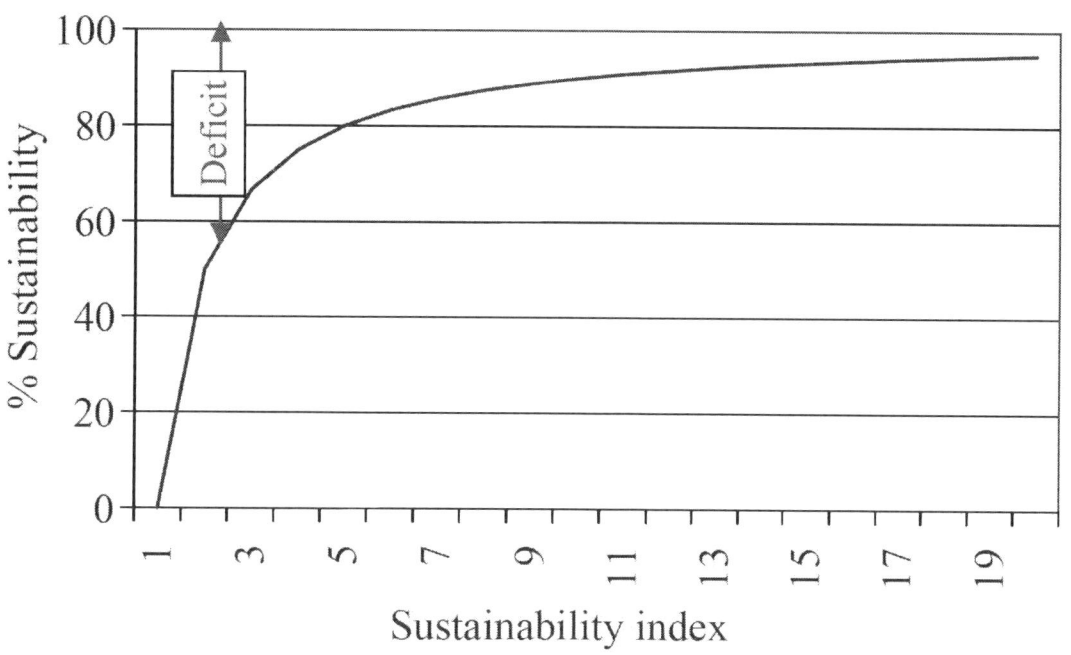

> What does being a "change agent" bring to the framework for our *Sustainable Lens*? Polistina (2009) points to the skills needed to "survive" as a change agent. She warns of a variety of mental, physical, psychological and emotional battles change agents will face with those seeking to sustain the status quo.

Dumaine (2008) and Robinson (2009) list attributes of change managers:

- People skilful in implementing change: action planning to produce a feasible and actionable strategy for organisational change
- Customer service focus
- Can conduct process reviews taking systems approach (including question setting and question posing to access information not available from a surface audit)
- Discipline of design
- Continuous improvement focus: every decision – how have we learnt from this decision?
- Recognition of a new business as usual.
- Accurate observation, monitoring and recording skills for the auditing of observable environmental and sustainability practices within an organisation
- Negotiation skills to agree an achievable and worthwhile action plan and influence practices and behaviour of individuals within an organisation
- Communication for the professional, confident and persuasive presentation of findings and action plans sustainability improvements

It is worth noting that this change agent view still has a core value set of critical and creative thinking, systemic thinking and sustainability.

Seeing through a *Sustainable Lens* does not imply over- enthusiastic gung-ho change for the sake of change. Instead, it is worth remembering AtKisson's (2008) advice that "doing sustainability requires, first and foremost, that we stop and think". To this end, and despite "the house appearing to be on fire", AtKisson reasons for the role of patience. I am reminded of the welcome sign at the Karori Wildlife Sanctuary in Wellington: "A journey that will take 500 years". Clearly there is urgency, but we also need to take the long view. (The Long Now Foundation hopes to creatively foster responsibility in the framework of the next 10,000 years. To emphasise this horizon, the group writes years using five digits instead of four: 02010 instead of 2010).

Interdisciplinary literacy (Tormey *et al.* 2009) is also an important aspect of the change agent lens. This means being open to valuing what other disciplines/cultures have to offer – their ways of seeing the world, of asking questions and of answering them. Darnton (2005) highlights another attribute of change agency: the audience for a change intervention should not be regarded as a passive target. Instead, our change agents should be learn how to facilitate partnership approaches and instead of understanding changing behaviour as a single event, it should be viewed as an ongoing process.

Such an ongoing process can be seen in this **management helix for sustainable organisation (Hargroves and Smith, 2005) "A mutually reinforcing process to achieve lasting competitive advantage" involves all aspects of an organisation.**

Lautensach (2004) argued for a "pedagogy of liberation" to specifically "help empower and motivate the learner towards taking action". This is different from merely "outraged" seen in the Oxfam Curriculum (Parker *et al.* 2004). The empowered change agent, then, should be able to visualise potential changes. These changes are in physical and organisational structures and in the transition pathways to get there.

Wearing a *Sustainable Lens*, we need to see ourselves making those changes.

seeing ourselves managing change

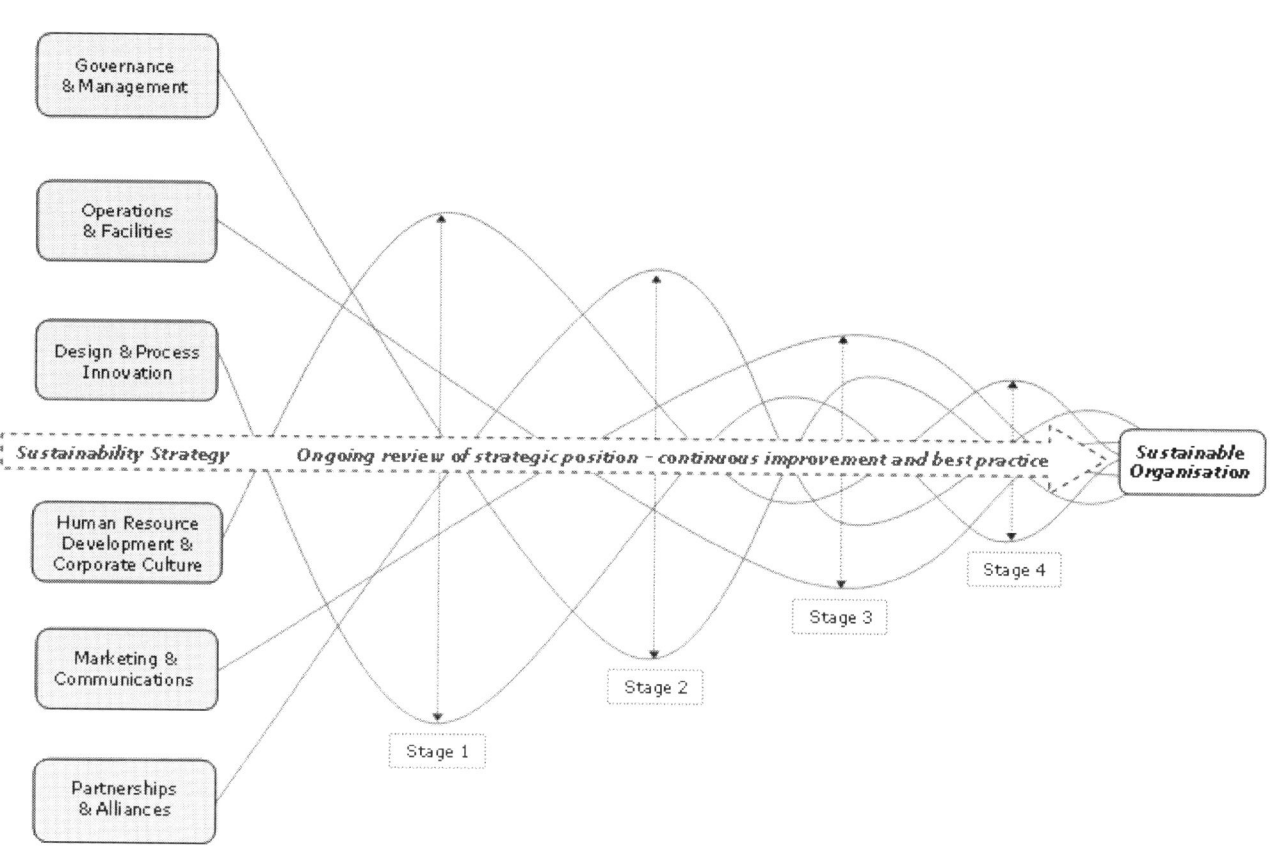

> It is not important who wins.

Fluxx, from Looney Labs is a card game that is all about change. It is a draw-play-discard game in which players try to win by meeting the conditions specified by the Goal card. How the game is played, and indeed how the game is won, constantly change during the game. There are four types of card: Rules, Goals, Actions, and Keepers (and a variant: Greepers.) At the start of the game the basic rules state that you pick up one card and play one card. If you play a Rule card, this may change how many cards are picked up, can be played, or many other variations – how many cards you may have in your hand; the order of play; bonus cards; and so on. Keepers are played to the table in front of the player. Action cards specify one-off actions: swap hands, pick up extra cards. How the game is won is specified by the current Goal card – usually, but not always stating that you win if you have a particular pair of Keepers.

So, a turn consists of drawing cards, playing cards, and discarding down to the current hand and Keeper limit. Players try manipulating the rules in their favour- if you have a hand-full of cards you might chose to play a card that increases the number of cards playable in each turn. The game though, usually defeats such attempts at manipulation – the next player changes it to something else, or conditions change so that having many cards is an advantage. There's little chance for long term game play strategy. Sometimes the winning is unexpected and the winner as surprised as the other players.

So, why am I writing about a game that surely sounds crazy and is, in practice chaotic and unpredictable? Why do I think it a useful basis for a *Sustainable Lens*?

Three reasons. First, unlike almost every other game, the winning conditions in Fluxx are not derivatives of "he who has the most gold wins". Whereas in Snakes and Ladders we delight in another player's slippery downfall, in Fluxx someone might lose all their cards but the next minute win the game largely on the basis of having the fewest cards. Whereas in Monopoly we build hotels on Parklane to extract money from our opponents, and success is driven by a mercenary purchase of the entire side of dark blue and all the green streets, in Fluxx while some goals need more cards, and winning is often about particular cards, which particular cards matter can change several times between your plays. Instead of accumulation of wealth and mercenary self interest, success is about good humour while adapting to changing conditions.

Second, soon the players realise that winning is really about having a good time with friends or family. It is wrong to say that Fluxx has no rules, it clearly has an underlying system – it is only the expression of the rules that really change. The deeper basics of taking turns, playing according to rules (albeit changing ones), and so on are still there and give a basis for this "good time" engagement. This might be a case of Robert Fulghum's *All I Really Need To Know I Learned In Kindergarten* (1999), but it really is a useful lesson in rethinking your style of engagement and measures of success. While we are playing to win individually, we put as much effort into the combined experience – if we are nasty to someone they stop playing and we all lose.

Third, Fluxx doesn't take itself too seriously. While I've described it here as useful as a basis for sustainability, Looney Labs has no such intention. **As one Fluxx reviewer stated "everyone had a good time, and it wasn't important who won" (Sarrett 1997). So long as "everyone" is taken widely and over the long term, wouldn't this be a great goal for humanity instead of national strategies entirely dependent on exploitation or growth?**

Sustainability - like Fluxx - does have a long term strategy, but it is bigger than the cards you have in front of you. Including a focus on both the obvious rules and the changing conditions, and with inclusive engagement at the core is a more than useful model for a *Sustainable Lens*.

inclusive and positive engagement

HOVERCRAFT EELS — ACTION
To play this card, do whatever it says, then place it on the discard pile.

My Hovercraft Is Full Of Eels

Choose any two players. On your cue, these players simultaneously call out a number between one and four. Add these, subtract one, then you do as follows:
one: Draw 1 card & play it.
two: Draw 2 cards.
three: Trash a Keeper.
four: Trash a New Rule.
five: Draw 3 cards.
six: There is no rule #6.
seven: Steal a Keeper.

GET ON WITH IT! — NEW RULE
Discard Your Hand & + Turn Redraw Ends

To play this card, place it face up in the center of the table. This rule goes into effect as soon as you play it.

Get On With It!

At any time before your final Play, you may discard your entire hand and draw a new hand of 3 cards. This is a free action but if you take it, your turn ends immediately.

THE CHEESE SHOP — GOAL
To play this card, place it face up in the center of the table. Discard previous Goal, if any.

The Cheese Shop

You win if you are the only player in possession of absolutely nothing, i.e. no Keepers, no Creepers, and no cards in your hand.

You Alone: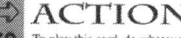

COCONUT-LADEN SWALLOW — GOAL
To play this card, place it face up in the center of the table. Discard previous Goal, if any.

Coconut-Laden Swallow

You win if you have Coconuts and a Swallow on the table in front of you.

OPENING CREDITS — GOAL
To play this card, place it face up in the center of the table. Discard previous Goal, if any.

Opening Credits

You win if you have the Foot and the Nude Organist on the table in front of you.

BRING THE GRENADE — GOAL
To play this card, place it face up in the center of the table. Discard previous Goal, if any.

Bring Forth the Holy Hand Grenade

You win if you have the Killer Rabbit and the Holy Hand Grenade on the table in front of you.

MUCH REJOICING — GOAL
To play this card, place it face up in the center of the table. Discard previous Goal, if any.

And There Was Much Rejoicing

You win if you have Robin's Minstrels and at least 2 Knights of the Round Table on the table.

RESTING PARROT — KEEPER
To play this card, place it face up on the table in front of you.

Resting Parrot

"He's pining for the fjords!"

KNIGHTS WHO SAY NI! — CREEPER
You cannot hold this card, but must place it face up in front of you as soon as you get it. If you drew it, immediately draw another card to replace it.

The Knights Who Say "NI!"

You cannot win if you have this unless the Goal says otherwise or a card is on the table with the word "It" (or "It's") in its *title*.

> This book has aimed to provide readers with a deeper understanding of sustainability as represented in its diagrams. The intention is to jointly improve our competence in visual thinking and in sustainability literacy. *Sustainable Lens* presents a model for seeing the world through a sustainability-driven perspective. It could be a design for augmented reality, or more simply, a way of seeing.

The second chapter, "**once upon a planet**" examined the development of sustainability. We observed that as the concepts that coalesced as sustainability evolved, they were represented in a variety of forms, from tabular to dehumanising representations of slave ships and an abstract balance. As the concept came together in words, so too did the diagrammatic representation. We explored how sustainability is both encapsulated and captured in the three pillars of social, environmental and economic concerns separate but together.

In "**the shape of things**" we concentrated on the impact of Barbier's Venn diagram. That sustainability only forms at the intersection has been overlooked by most subsequent authors. In the same way that red is not purple, economic development is not sustainability, and "environmental sustainability" is a nonsense. We discovered that although the pillars approach pulls together an understanding of sustainability, it brings with it an inherent contradiction - here are these separate things, now think of them together. Despite this problem, the pillars model is represented in several forms and sometimes the three pillars are four, five or more things. Adding pillars doesn't help either, the model crumbles in complexity. The bullseye model of Strong Sustainability is still based upon the pillars, but instead of sustainability forming in an amorphous blob at the intersection, it is the nature of the relationship - one of encapsulation - that defines sustainability.

In "**all the world's a stage**" we explored alternative approaches to that of the pillars. We first explored alternative models - a journey, a spaceship and Gaia. These led us to the notion that seeing through a *Sustainable Lens* is not just a matter of optics and augmentation, it requires a way of thinking to organise what we see. In doing so we moved from diagrams that attempt to define sustainability, to ones that reflect sustainable thinking.

In "**visual thinking**" I presented diagrams that describe sustainable thinking without reference to a Brundtland definition (or its pillars based visual representations). The attributes of such thinking include systems thinking, critical and creative thinking, change agent thinking, and ethical thinking.

"Sustainable Lens" describes the concept of the *Sustainable Lens*. I presented the argument for why anyone would want to see such a view of the world. I then described the two elements that together comprise the *Sustainable Lens*: sustainability and diagrams. We soon discover that simple visualisations of single parameter resource consumption - representing values of sustainability or perhaps unsustainability, while informative, do not provide sufficient depth to provide a basis for the *Sustainable Lens*. Instead we need to build our visual sustainability literacy.

In "**visual thinking**" I identified the tasks for the *Sustainable Lens*. Beyond visualisation of simple resources the problem becomes one of dimensions - we need to ask "so what do we actually see through our *Sustainable Lens*?" How might we look at a scene and see the dimensions of time or space, or even risk, uncertainty, ambiguity and ignorance? How do we see the effects of scaling? or emergent properties? We explored an approach to sustainability, one that recognises that as a society we have to learn to live in a complex world of interdependent systems with high uncertainties and multiple legitimate interests (Stagl 2007). We considered how the thinking behind the *Sustainable Lens* might be represented by diagrams of ethics, values, systems thinking, a connected socio-ecosystem, and participatory approaches to engagement.

"**green is a verb**" presented a series of examples of visual representation of sustainability in different contexts. We looked at how existing frameworks support this way of thinking and how they might provide us with frameworks with which to organise what we see with a *Sustainable Lens*. Representations of sustainability (and related concepts) in different belief systems - religions, cultural understandings and new approaches to science lead us to look at different organising themes.

"**caring to act**" returns to the personal imperative - we have to care.

full circle

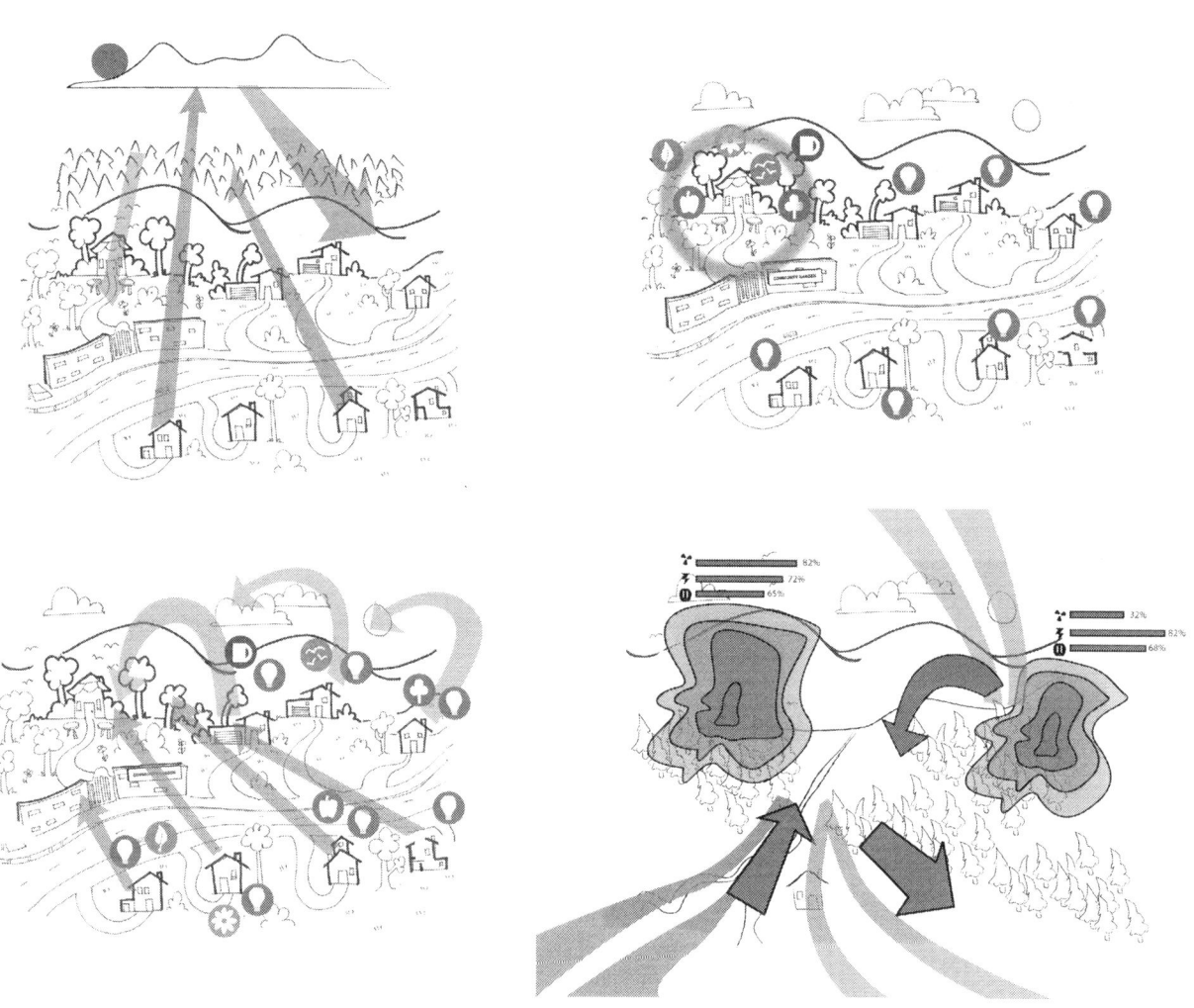

In the introduction to this book I invited you to take the sustainability visualisation challenge. I asked what sustainability means to you in diagrammatic form. In the intervening pages I have presented 146 different diagrams. None of these diagrams are the perfect answer. Nor is this an exhaustive collection - I have collected at least as many such diagrams again. If pushed, and since you asked, Sam's favourite is the people, time and space diagram from Iribarnegaray and Seghezzo (2011).

Viewing the world through a *Sustainable Lens* is resolutely positive. It is easy to become negative about sustainability. To do so, however, is to miss the point. The focus of sustainability is on the solutions, not the problems.

Seeing through a *Sustainable Lens* means recognising hidden threats. In the absence of augmented reality and in-built pollution detectors this means being aware of systems. A *Sustainable Lens* means "seeing" the impacts of our actions - both negative and positive and the more usual somewhere in-between. By thinking across time and space we can begin to appreciate the how our way of living affects systems in places unseen or in times to come. By using spatial and temporal scales as dimensions we can recognise the potential we have to make a difference.

What you see through your *Sustainable Lens* will differ according to your background, your world perspective, your disciplinary focus, and where you are on this sustainability continuum:

1. Ecosystems are under stress and are declining, and this is affecting human conditions and futures.

2. Sustainability - defined broadly as meeting the needs of all current and future generations is a reasonable approach to addressing this decline.

3. Sustainability is the responsibility of everyone, in their whole lives – including work (this work component we call sustainable practice).

4. This work component – the sustainable practitioner – applies to every career, every discipline.

5. Acting as a sustainable practitioner means both reducing my footprint (reducing harm) and increasing my handprint (actions towards sustainability).

6. I am currently integrating sustainable practice into my life and work as a sustainable practitioner.

No matter where you are on this continuum, there are opportunities to open your eyes to seeing sustainably. It is critical that the *Sustainable Lens* not be an encyclopedic display of doom. Information, though, is clearly a requirement of acting as a sustainable practitioner. Information is the basis of intelligent decisions. Yet there is a lot of information about the state of our systems but still we wander perilously close to disaster. But information alone is most clearly not the entire answer.

So, the *Sustainable Lens* needs to see the problems, but to do so in a way that frames solutions. This framing might be on the basis of appreciating the complexity of interconnected systems worth valuing and appreciating. In other words, seeing beauty and with a pathway forward.

We started with a visualisation challenge. We finish with a bigger challenge. As you go about your life, stop occasionally, put up a frame (thumbs and fingers work well), and ask yourself how much difference you could make by seeing this scene through a *Sustainable Lens*?

positive action

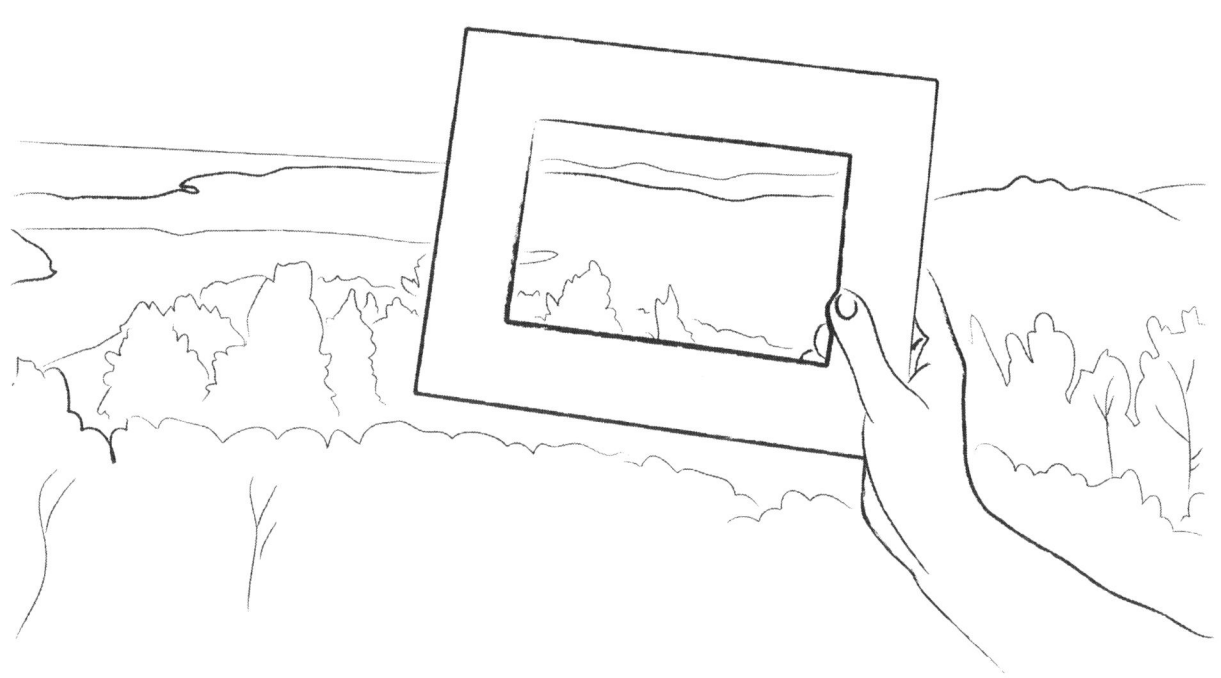

references

Diagrams are with the permissions of cited authors. and/or publishers. Copyright remains with them. We have endeavoured to contact everyone, please contact samuel.mann@op.ac.nz so any errors or omissions can be corrected in future editions.

Images identified as Mann/NewSplash are CC BY.

Page 7:

Maery, É. J. (1878). *La Méthode graphique*. Paris. (public domain).

Page 9:

NewSplash, & Mann, S. (2011). Otago Polytechic. (self). CC BY

Page 11:

United Nations Environment Programme. (2007). *Global Environmental Outlook 4*. (with permission)

Simms, A., Johnston, V., Smith, J., Mitchell, S., & Staff, N. E. F. (2009). *The Consumption Explosion: The third UK Interdependence Report*: New Economics Foundation. (with permission)

Page 13:

NewSplash, & Mann, S. (2011). Otago Polytechic. (self). CC BY

Page 15:

Plymouth Chapter of the Society for Effecting the Abolition of the Slave Trade. (1788). Slaveship Brooks http://commons.wikimedia.org/wiki/File:Slaveshipplan.jpg (public domain)

Page 17:

Lewis, E. P. (1811). *Historical inquiries, concerning forests and forest laws: With topographical remarks, upon the ancient and modern state of the New Forest, in the county of Southampton*. London: Printed for T. Payne by J. M'Creery. (public domain)

Page 19:

Hubbert, M. K. (1949). Energy from fossil fuels. *Science, 109*(2823), 103-109. (with permission)

Meadows, D. H., Randers, J., & Meadows, D. L. (2005). *Limits to growth: the 30-year update:* Chelsea Green.)   Diagrams from original Meadows, D. H., Meadows, D. L., Randers, J., & Behrens, W. W. (1972). The Limits to Growth; a report for the Club of Rome's project on the Predicament of Mankind. NY: Universe Books. (with permission).

Page 21:

International Union for Conservation of Nature and Natural Resources, United Nations Environment Programme, & World Wildlife Fund. (1980). *World Conservation Strategy: Living Resource Conservation for Sustainable Development. International Union for Conservation of Nature and Natural Resources, Gland.* . Retrieved from http://data.iucn.org/dbtw-wpd/edocs/WCS-004.pdf. (fair use, historical document).

Page 23:

NewSplash, & Mann, S. (2011). Otago Polytechic. (self). CC BY

Ingold, T. (1980). *Hunters, pastoralists, and ranchers: reindeer economies and their transformations*. Cambridge: Cambridge University Press. (with permission)

Page 25:, 27:

NewSplash, & Mann, S. (2011). Otago Polytechic. (self). CC BY

Page 27:

Storck, I. (2006). The Triple Bottom Line Still Includes People, from http://www.ivanenviroman.com/the-triple-bottom-line-still-includes-people/ (with permission)

Page 29:

Barbier, E. B. (1989). The Concept of Sustainable Economic Development. *Environmental Conservation, 14*(02), 101-110. doi: doi:10.1017/S0376892900011449 (with permission)

Page 31:

Dalal-Clayton, D., Bass, S., Sadler, B., Tomson, K., Sandbrook, R., Robins, N., & R., H. (1994). *National sustainable development strategies: experience and dilemmas*: International Institute for Environment and Development: Environmental Planning Group. (with permission)

image references

Page 33:

NewSplash, & Mann, S. (2011). Otago Polytechic. (self). CC BY

Page 35:

Morrison, J. (2010). Certificate IV in Understanding and Negotiating Sustainability Issues Retrieved 26/11/2010, from http://sustainabilitytraining.net.au/ (with permission)

Schlange, L. E. (2009). Stakeholder Identification in Sustainability Entrepreneurship. [Article]. *Greener Management International*(55), 13-32. (with permission)

Flint, R. W. (2002). Sustainable Development: What does sustainability mean to individuals in the conduct of their lives and businesses. In G. M. Mudacumura & M. S. S. Haque (Eds.), *Handbook of Development Policy Studies* (pp. 67-87 754 p). NY: Marcel Dekker Inc. (with permission Dr R. Warren Flint Five E's Unlimited)

Page 37:

NewSplash, & Mann, S. (2011). Otago Polytechic. (self). CC BY

After Välimäki. (2002). Sustainable development reporting: aggregated indicators. Background paper for discussion at EEA SoE Expert Group Workshop, December 16-17, Helsinki, Finland. (unable to contact) this version NewSplash, & Mann, S. (2011). Otago Polytechic.

Greenwood, T. (2010). Sustainable Design Guide: Triple Bottom Line, from http://www.espdesign.org/sustainability-definition/triple-bottom-line/ (with permission)

Page 39:

Landcare Research. (nd). Our approach to Triple Bottom Line reporting, from http://www.landcareresearch.co.nz/about/principles/tbl_reporting.asp (with permission)

Runnalls, C. R. (2006). *Choreographing community sustainability: The importance of cultural planning to community viability*. Royal Rhodes University, Victoria, BC.

NZ Ministry for Culture and Heritage. (2002). *Cultural Well-being - What is it?*, . Retrieved from http://www.culturalwellbeing.govt.nz/files/WhatIsCulturalWellbeingBrochure.pdf. (with permission)

Di Castri, F. (1995). The chair of sustainable development. *Nature and Resources, 31*(3), 2-7. (with permission)

Page 41:

Nijkamp, P., van den Bergh, J., & Soeterman, F. (1990). *Regional Sustainable Development and Natural Resource Use*. Paper presented at the World Bank Annual Conference on Development Economics. , Washington D.C. http://www-wds.worldbank.org/external/default/main?print=Y&pagePK=64193027&piPK=64187937&theSitePK=523679&menuPK=64187510&searchMenuPK=64187283&siteName=WDS&entityID=000178830_98101911514472 153-189 (with permission) Note: The figures were left out of the 1990 publication but were widely circulated and cited as Nijkamp *et al.* 1990 (eg Dourojeanni 1997).

NewSplash, & Mann, S. (2011). Otago Polytechic. after McDonough, W., & Braungart, M. (2002). *Cradle to cradle: remaking the way we make things*. San Francisco: North Point Press.

Page 43:

Munasinghe, M. (1992). *Environmental Economics and Sustainable Development*. Paper presented at the Paper presented at the UN Earth Summit, Rio de Janeiro. 463 (with permission http://www.mohanmunasinghe.com/ and www.mindlanka.com)

Wijayadasa, K. H. J. (1997). Integrating Environmental Considerations into Economic Decision Making Processes in South Asia: Synthesis Paper: Sri Lanka. (United Nations acknowledged).

Page 45:

Meadows, D. (1998). *Indicators and information systems for sustainable development: a report to the Balaton Group, September 1998*: The Sustainability Institute. (with permission)

NewSplash, & Mann, S. (2011). Otago Polytechic. (self). CC BY after Daly, H. E. (2007). Ecological Economics and Sustainable Development, Selected Essays of Herman Daly. Cheltenham, UK: Edward Elgar.

Page 47:

Dodds, R., & Venables, R. (2005). Principles of engineering for sustainable development Retrieved 13/3/07, from www.raeng.org.uk/education/vps/pdf/Engineering_for_Sustainable_Development.pdf (with permission)

Page 49:

Spangenberg, J. H., & Bonniot, O. (1998). *Sustainability Indicators - A Compass on the Road Towards Sustainability*: Wuppertal Institut für Klima, Umwelt, Energie (ed.), Wuppertal Paper No. 81. (with permission)

SIGMA project. (2003), from http://www.projectsigma.co.uk/default.asp (unable to contact)

Page 51:

South Glousterschire Council. (2008). *South Gloucestershire Core Strategy - Issues and Options consultation: Issues and Options document*. Retrieved from https://consultations.southglos.gov.uk/inovem/consult.ti/CSissuesandoptions/printCompoundDoc?docid=109780. (with permission)

Ecotrust. (nd). Reliable Prosperity Framework Retrieved 2/12/10, from http://www.reliableprosperity.net (with permission)

Page 53:

Steward, W. C. (nd). The 5 Domains & EcoSTEP: An Introduction Retrieved 3/12/10, from http://www.ecospheres.com/5Domains_EcoStep_introduction.pdf also Steward, W. C., & Kuska, S. (2011). Sustainometrics: Measuring Sustainability - Design, Planning, and Public Administration for Sustainable Living. Omaha: Joslyn Institute for Sustainable Communities. (with permission. With acknowledgement to the authors, the Joslyn Institute for Sustainable Communities, and the Ostberg Press)

Auckland City Council. (2008). Keeping Auckland's future bright: Our long-term plan for a sustainable Auckland city Retrieved 2/12/10, from http://www.aucklandcity.govt.nz/council/documents/bright/themes.asp (with permission)

Office of the Deputy Prime Minister (UK). (2004). *The Egan Review: Skills for Sustainable Communities*. London: Retrieved from http://www.communities.gov.uk/publications/communities/eganreview. (UK Crown copyright)

Page 55:

Encyclopedia of Life Support Systems. (2004). GLOBAL CRISIS AND SUSTAINABLE DEVELOPMENT: THE INSPIRATION FOR THE EOLSS, from http://www.eolss.net/Eolss-Inspiration.aspx (with permission)

Page 57:

NewSplash, & Mann, S. (2011). Otago Polytechic. (self). CC BY

Page 59:

Blackburn, W. R. (2007). *The Sustainability Handbook: The Complete Management Guide to Achieving Social, Economic, and Environmental Responsibility*. Washington: Island Press. (with permission)

Page 61:

Fuller, R. B. (2008 (first published 1969)). *Operating Manual For Spaceship Earth*. Baden: Lars Müller Publishers. (with permission)

Page 63:

Johnson, S. P., & Finn, J., C. (1963). Ecological Considerations of a Permanent Lunar Base. *American Biology Teacher*, 530. (with permission)

Page 65:

Harding, S. (2006). *Animate earth: science, intuition and Gaia*. Totnes: Green Books. (with permission)

Page 67, 69

NewSplash, & Mann, S. (2011). Otago Polytechic. (self). CC BY

Page 71

Bonanni, L., Hockenberry, M., Zwarg, D., Csikszentmihalyi, C., & Ishii, H. (2010). *Small business applications of sourcemap: a web tool for sustainable design and supply chain transparency*. Paper presented at the Proceedings of the 28th international conference on Human factors in computing systems, Atlanta, Georgia, USA. (with persmission, this updated image from http://sourcemap.com/)

Page 73:

NewSplash, & Mann, S. (2011). Otago Polytechic. (self). CC BY

Page 75:

Rockstrom, J., Steffen, W., Noone, K., Persson, A., Chapin, F. S., III, Lambin, E. F., Lenton, T. M., Scheffer, M., Folke, C., Schellnhuber, H. J., Nykvist, B., de Wit, C. A., Hughes, T., van der Leeuw, S., Rodhe, H., Sorlin, S., Snyder, P. K., Costanza, R., Svedin, U., Falkenmark, M., Karlberg, L., Corell, R. W., Fabry, V. J., Hansen, J., Walker, B., Liverman, D., Richardson, K., Crutzen, P., & Foley, J. A. (2009). A safe operating space for humanity: identifying and quantifying planetary boundaries that must not be transgressed could help prevent human activities from causing unacceptable environmental change, argue Johan Rockstrom and colleagues. *Nature, 461*(7263), 472(474). (with permission).

Page 77:

NewSplash, & Mann, S. (2011). Otago Polytechic. (self). CC BY

Saito, O. (2007). Pathways to sustainable industrial societies. *Encyclopedia of the Earth*, from http://www.eoearth.org/article/Pathways_to_sustainable_industrial_societies (with permission and credit for Saito for an updated version)

Page 79:

Taylor, D. M. (1994). *Off course: restoring balance between Canadian society and the environment*: International Development Research Centre. (with permssion)

Page 81:

Cherp, A. (nd). Five Mindsets Retrieved 8/12/10, from http://5minds.mespom.eu/files/mindsets_leaflet.pdf (with permission)

Page 83:

Odum, E. P., & Barrett, G. W. (2004). Redesigning Industrial Agroecosystems. *Journal of Crop Improvement, 11*(1-2), 45-60. doi: 10.1300/J411v11n01_03 (with permission)

Page 85:

Public domain

Page 87:

Anthony, J. N. J. (1992). Configuring globally and contending locally: Shaping the global network of local bargins by decoding and maping Earth Summit intersectoral issues *Prepared for the International Facilitating Committee for the Independent Sectors in the UNCED process* Geneva. (with permission)

Page 89:

Daly, H. E. (2007). *Ecological Economics and Sustainable Development, Selected Essays of Herman Daly*. Cheltenham, UK: Edward Elgar. (with permission)

Page 91:

Kesavan, P. C., & Swaminathan, M. S. (2006). Managing extreme natural disasters in coastal areas. *Philosophical Transactions of the Royal Society A: Mathematical, Physical and Engineering Sciences, 364*(1845), 2191-2216. (with permission)

Hinton, S. (2010). Connecting people to sustainability: the uncomfortable truths Retrieved 8/12/10, from http://avbp.net/ (with permission)

Page 93:

Machlis, G. E., Force, J. E., & Burch, W. R. (1997). The human ecosystem Part I: The human ecosystem as an organizing concept in ecosystem management. *Society & Natural Resources, 10*(4), 347-367. doi: 10.1080/08941929709381034 (with permision and credit for updated version)

Page 95:

United Nations Environment Programme. (2007). *Global Environmental Outlook 4*. (United Nations acknowledgement).

Page 97:

Naveh, Z. (1982). Landscape Ecology as an Emerging Branch of Human Ecosystem Science. In A. Macfadyen & E. D. Ford (Eds.), *Advances in Ecological Research* (Vol. Volume 12, pp. 189-237): Academic Press. (with permission)

Page 99:

With kind permission of Navajo Flexcrete. www.navajoflexcrete.biz

Page 101:

Baudot, B. (1993). Environmental Security and the Res Publica: An Analysis of Environmentalism and an Alternative for the Future. Presented International Consortium for the Study of Environmental Security, Held January 6-9, 1993, Chantilly, France. Geopolitics of the Environment and the New World Order: Limits, Conflicts, and Insecurity. (with permission)

Milne, M. J., Tregidga, H., & Walton, S. (2009). Words not actions! The ideological role of sustainable development reporting. *Accounting, Auditing & Accountability Journal, 22*(8), 1211-1257. (with permission)

Page 103:

NewSplash, & Mann, S. (2011). Otago Polytechic. (self). CC BY

Page 105:

Isaksson, R., & Steimle, U. (2008). *What does GRI-reporting tell us about corporate sustainability?* Paper presented at the Proceedings of the 11th International Conference on Quality Management and Organisational Development, Helsingborg. (with permission)

Page 107:

NewSplash, & Mann, S. (2011). Otago Polytechic. (self). CC BY after National Research Council . Policy Division. Board on Sustainable Development. (1999). *Our common journey: a transition toward sustainability*: National Academy Press.

Page 109:

NewSplash, & Mann, S. (2011). Otago Polytechic. (self). After Wilber, K. (2007). *A Brief History of Everything*. Boston, MA: Shambhala.

Page 111:

Daly, H. E. (1996). *Beyond Growth: The Economics of Sustainable Development*. Boston: Beacon Press. (with permission)

Abbott, E. A. (1885). *Flatland*. Boston: Roberts brothers. (Public domain)

Daly, H. E. (1996). *Beyond Growth: The Economics of Sustainable Development*. Boston: Beacon Press. (with permission)

Page 113:

Meredith, T. C. (2000). *Community Participation in Environmental Information Management: Exploring Tools for Developing an Impact Assessment Preparedness Program* (Vol. Catalog No. En105-3/81-2004E): Canadian Environmental Assessment Agency's Research and Development Program. (Reproduced with the permission of the Minister of Public Works and Government Services)

Martens, P. (2006). Sustainability: science or fiction? *Sustainability: Science, Practice, & Policy 2*(1), 36-41. (with permission)

Page 115:

Vugteveen, P. e., Leuven, R. S. E. W., Huijbregts, M. A. J., & Lenders, H. J. R. (2006). Redefinition and Elaboration of River Ecosystem Health: Perspective for River Management. [Article]. *Hydrobiologia, 565*, 289-308. (with permission and credit for updated version)

Page 117:

Gasto, J., Vera, L., Vieli, L., & Montalba, R. (2009). Sustainable Agriculture: unifying concepts. *Cien. Inv. Agr., 36*(1), 5-26. (with permission)

Page 119:

Ranville, J. (nd). The Human Life Project: Sustainable Patterns in Nature, Family, and Community, from http://www.humanlifeproject.com/ (with permission)

Page 121:

Australian Government. (2010). *Australia to 2050: future challenges* (The 2010 intergenerational report). (ISBN 978-0-642-74576-7). Retrieved from http://www.treasury.gov.au/igr/igr2010/report/pdf/IGR_2010.pdf. (Australian Crown Copyright)

Page 123:

Evans, G. R. (2008). Transformation from "Carbon Valley" to a "Post-Carbon Society" in a climate change hot spot: the coalfields of the Hunter Valley, New South Wales, Australia. *Ecology and Society 13*(1), 39 [online] http://www.ecologyandsociety.org/vol13/iss31/art39/. (with permission - and with grateful thanks to the assistance of Gunderson)

Page 125:

United Nations Environment Programme. (2007). *Global Environmental Outlook 4*. (United Nations acknowledgment).

Page 127:

Loh, J. (Ed.). (2010). *2010 and Beyond: Rising to the biodiversity challenge*. Gland Switzerland: WWF International. (with permission)

Page 129:

Tett, P., Portilla, E., Gillibrand, P. A., & Inall, M. (2011). Carrying and assimilative capacities: the ACExR-LESV model for sea-loch aquaculture. *Aquaculture Research, 42*, 51-67. doi: 10.1111/j.1365-2109.2010.02729.x (with permission)

Page 131:

Center for a New American Dream. New Dream Puzzle Retrieved 20/9/11, 2011, from http://whitedwarf.org/affluenza/cnad/tour.html (with permission)

Fiddler, H. (2008). Plan S, Sustainable Living for the Long Term Retrieved 20/9/11, from http://plan-s.htfiddler.net/ (with permission)

Page 133:

Puthli, H. (2010). HPA Perspective on Sustainability: FAQs – 3 Retrieved 20/9/11, from http://hemantputhli.com/2010/02/01/hpa-perspective-on-sustainability-faqs-%E2%80%93-3/

WWF/ZSL/GFN, Humphrey, S., Loh, J., & Goldfinger, S. (Eds.). (2008). *Living planet report*. Gland Switzerland: WWF International. (with permission)

Page 135:

Moffatt, S., & Kohler, N. (2008). Conceptualising the built environment as a social-ecological system. *Building and research information, 36*(3), 248-268. (with permission and credit for updated version)

Page 137:

Dow, A. B. *A way of life cycle*. Courtesy of the Alden B. Dow Archives. www.abdow.org

Page 139:

International Network for Acid Prevention. (nd). The Global Acid Rock Drainage (GARD) Guide, Chapter 3 Corporate, Regulatory, and Community Framework, http://www.gardguide.com/index.php/Chapter_3 Retrieved 9/12/10 (with permission)

Page 141:

van Mansvelt, J. D., & van der Lubbe, M. J. (1999). *Checklist for sustainable landscape management: final report of the EU concerted action AIR3-CT93-1210 : the landscape and nature production capacity of organic/sustainable types of agriculture*. Amsterdam: Elsevier. (with permission)

IDEO. (nd). *Using Life Cycle Awareness Tools*. (with permission)

Page 143:

Taplin, J. R. D., Bent, D., & Aeron-Thomas, D. (2006). Developing a sustainability accounting framework to inform strategic business decisions: a case study from the chemicals industry. [Article]. *Business Strategy & the Environment (John Wiley & Sons, Inc), 15*, 347-360. (with permission and thnaks to Forum for the Future for updated version)

Page 145:

Reed, B. (nd). Integrating the Whole System, The practice of Living System (Regenerative) Design, from http://integrativedesign.net/images/whole_systems_regenerative_development.pdf (with perssmission and acknowledgement to Reed for updated version).

Page 147:

NewSplash, & Mann, S. (2011). Otago Polytechic. (self). Derived from text in Willard, B. (2005). The Next Sustainability Wave: Building Boardroom Buy-in (Conscientious Commerce). Gabriola Island, British Columbia, Canada: New Society Publishers.

Page 149:

Young, W., & Tilley, F. (2006). Can businesses move beyond efficiency? The shift toward effectiveness and equity in the corporate sustainability debate. *Business Strategy and the Environment, 15*(6), 402-415. doi: 10.1002/bse.510 (with permission)

Page 151:

Augenbroe, G., & Pearce, A. R. (1998). Sustainable Construction in the United States of America: a perspective to the year 2010 (pp. 31): College of Architecture, Georgia Institute of Technology. (with permission)

Page 153:

Anderson, R. C. (2003). Introduction: Envisioning the prototypical company of the 21st century. In S. A. Waage (Ed.), *Ants, Galileo & Gandhi: designing the future of business through nature, genius, and compassion* (pp. 18-31). Sheffield: Greenleaf. (with permission)

Page 155:

NewSplash, & Mann, S. (2011). Otago Polytechic. (self). CC BY after Arnstein, S. R. (1969). A Ladder of Citizen Participation. *Journal of the American Planning Association, 35*(4), 216-224.

Regional Planning Canada. (nd, 8/12/10). Plans, from http://www.regionalplanning.ca/plans.html (with permission)

Page 157:

Wals, A. E. J., & Jickling, B. (2002). "Sustainability" in higher education: From doublethink and newspeak to critical thinking and meaningful learning. *International Journal of Sustainability in Higher Education, 3*(3), 221-232. (with permission)

Macgregor, C. (2000). *Applying an Analytical Model for Assessing Community Sustainability: some preliminary results from northern Australian remote towns*. Paper presented at the Paper presented to the First National Conference on the Future of Australia's Country Towns, Bendigo, Victoria. http://www.regional.org.au/au/countrytowns/global/macgregor.htm (with permission)

Page 159:

Iribarnegaray, M., & Seghezzo, L. (2011, 1-30 November 2011). *Governance, sustainability and decision making in water and sanitation management systems*. Paper presented at the Proceedings of the 1st World Sustainability Forum. (with permission)

Page 161:

Madden, P., & Weißbrod, I. (2008). *Connected: ICT and sustainable development*. London: Forum for the Future. (with permission)

Page 163:

Seedhouse, D. (2009). *Ethics: the heart of health care*. Wiley-Blackwell. (with permission and credit for updated version Seedhouse)

Page 165:

Langhelle, O. (1999). Sustainable Development: Exploring the Ethics of Our Common Future. *International Political Science Review/ Revue internationale de science pol, 20*(2), 129-149. doi: 10.1177/0192512199202002 (fair use table).

NewSplash, & Mann, S. (2011). Otago Polytechic. (self). CC BY after (United Nations acknowledgement).

Page 167:

NewSplash, & Mann, S. (2011). Otago Polytechic. (self). CC BY after Marshall, J. D., & Toffel, M. W. (2005). Framing the Elusive Concept of Sustainability: A Sustainability Hierarchy. [Article]. *Environmental Science & Technology, 39*, 673-682.

Spangenberg, J. H. (2005). Will the information society be sustainable? Towards criteria and indicators for a sustainable knowledge society. *Int. J. Innovation & Sustainable Development* 1(1-2), 85-102. (with permission. Also Irish Open Government).

Page 169:

Quisumbing, L. R., & de Leo, J. (2005). *Learning to Do: Values for Learning and Working Together in a Globalized World: An integrated Approach to Incorporating Values Education in in Technical and Vocational Education and Training*. Bonn: UNESCO-APNIEVE and UNESCO-UNEVOC International Centre for Technical and Vocational Education and Training. (with permission)

Page 171:

Reagan, D. R. (nd). 2012 The end of the world? Retrieved 20/9/11, from http://www.lamblion.com/articles/articles_signs12.php (with permission)

Page 173:

Turner, N. J., Gregory, R., Brooks, C., Failing, L., & Satterfield, T. (2008). From invisibility to transparency: identifying the implications. *Ecology and Society, 13*(2), 7. (with permission)

Page 175:

Næss, A. (2005). *The selected works of Arne Næss*. Dordrecht: Springer. This version public domain (wikicommons).

Page 177:

Onwueme, I., & Borsari, B. (2007). The sustainability asymptogram. *International Journal of Sustainability in Higher Education, 8*(1), 44-52. (with permission)

Page 179:

Hargroves, K., & Smith, M. (2005). *The natural advantage of nations: business opportunities, innovation, and governance in the 21st century*. London: Earthscan. (with permission)

Page 181:

Looney, A. (1996). Fluxx http://www.looneylabs.com/games/fluxx. (with permission)

Page 183, 185

NewSplash, & Mann, S. (2011). Otago Polytechic. (self). CC BY

Abbott, E. A. (1885). *Flatland*. Boston: Roberts brothers.

Adam, B. (1998). *Timescapes of modernity: the environment and invisible hazards*. London: Routledge.

Adam, B. (2000). Time and the environment. In M. Redclift & G. Woodgate (Eds.), *The international handbook of environmental sociology* (pp. 169-179). Cheltenham, UK: Edward Elgar.

Adam, B. (2006). *Minding Futures. Working Paper* 67. Cardiff Retrieved from http://www.cardiff.ac.uk/socsi/research/publications/workingpapers/paper-67.html

Albrecht, G. (2010). Solastalgia and the creation of new ways of living. In S. Pilgrim & J. N. Pretty (Eds.), *Nature and culture: rebuilding lost connections* (pp. 215-234). London: Earthscan.

Alexander, C. (1979). *The timeless way of building*: Oxford University Press.

Alexander, C., Ishikawa, S., & Silverstein, M. (1977). *A pattern language: towns, buildings, construction*: Oxford University Press.

Anderson, R. C. (1998). *Mid-course correction: toward a sustainable enterprise :The Interface model*. Atlanta: Peregrinzilla Press.

Anderson, R. C. (2003). Introduction: Envisioning the prototypical company of the 21st century. In S. A. Waage (Ed.), *Ants, Galileo & Gandhi: designing the future of business through nature, genius, and compassion* (pp. 18-31). Sheffield: Greenleaf.

Ankler, P. (2005). The Ecological Colonization of Space. *Environmental History*, 10, 239-268.

Anonymous. (1853). *English forests and forest trees, historical, legendary, and descriptive*. London: Ingram, Cooke, and co.

Anthony, J. N. J. (1992). Configuring globally and contending locally: Shaping the global network of local bargins by decoding and maping Earth Summit intersectoral issues Prepared for the International Facilitating Committee for the Independent Sectors in the UNCED process Geneva.

Arnstein, S. R. (1969). A Ladder of Citizen Participation. *Journal of the American Planning Association*, 35(4), 216-224.

AtKisson, A. (2008). *The ISIS agreement: how sustainability can improve organizational performance and transform the world*. London: Earthscan.

Auckland City Council. (2008). Keeping Auckland's future bright: Our long-term plan for a sustainable Auckland city Retrieved 2/12/10, from http://www.aucklandcity.govt.nz/council/documents/bright/themes.asp

Augenbroe, G., & Pearce, A. R. (1998). Sustainable Construction in the United States of America: a perspective to the year 2010 (pp. 31): College of Architecture, Georgia Institute of Technology.

Australian Government. (2010). *Australia to 2050: future challenges (The 2010 intergenerational report)*. (ISBN 978-0-642-74576-7). Retrieved from http://www.treasury.gov.au/igr/igr2010/report/pdf/IGR_2010.pdf.

Bailey, R. G. (1985). The factor of scale in ecosystem mapping. *Environmental Management*, 9, 271-276.

Baker, W. L. (1989). A review of models of landscape change. *Landscape Ecology*, 2(2), 111-113.

Barash, D. P., & Webel, C. (2008). *Peace and Conflict Studies* (2 ed.). Thousand Oaks, California: SAGE

Barbier, E. B. (1989). The Concept of Sustainable Economic Development. *Environmental Conservation*, 14(02), 101-110. doi: doi:10.1017/S0376892900011449

Barnes, P. (2006). *Capitalism 3.0: a guide to reclaiming the commons*. San Francisco: Berrett-Koehler Publishers.

Baudot, B. (1993). Environmental Security and the Res Publica: An Analysis of Environmentalism and an Alternative for the Future. Presented International Consortium for the Study of Environmental Security, Held January 6-9, 1993, Chantilly, France. Geopolitics of the Environment and the New World Order: Limits, Conflicts, and Insecurity.

Bell, S. (2008). Green is the new sex – in a marketing sense. *ComputerWorld*, http://computerworld.co.nz/news.nsf/news/6250EE6252BF5686 09FCC525748D560008B568604A568608?opendocument&utm_source=topnews&utm_medium=email&utm_campaign=topnews.

Benford, S., Giannachi, G., Koleva, B., & Rodden, T. (2009). *From interaction to trajectories: designing coherent journeys through user experiences. Paper presented at the Proceedings of the 27th international conference on Human factors in computing systems*, Boston, MA, USA.

Bergandi, D. (2000). Frank H. George Research Award Highly Commended Paper: Eco-cybernetics: the ecology and cybernetics of missing emergences. *Kybernetes*, 29(7), 928-942.

Berkes, F. (2009). Indigenous ways of knowing and the study of environmental change. *Journal of the Royal Society of New Zealand*, 39(4), 151-156. doi: 10.1080/03014220909510568

Berry, T. (2000). *The Great Work*. New York: Harmony Books.

references

Berry, T. (2009). *The Sacred Universe: Earth, Spirituality, and Religion in the Twenty-first Century*: Columbia University Press.

Betjeman, J., & Auden, W. H. (1947). *Slick but not streamlined: poems & short pieces*: Doubleday.

Blackburn, W. R. (2007). *The Sustainability Handbook: The Complete Management Guide to Achieving Social, Economic, and Environmental Responsibility*. Washington: Island Press.

Blevis, E. (2007). *Sustainable Interaction Design: Invention and disposal, renewal and reuse*. Paper presented at the Conference on Human Factors in Computing Systems, San Jose, California.

Bonanni, L., Hockenberry, M., Zwarg, D., Csikszentmihalyi, C., & Ishii, H. (2010). *Small business applications of sourcemap: a web tool for sustainable design and supply chain transparency*. Paper presented at the Proceedings of the 28th international conference on Human factors in computing systems, Atlanta, Georgia, USA.

Bosselmann, K. (2008). *The principle of sustainability: transforming law and governance*. Farnham, Surrey: Ashgate Publ.

Boulding, K. (1965). *Earth as a Space Ship,* May 10, 1965. Washington State University Committee on Space Sciences. http://www.colorado.edu/econ/Kenneth.Boulding/spaceship-earth.html.

Brooks, L., & Atkinson, C. (2008). *Exploring the Potential of the Ethical Grid for Informing Decision-Taking Practices in the Soft Information Systems and Technologies, Methodology*. Paper presented at the ICIS 2008 Proceedings, Paper 174.

Brown, B. C. (2005). Integral Communications for Sustainability. *Kosmos, 4*(2), 17-22.

Burrough, P. A. (1986). *Principles of geographic information systems for land resources assessment*. Oxford: Clarendon Press.

Butcher, T. (2008). *Blood River: A Journey to Africa's Broken Heart:* Grove Press.

Butler, R. (1991). *Designing Organizations, A decision-making perspective*. London: Routledge.

Carpenter, R. A. (1995). Risk Assessment. In F. Vanclay & D. A. Bronstein (Eds.), *Environmental and Social Impact Assessment* (pp. 194-219). Chichester: John Wiley.

Carson, R. (1962). *Silent Spring*. Boston: Houghton Mifflin.

Center for a New American Dream. New Dream Puzzle Retrieved 20/9/11, 2011, from http://whitedwarf.org/affluenza/cnad/tour.html

Cherp, A. (nd). Five Mindsets Retrieved 8/12/10, from http://5minds.mespom.eu/files/mindsets_leaflet.pdf

Clark, B., Foster, J. B., & Marsh, G. P. (2002). George Perkins Marsh and the transformation of earth: An introduction to Marsh's Man and Nature / Excerpts from Man and Nature. *Organization & Environment, 15*(2), 164.

Colby, M. E. (1991). Environmental management in development: the evolution of paradigms. *Ecological Economics, 3*(3), 193-213. doi: 10.1016/0921-8009(91)90032-a

Cotta, H. (1817). *Anweisung zum Waldbau*. translated in Forestry Quarterly Volume 1 1902-1903 preface reprinted in Forest History Today Fall 2000: 27-28.

Crowe, R. (2002). *Developing Value The business case for sustainability in emerging markets* London: SustainAbility.

Cumming, R. (2007). *Art Explained*: Dk Pub.

Dalal-Clayton, D., Bass, S., Sadler, B., Tomson, K., Sandbrook, R., Robins, N., & R., H. (1994). *National sustainable development strategies: experience and dilemmas*: International Institute for Environment and Development: Environmental Planning Group.

Daly, H. (1973). *Toward a steady-state economy:* W. H. Freeman.

Daly, H. E. (1996). *Beyond Growth: The Economics of Sustainable Development*. Boston: Beacon Press.

Daly, H. E. (2007). *Ecological Economics and Sustainable Development, Selected Essays of Herman Daly*. Cheltenham, UK: Edward Elgar.

Darnton, A., Elsster-Jones, J., Lucas, K., & Brooks, M. (2005). Promoting Pro-Environmental Behaviour: Existing Evidence to Inform Better Policy Making: Chapter 1: Theory (pp. 84). London: A study for the department for environment, food and rural affairs

Davell, B., & Sessions, G. (1985). *Deep Ecology: Living as if Nature Mattered*. Salt Lake City:: Peregrine Smith Books.

Dean, R. H. (2008). Optimising Uncertainty. In W. Vitek & W. Jackson (Eds.), *The virtues of ignorance: complexity, sustainability, and the limits of knowledge* (pp. 81-100). Lexington: University Press of Kentucky.

Dearing, J. A. (2007). Human–Environment Interactions: Learning from the Past. In R. Costanza, L. J. Graumlich & W. Steffen (Eds.), *Sustainability or Collapse? An Integrated History and Future of People on Earth* (pp. 19-37). Cambridge, Massachusetts: The MIT Press.

Deese, R. S. (2009). The artifact of nature: 'Spaceship Earth' and the dawn of global environmentalism. *Endeavour, 33*(2), 70-75.

Deffeyes, K. S. (2008). *Hubbert's peak: the impending world oil shortage*: Princeton University Press.

Deng, R., Williams, E., & Babbitt, C. (2009). *Hybrid Assessment of the Life Cycle Energy Intensity of a Laptop Computer*. Paper presented at the Joimt North American Life Cycle Assessment IX, Boston.

Design Council. (2008). *The Good Design Plan* (pp. 39). London.

Di Castri, F. (1995). The chair of sustainable development. *Nature and Resources, 31*(3), 2-7.

Dickison, M. (2009). The asymmetry between science and traditional knowledge. *Journal of the Royal Society of New Zealand, 39*(4), 171-172. doi: 10.1080/03014220909510573

Doak, K. M. (1994). *Dreams of Difference: The Japan Romantic School and the Crisis of Modernity*. Berkeley, CA.: University of California Press.

Dodds, R., & Venables, R. (2005). *Principles of engineering for sustainable development* Retrieved 13/3/07, from www.raeng.org.uk/education/vps/pdf/Engineering_for_Sustainable_Development.pdf

Dourojeanni, A. (1997). Management procedures for sustainable development (applicable to municipalities, micro-regions and river basins) (pp. 71). Santiago, Chile: UN Economic Commission for Latin America and the Caribbean.

Dow Alden B. *A way of life cycle* www.abdow.org

Dumaine, B. (2008). *The plot to save the planet: How visionary entrepreneurs and corporate Titans are creating real solutions to global warming*. New York: Crown Business.

ECASA. (2007). Ecasa Toolbox (Ecosystem Approach for Sustainable Aquaculture), from http://www.ecasatoolbox.org.uk/the-toolbox/informative/key-ideas/management-for-sustainability

Ecotrust. (nd). *Reliable Prosperity Framework* Retrieved 2/12/10, from http://www.reliableprosperity.net

Edwards, C. A., Grove, T. L., Harwood, R. R., & Colfer, C. J. P. (1993). The role of agroecology and integrated farming systems in agricultural sustainability. 46, 99-121.

Ehrlich, A., & Ehrlich, P. (1987). *Earth:* Thames Methuen.

Encyclopedia of Life Support Systems. (2004). Global crisis and sustainable development: the inspiration for the eolss, from http://www.eolss.net/Eolss-Inspiration.aspx

Engster, D. (2008). T*he Heart of Justice: Care Ethics and Political Theory.* Oxford: Oxford University Press.

Entwistle, A., & Dunstone, N. (2000). *Priorities for the conservation of mammalian diversity: has the panda had its day?* Cambridge: Cambridge University Press.

Erekson, J. A. (Writer). (2009). Putting Humpty Dumpty together again: When illustration shuts down interpretation [Article], *Journal of Visual Literacy:* International Visual Literacy Association.

Esbjörn-Hargens, S. (2005). Integral ecology: the what, who, and how of environmental phenomena. *World Futures, 61*(1-2), 5-49. doi: 10.1080/02604020590902344

Esbjörn-Hargens, S., & Zimmerman, M. E. (2009). *Integral ecology: uniting multiple perspectives on the natural world*. Boston: Integral Books.

Evans, G. R. (2008). Transformation from "Carbon Valley" to a "Post-Carbon Society" in a climate change hot spot: the coalfields of the Hunter Valley, New South Wales, Australia. *Ecology and Society* 13(1), 39 [online] http://www.ecologyandsociety.org/vol13/iss31/art39/.

Fagan, G. (2009). The Emerging Paradigm. In A. Stibbe (Ed.), The Handbook of Sustainability Literacy: Skills for a Changing World (pp. online). Foxhole, Dartington, Totnes: Green Books.

Fedra, K., & Reitsma, R. F. (1990). Decision Support and Geographical Information Systems. In H. J. Scholten & J. C. H. Stillwell (Eds.), Geographical Information Systems for Urban and Regional Planning (Vol. 17, pp. 177-188). Dordrecht: Kluwer.

Fiddler, H. (2008). Plan S, Sustainable Living for the Long Term Retrieved 20/9/11, from http://plan-s.htfiddler.net/

Flint, R. W. (2002). Sustainable Development: What does sustainability mean to individuals in the conduct of their lives and businesses. In G. M. Mudacumura & M. S. S. Haque (Eds.), Handbook of Development Policy Studies (pp. 67-87 754 p). NY: Marcel Dekker Inc.

Foot, P. (1978). Virtues and vices and other essays in moral philosophy. Berkeley: University of California Press.

Freidel, M. H. (1991). Range condition assessment and the concept of thresholds: a viewpoint. Journal of Range Management, 44, 422-426.

Freire, P., & Freire, A. M. A. (2000). Pedogogy of the Heart New York, NY: Continuum International Publishing.

Freyfogle, E. T. (1996). Justice and the Earth: images for our planetary survival: University of Illinois Press.

Fulghum, R., Caldwell, D., & Zulia, E. (1999). *Robert Fulghum's All I really need to know I learned in kindergarten*: Dramatic Pub.

Fuller, B. (1965). *Statement of 1965, in reference to Operating Manual for Spaceship Earth <http://en.wikipedia.org/wiki/Operating_Manual_for_Spaceship_Earth> (1963) by Buckminster Fuller <http://en.wikiquote.org/wiki/Buckminster_Fuller>, as quoted by Vallero,D.A. (2005) Paradigms Lost: Learning from Environmental Mistakes, Mishaps and Misdeeds 367.*

Fuller, R. B. (1969). *Operating Manual For Spaceship Earth*. Carbondale: Southern Illinois University Press.

Fuller, R. B. (2008 (first published 1969)). *Operating Manual For Spaceship Earth*. Baden: Lars Müller Publishers.

Gardner, H. (1993). *Frames of Mind: The theory of multiple intelligences* (2nd ed.). NY: Basic Books.

Gasto, J., Vera, L., Vieli, L., & Montalba, R. (2009). Sustainable Agriculture: unifying concepts. *Cien. Inv. Agr., 36*(1), 5-26.

Geczi, E. (Writer). (2007). Sustainability and public participation: toward an inclusive model of democracy [Article], *Administrative Theory & Praxis (Administrative Theory & Praxis)*: Administrative Theory & Praxis.

George, H. (2005). *Progress and Poverty*. New York: Cosimo (EP Dutton 1879).

Gerber, J. M. (2005). Sustainability Studies Retrieved 30/11/10, from http://www.umass.edu/umext/jgerber/bdicrecommends.htm

Gilpin, M., Gall, G. A. E., & Woodruff, D. S. (1992). Ecological dynamics and agricultural landscapes. *Agriculture, Ecosystems and the Environment, 42*, 27-52.

Global Action Plan. (2007). An Inefficient Truth. London.

Goleman, D. (2009). *Ecological Intelligence: How Knowing the Hidden Impacts of What We Buy Can Change Everything*: Broadway Business.

Goodwin, C. (1994). Professional vision. *American Anthropologist, 96*(3), 606.

Government, T. S. (2006). *Sustainable Development: A Review of International Literature*.

Greenwood, T. (2010). Sustainable Design Guide: Triple Bottom Line, from http://www.espdesign.org/sustainability-definition/triple-bottom-line/

Grimm, V., Schmidt, E., & Wissel, C. (1992). On the application of stability concepts in ecology. *Ecological Modelling, 63*, 143-161.

Grossman, W. D. (1994). Socio-economic ecological models: criteria for evaluation of state-of-the-art models shown on four case studies. *Ecological Modelling, 75/76*, 21-36.

Guijt, I., Moiseev, A., Prescott-Allen, R., IUCN/IDRC Sustainability Assessment Team, IUCN--The World Conservation Union, International Development Research Centre, . . . Evaluation Initiative. (2001). *IUCN resource kit for sustainability assessment*: IUCN-The World Conservation Union.

Gunderson, L. H., & Holling, C. S. (2002). *Panarchy: understanding transformations in human and natural systems*: Island Press.

Hanns Carl von Carlowitz. (1713). *Sylvicultura Oeconomics - Anweisung zur wilden Baum-Zucht*. Leipzig: Johann Friedrich Braun.

Harding, S. (2006). *Animate earth: science, intuition and Gaia*. Totnes: Green Books.

Hargroves, K., & Smith, M. (2005). *The natural advantage of nations: business opportunities, innovation, and governance in the 21st century*. London: Earthscan.

Hart, R. D. (1984). Agroecosystem determinants. In R. Lowrance, B. R. Stinner & G. J. House (Eds.), *Agricultural ecoystems: unified concepts* (pp. 105-119). New York: Wiley.

Hawkes, J. (2001). *The Fourth Pillar of Sustainability: Culture's essential role in public planning*. Melbourne. : Common Ground, Published by The Humanities,.

Healey, M. (2009). An Inconvenient Data Center *Information Week*, http://www.informationweek.com/news/infrastructure/showArticle.jhtml?articleID=212900868.

Heltne, P. G. (2008). Imposed ignorance and humble ignorance - two worldviews. In W. Vitek & W. Jackson (Eds.), *The virtues of ignorance: complexity, sustainability, and the limits of knowledge* (pp. 135-149). Lexington: University Press of Kentucky.

Hinton, S. (2010). Connecting people to sustainability: the uncomfortable truths Retrieved 8/12/10, from http://avbp.net/?p=466%20Stephen%20Hinton

Holmberg, J., & Samuelsson, B. E. (2006). Drivers and Barriers for Implementing Sustainable Development in Higher Education: Executive Summary. In J. Holmberg & B. E. Samuelsson (Eds.), *Drivers and Barriers for Implementing Sustainable Development in Higher Education* (pp. 7-11). Paris: UNESCO Education.

Homer-Dixon, T. F. (2009). Our panarchic future. *World Watch, 22*(2), 8+.

Hossay, P. (2006). *Unsustainable: A primer for global environmental and social justice*. London: Zed Books.

Hubbel, S. P., & Foster, R. B. (1986). Canopy gaps and the dynamics of a neotropical forest. In M. J. Crawley (Ed.), *Plant Ecology* (pp. 77-96). Oxford: Blackwell Scientific.

Hubbert, M. K. (1949). Energy from fossil fuels. *Science, 109*(2823), 103-109.

Hunt, J. D., & Holland, F. M. (1982). *The Ruskin polygon: essays on the imagination of John Ruskin*: Manchester University Press.

Hunter, G. J., & Goodchild, M. F. (1995). *The treatment of vector data error in Geographic Information Systems*. Paper presented at the Proceedings of the 23rd Annual International Conference of the Australasian Urban and Regional Information Systems Assocaiation Incorporated, Melbourne.

Hutchinson, G. E. (1965). *The Ecological Theater and the Evolutionary Play*. New Haven, Connecticut: Yale University Press.

IDEO. (nd). *Using Life Cycle Awareness Tools*.

Industrial Designers Society of America. (2001). IDSA recognizes the following ecological principles Retrieved 13/1/11, 2011, from http://www.idsa.org/content/content1/idsa-recognizes-following-ecological-principles

Ingold, T. (1980). *Hunters, pastoralists, and ranchers: reindeer economies and their transformations*. Cambridge: Cambridge University Press.

Interface. (2011). The Interface Model Retrieved 16/9/11, 2011, from http://www.interfaceglobal.com/Sustainability/Our-Journey/Interface-Model.aspx

International Commission on the Development of Education, & Faure, E. (1972). *Learning to be: the world of education today and tomorrow*: Unesco.

International Network for Acid Prevention. (nd). The Global Acid Rock Drainage (GARD) Guide, Chapter 3 Corporate, Regulatory, and Community Framework, http://www.gardguide.com/index.php/Chapter_3 Retrieved 9/12/10

International Union for Conservation of Nature and Natural Resources, United Nations Environment Programme, & World Wildlife Fund. (1980). *World Conservation Strategy: Living Resource Conservation for Sustainable Development*. International Union for Conservation of Nature and Natural Resources, Gland. . Retrieved from http://data.iucn.org/dbtw-wpd/edocs/WCS-004.pdf.

Iribarnegaray, M., & Seghezzo, L. (2011, 1-30 November 2011). *Governance, sustainability and decision making in water and sanitation management systems*. Paper presented at the Proceedings of the 1st World Sustainability Forum.

Isaksson, R., & Steimle, U. (2008). *What does GRI-reporting tell us about corporate sustainability?* Paper presented at the Proceedings of the 11th International Conference on Quality Management and Organisational Development, Helsingborg.

Isaksson, R., & Steimle, U. (2009). What does GRI-reporting tell us about corporate sustainability? [DOI: 10.1108/17542730910938155]. *The TQM Journal, 21*(2), 168-181.

Jalas, M. (2006). *Sustainable consumption innovations – instrumentalization and integration of emergent patterns of everyday life*. Paper presented at the Perspectives on Radical Changes to Sustainable Consumption and Production (SCP), Copenhagen.

Jensen, B. B., & Schnack, K. (1997). The Action Competence Approach in Environmental Education. *Environmental Education Research, 3*(2), 163-179.

Jickling, B., Lotz-Sisitka, H., O'Donoghue, R., & A., O. (2006). *Environmental Education, Ethics, and Action: A Workbook to Get Started*. Nairobi: United Nations Environment Programme.

Johnson, S. P., & Finn, J., C. (1963). Ecological Considerations of a Permanent Lunar Base. *American Biology Teacher*, 530.

Jones, P., & Powell, J. (1999). Gary Anderson has been found. *Resource Recycling, May 1999*, 1-2.

Kennedy, J. J., & Koch, N. E. (2004). Viewing and managing natural resources as human-ecosystem relationships. *Forest Policy and Economics, 6*(5), 497-504.

Kesavan, P. C., & Swaminathan, M. S. (2006). Managing extreme natural disasters in coastal areas. *Philosophical Transactions of the Royal Society A: Mathematical, Physical and Engineering Sciences, 364*(1845), 2191-2216.

Kira, M., & Eijnatten, F. M. v. (Writers). (2008). Socially sustainable work organizations: A chaordic systems approach [Article], *Systems Research & Behavioral Science*: John Wiley & Sons, Inc. / Business.

Koutsouris, A. (2009). Sustainability, cross disciplinarity and higher education: An agronomic point of view. *US China Education Review, 6*(3), http://www.teacher.org.cn/doc/ucedu200903/ucedu20090302.pdf.

Kraft, M. (2007). *Environmental policy and politics*. NY: Pearson/Longman.

Landcare Research. (nd). Our approach to Triple Bottom Line reporting, from http://www.landcareresearch.co.nz/about/principles/tbl_reporting.asp

Langhelle, O. (1999). Sustainable Development: Exploring the Ethics of Our Common Future. *International Political Science Review/ Revue internationale de science pol, 20*(2), 129-149. doi: 10.1177/0192512199202002

Lautensach, A. K. (2004). *A tertiary curriculum for sustainability*. Paper presented at the Australian Association of Research in Education Conference, Melbourne Nov 29 - Dec 2, 2004. http://www.aare.edu.au/04pap/lau04260.pdf

Laycock, W. A. (1991). Stable states and thresholds of range condition on North American rangelands, a viewpoint. *Journal of Range Management, 44*(5), 427-433.

Lee, J. A. (2005). GREAT GEOGRAPHERS: George Perkins Marsh. *Focus On Geography, 48*(3), 35.

Lee, K. N. (1993). Greed, scale mismatch, and learning. *Ecological Applications, 3*(4), 560-564.

Leopold, A. (1949). *A Sand County Almanac*: Oxford University Press.

Lewis, E. P. (1811). *Historical inquiries, concerning forests and forest laws: With topographical remarks, upon the ancient and modern state of the New Forest, in the county of Southampton*. London: Printed for T. Payne by J. M'Creery.

Lockwood, J. A., & Lockwood, D. R. (1993). Catastrophe theory: a unified paradigm for rangeland ecosystem dynamics. *Journal of Range Management, 46*(4), 282-288.

Loh, J. (Ed.). (2010). *2010 and Beyond: Rising to the biodiversity challenge*. Gland Switzerland: WWF International.

Looney, A. (1996). Fluxx http://www.looneylabs.com/games/fluxx.

Lovelock, J. (1995). *The ages of Gaia: a biography of our living earth*: Norton.

Lovelock, J. (2000). *Gaia: a new look at life on earth*. Oxford: Oxford University Press.

Lovelock, J. (2006). *The Revenge of Gaia*. London: Allen Lane.

Lowes, D., & Walker, D. (1995). *Environmental Management: Opportunities and Challenges in the Application of AI*. Paper presented at the Proceedings of the Workshop on AI and the Environment: Eigth Australasian Joint Conference on Artificial Intelligence, Australian Defence Force Academy, Canberra.

Lyons, M., Smuts, C., & Stephens, A. (2001). Participation, Empowerment and Sustainability: (How) Do the Links Work? [Article]. *Urban Studies, 38*(8), 1233-1251.

Macgregor, C. (2000). *Applying an Analytical Model for Assessing Community Sustainability: some preliminary results from northern Australian remote towns*. Paper presented at the Paper presented to the First National Conference on the Future of Australia's Country Towns, Bendigo, Victoria. http://www.regional.org.au/au/countrytowns/global/macgregor.htm

Machlis, G. E., Force, J. E., & Burch, W. R. (1997). The human ecosystem Part I: The human ecosystem as an organizing concept in ecosystem management. *Society & Natural Resources, 10*(4), 347-367. doi: 10.1080/08941929709381034

Machlis, G. E., Force, J. E., & Dalton, S. E. (1994). Monitoring Social Indicators for Ecosystem Management *Technical paper submitted to the Interior Columbia River Basin Project*.: University of Idaho.

Madden, P., & Weißbrod, I. (2008). *Connected: ICT and sustainable development*. London: Forum for the Future.

Maddex, D. (2007). *Alden B. Dow: midwestern modern*: Alden B. Dow Home and Studio.

Maery, É. J. (1878). *La Méthode graphique*. Paris.

Maik, A., Jasmin, G., & Gerd, M. (2007). Transferability of approaches to sustainable development at universities as a challenge. *International Journal of Sustainability in Higher Education, 8*(4), 385.

Maiteny, P. (2009). Finding meaning without consuming: the ability to experience meaning, purpose and satisfaction through non-material wealth. In A. Stibbe (Ed.), *The Handbook of Sustainability Literacy: Skills for a Changing World* (pp. 224). Totnes: Green Books.

Markevich, A. (2009). The Evolution of Sustainability. *MIT Sloan Management Review, 51*(1), 13.

Marsh, G. P. (1864). *Man and Nature; or Physical Geography as Modified by Human Action*. New York: Charles Scribner.

Marshall, J. D., & Toffel, M. W. (2005). Framing the Elusive Concept of Sustainability: A Sustainability Hierarchy. [Article]. *Environmental Science & Technology, 39*, 673-682.

Marten, G. G. (1988). Productivity, stability, sustainability, equitability and autonomy as properties for agroecosystem assessment. *Agricultural Systems, 26*, 291-316.

Martens, P. (2006). Sustainability: science or fiction? *Sustainability: Science, Practice, & Policy 2*(1), 36-41.

Martin, S. (2005). Sustainability, Systems Thinking and Professional Practice. *Systemic Practice and Action Research, 18*(2), 163-171.

McDonough, W., & Braungart, M. (2002). *Cradle to cradle: remaking the way we make things*. San Francisco: North Point Press.

McDonough, W., Braungart, M., Anastas, P. T., & Zimmerman, J. B. (2003). Applying the principle of Green Engineering to cradle-to-cradle design. *Environmental Science & Technology, 37*(23), A434.

McEvoy, T. J. (2004). *Positive impact forestry: a sustainable approach to managing woodlands*: Island Press.

McEwan, C. A., & Schmidt, J. D. (2007). *Mindsets in Action: Leadership and the Corporate Sustainability Challenge*. Roswell, GA: Avastone Consulting.

McKeown, R. (2002). Education for sustainable development toolkit 2. Retrieved 15/3/7, 2007, from http://www.esdtoolkit.org

McNamee, P. J., Bunnell, P., & Sonntag, N. C. (1986). Dealing with wicked problems: a case study of models and resource management in southeast Alaska. In J. Verner, M. L. Morrison & C. J. Ralph (Eds.), *Wildlife 2000: modelling habitat relationships of terrestrial vertebrates* (pp. 395-399). Wisconsin: UWP.

Meadows, D. (1998). *Indicators and information systems for sustainable development: a report to the Balaton Group, September 1998*: The Sustainability Institute.

Meadows, D. H., Meadows, D. L., Randers, J., & Behrens, W. W. (1972). *The Limits to Growth; a report for the Club of Rome's project on the Predicament of Mankind*. NY: Universe Books.

Meadows, D. H., Randers, J., & Meadows, D. L. (2005). *Limits to growth: the 30-year update*: Chelsea Green.

Meredith, T. C. (2000). *Community Participation in Environmental Information Management: Exploring Tools for Developing an Impact Assessment Preparedness Program* (Vol. Catalog No. En105-3/81-2004E): Canadian Environmental Assessment Agency's Research and Development Program.

Messerschmitt, D., & Szyperski, C. (2003). *Software Ecosystem: Understanding an Indispensable Technology and Industry*. Cambridge, MA.: MIT Press.

Millenium Ecosystem Assessment. (2005). Ecosystems and Human Well-Being: Opportunities and Challenges for Business and Industry. Washington, DC.: World Resources Institute.

Milne, M. J., Tregidga, H., & Walton, S. (2009). Words not actions! The ideological role of sustainable development reporting. *Accounting, Auditing & Accountability Journal, 22*(8), 1211-1257.

Ministry for the Environment. (2009). *Re-thinking our built environments: Towards a sustainable future*. Wellington: NZ Government.

Moffatt, S., & Kohler, N. (2008). Conceptualising the built environment as a social-ecological system. *Building and research information, 36*(3), 248-268.

Morris, D., & Martin, S. (2009). Complexity, systems thinking and practice: skills and techniques for managing complex systems. In A. Stibbe (Ed.), *The Handbook of Sustainability Literacy: Skills for a Changing World* (pp. 156-164). Totnes, Devon: Green Books.

Morrison, J. (2010). Certificate IV in Understanding and Negotiating Sustainability Issues Retrieved 26/11/2010, from http://sustainabilitytraining.net.au/

Munasinghe, M. (1992). *Environmental Economics and Sustainable Development*. Paper presented at the Paper presented at the UN Earth Summit, Rio de Janeiro.

Munasinghe, M. (2010). *Making Development More Sustainable: Sustainomics Framework and Practical Applications, . URL:* (2nd ed.). Colombo: MIND Press, Munasinghe Institute for Development, www.mindlanka.org.

Munasinghe, M., Sunkel, O., & Miguel, C. (2001). *The sustainability of long-term growth: socioeconomic and ecological perspectives*. Cheltenham: Edward Elgar.

Myers, J. (1963). Introductory Remarks. *American Biology Teacher*, 409-411.

Næss, A. (1973). The Shallow and the Deep, Long Range Ecology Movements. *Inquiry (Oslo)*.

Næss, A. (2005). *The selected works of Arne Næss*. Dordrecht: Springer.

National Research Council . Policy Division. Board on Sustainable Development. (1999). *Our common journey: a transition toward sustainability*: National Academy Press.

Naveh, Z. (1980). Landscape Ecology as a Scientific and Educational Tool for Teaching The Total Human Ecosystem. In T. S. Bakshi & Z. Naveh (Eds.), *Environmental education: principles, methods, and applications* (pp. 149-163). NY: Plenum Press.

Naveh, Z. (1982). Landscape Ecology as an Emerging Branch of Human Ecosystem Science. In A. Macfadyen & E. D. Ford (Eds.), *Advances in Ecological Research* (Vol. Volume 12, pp. 189-237): Academic Press.

Naveh, Z. (2000). What is holistic landscape ecology? A conceptual introduction. *Landscape and Urban Planning, 50*(1-3), 7-26. doi: 10.1016/s0169-2046(00)00077-3

Naveh, Z. (2004). Sustainability and public participation: toward an inclusive model of democracy. *World Futures, 60*(7), 469-502. doi: 10.1080/02604020490518324

Naveh, Z., & Lieberman, A. S. (1994). *Landscape Ecology: Theory and Application* (2nd ed.). New York: Springer-Verlag.

NewSplash, & Mann, S. (2011). Otago Polytechic.

Nijkamp, P., van den Bergh, J., & Soeterman, F. (1990). *Regional Sustainable Development and Natural Resource Use*. Paper presented at the World Bank Annual Conference on Development Economics. , Washington D.C. http://www-wds.worldbank.org/external/default/main?print=Y&pagePK=64193027&piPK=64187937&theSitePK=523679&menuPK=64187510&searchMenuPK=64187283&siteName=WDS&entityID=000178830_98101911514472

Niu, W.-Y., Lu, J. J., & Khan, A. A. (1993). Spatial systems approach to sustainable development: a conceptual framework. *Environmental Management, 17*(2), 179-186.

Nkhata, B., Breen, C., & Abacar, A. (2009). Social capital, community-based governance and resilience in an African artisanal river fishery. *Water SA, 35*, 45-53.

NZ Ministry for Culture and Heritage. (2002). *Cultural Well-being - What is it?, .* Retrieved from http://www.culturalwellbeing.govt.nz/files/WhatIsCulturalWellbeingBrochure.pdf.

O'Neill, R. V. (1988). Hierarchy theory and global change. In T. Rosswall, R. G. Woodmansee & P. G. Risser (Eds.), *Scales and Global Change* (pp. 29-45). New York: Wiley and Sons.

O'Neill, S., & Nicholson-Cole, S. (2009). "Fear Won't Do It": Promoting Positive Engagement With Climate Change Through Visual and Iconic Representations. *Science Communication, 30*(3), 355-379. doi: 10.1177/1075547008329201

Odum, E. P. (1971). *Fundamentals of ecology*: Saunders.

Odum, E. P., & Barrett, G. W. (2004). Redesigning Industrial Agroecosystems. *Journal of Crop Improvement, 11*(1-2), 45-60. doi: 10.1300/J411v11n01_03

Odum, H. T. (1974). Energy, Ecology, & Economics.

OECD. (2009). Green at Fifteen? How 15-year-olds perform in environmental science and geoscience and geoscience in PISA 2006 (pp. 117). Paris: OECD Publications.

Office of the Deputy Prime Minister (UK). (2004). *The Egan Review: Skills for Sustainable Communities.* London: Retrieved from http://www.communities.gov.uk/publications/communities/eganreview.

Onwueme, I., & Borsari, B. (2007). The sustainability asymptogram. *International Journal of Sustainability in Higher Education, 8*(1), 44-52.

Organisation for Economic Co-operation and Development. (2004). *OECD environmental strategy: 2004 review of progress*: OECD.

Orr, D. W. (1992). *Ecological Literacy: Education and the Transition to a Postmodern World*. Albany: State University of New York Press.

Orr, D. W. (2004a). *Earth in mind: on education, environment, and the human prospect* (Vol. 221). Washington, D.C.: Island Press

Orr, D. W. (2004b). The Learning Curve. *Resurgance, 226*, http://ecoliteracy.org/publications/ecodesign.html.

Osbaldiston, R., & Sheldon, K. (2002). Social dilemmas and sustainability: promoting peoples' motivation to cooperate *Psychology of sustainable development* (pp. 37-57).

Parker, J., Wade, R., & Atkinson, H. (2004). Citizenship and Community from Local to Global: Implications for Higher Education of a Global Citizenship Approach. In J. Blewitt & C. Cullingford (Eds.), *The Sustainability Curriculum: The Challenge for Higher Education* (pp. 63-77). London: Earthscan.

Parr, A. (2009). *Hijacking Sustainability*. Camridge, Mass: The MIT Press.

Pickett, S. T. A., Kolasa, J., Armesto, J. J., & Collins, S. L. (1989). The ecological concept of disturbance and its expression at various hierarchical levels. *Oikos, 54*, 129-136.

Pilgrim, S., & Pretty, J. N. (2010). *Nature and culture: rebuilding lost connections*: Earthscan.

Polistina, K. (2009). Cultural Literacy: *understanding and respect for the cultural aspects of sustainability*. In A. Stibbe (Ed.), *The Handbook of Sustainability Literacy: Skills for a Changing World* (pp. 117-123). Totnes, Devon: Green Books.

Poole, R., & Poole, R. (2008). *Earthrise: how man first saw the Earth*: Yale University Press.

Preston, N. (2007). *Understanding Ethics* (3rd ed.). Sydney: The Federation Press.

Puthli, H. (2010). HPA Perspective on Sustainability: FAQs – 3 Retrieved 20/9/11, from http://hemantputhli.com/2010/02/01/hpa-perspective-on-sustainability-faqs-%E2%80%93-3/

Queensland Government, Q. G. (2009). *Queensland Design Strategy 2020*. Brisbane: Retrieved from http://cdx.dexigner.com/article/18061/The_Queensland_Design_Strategy_2020.pdf.

Quisumbing, L. R., & de Leo, J. (2005). *Learning to Do: Values for Learning and Working Together in a Globalized World: An integrated Approach to Incorporating Values Education in in Technical and Vocational Education and Training*. Bonn: UNESCO-APNIEVE and UNESCO-UNEVOC International Centre for Technical and Vocational Education and Training.

Ranville, J. (nd). The Human Life Project: Sustainable Patterns in Nature, Family, and Community, from http://www.humanlifeproject.com/

Rastetter, E. B., King, A. W., Cosby, B. J., Hornberger, G. M., O'Neill, R. V., & Hobbie, J. E. (1992). Aggregating fine-scale ecological knowledge to model coarser-scale attributes of ecosystems. *Ecological Applications, 2*(1), 55-70.

Reagan, D. R. (nd). 2012 The end of the world? Retrieved 20/9/11, from http://www.lamblion.com/articles/articles_signs12.php

Reed, B. (2007). Shifting from 'sustainability' to regeneration. *Building Research & Information, 35*(6), 674-680. doi: 10.1080/09613210701475753

Reed, B. (nd). Integrating the Whole System, The practice of Living System (Regenerative) Design, from http://integrativedesign.net/images/whole_systems_regenerative_development.pdf

Robinson, Z. (2009). Greening Business: the ability to drive environmental and sustainability improvements in the workplace. In A. Stibbe (Ed.), *The Handbook of Sustainability Literacy: Skills for a Changing World* (pp. 130-136). Totnes, Devon: Green Books.

Robson, J. P., & Berkes, F. (2010). Sacred nature and community conserved areas. In S. Pilgrim & J. N. Pretty (Eds.), *Nature and culture: rebuilding lost connections* (pp. 197-216). London: Earthscan.

Rockstrom, J., Steffen, W., Noone, K., Persson, A., Chapin, F. S., III, Lambin, E. F., . . . Foley, J. A. (2009). A safe operating space for humanity: identifying and quantifying planetary boundaries that must not be transgressed could help prevent human activities from causing unacceptable environmental change, argue Johan Rockstrom and colleagues. *Nature, 461*(7263), 472(474).

Rodríguez, J. P., T. D. Beard, J., Bennett, E. M., Cumming, G. S., Cork, S., Agard, J., . . . Peterson., G. (2006). Trade-offs across space, time, and ecosystem service. *Ecology and Society, 11*(28), http://www.ecologyandsociety.org/vol11/iss11/art28/.

Root-Bernstein, R. (2008). I Don't Know! In W. Vitek & W. Jackson (Eds.), *The virtues of ignorance: complexity, sustainability, and the limits of knowledge* (pp. 233-250). Lexington: University Press of Kentucky.

Rowledge, L., Barton, R., Brady, K., & Fava, J. (1999). *Mapping the journey: case studies in strategy and action toward sustainable development*. Sheffield: Greenleaf.

Runnalls, C. R. (2006). *Choreographing community sustainability: The importance of cultural planning to community viability*. Royal Rhodes University, Victoria, BC.

Saito, O. (2007). Pathways to sustainable industrial societies. *Encyclopedia of the Earth*, from http://www.eoearth.org/article/Pathways_to_sustainable_industrial_societies

Samuel, J. (2011). James Samuel, from http://sustainablelens.org/?p=148

Sarrett, P. (1997). Fluxx, from http://www.gamereport.com/tgr17/fluxx.html

Schendler, A. (2009). *Getting Green Done: Hard Truths from the Front Lines of the Sustainability Revolution*. New York: Public Affairs.

Schlange, L. E. (2009). Stakeholder Identification in Sustainability Entrepreneurship. [Article]. *Greener Management International*(55), 13-32.

Seedhouse, D. (2009). *Ethics: the heart of health care*: Wiley-Blackwell.

Seghezzo, L. (2009). The five dimensions of sustainability. *Environmental Politics, 18*(4), 539-556.

Semple, E. C. (2005). *Influences of Geographic Environment On the Basis of Ratzel's System of Anthropo-Geography* BiblioBazaar.

Senge, P. M., Laur, J., Schley, S., & Smith, B. (2006). *Learning for Sustainability*. Cambridge, Mass: Society for Organisational Learning.

Senge, P. M., Smith, B., Schley, S., Laur, J., & Kruschwitz, N. (2008). *The Necessary Revolution: How individuals and organizations are working together to create a sustainable world*.: Doubleday Publishing.

SIGMA project. (2003), from http://www.projectsigma.co.uk/default.asp

Simms, A., Johnston, V., Smith, J., Mitchell, S., & Staff, N. E. F. (2009). *The Consumption Explosion: The third UK Interdependence Report*: New Economics Foundation.

Singer, P. (Producer). (2007). Gloabl Poverty, Lecture 1. *Uehiro Lectures*. Retrieved from http://www.practicalethics.ox.ac.uk/Events/Uehiro%20Lectures/Video/Uehiro-1w.mov

Singer, P. (2010). *The Life You Can Save: Acting Now to End World Poverty*. Melbourne: Text Publishing Company.

Smaling, E. M. A., & Fresco, L. O. (1993). A decision-support model for monitoring nutrient balances under agricultural land-use (Nutmon). *Geoderma, 60*, 235-256.

South Gloustershire Council. (2008). *South Gloucestershire Core Strategy - Issues and Options consultation: Issues and Options document*. Retrieved from https://consultations.southglos.gov.uk/inovem/consult.ti/CSissuesandoptions/printCompoundDoc?docid=109780.

Spaling, H., & Smit, B. (1993). Cummulative environmental change: conceptual frameworks, evaluation approaches, and institional perspectives. *Environmental Management, 17*(5), 587-600.

Spangenberg, J. H. (2007). The institutional dimension of sustainable development. In T. Hák, B. Moldan & A. L. Dahl (Eds.), *Sustainability indicators: a scientific assessment* (Vol. 67, pp. 107-124). Washington: Island Press.

Spangenberg, J. H., & Bonniot, O. (1998). *Sustainability Indicators - A Compass on the Road Towards Sustainability*: Wuppertal Institut für Klima, Umwelt, Energie (ed.), Wuppertal Paper No. 81.

Sprugel, D. (1991). Disturbance, equilibrium and environmental variability: what is 'natural' vegetation in a changing environment. *Biological Conservation, 58*, 1-18.

Stagl, S. (2007a). Theoretical foundations of learning processes for sustainable development. *International Journal of Sustainable Development and World Ecology, 14*, 52-62.

Stagl, S. (2007b). Theoretical foundations of learning processes for sustainable development. *International Journal of Sustainable Development and World Ecology, 14*(1), 52-62.

Stanners, D., Dom, A., Gee, D., Martin, J., Ribeiro, T., Rickard, L., & Weber, J.-L. (2007) Bridging the gaps between theory and practice: a service niche approach to urban sustainability indicators. In T. Hák, B. Moldan & A. L. Dahl (Eds.), *Sustainability indicators: a scientific assessment* (Vol. 67, pp. 329-340). Washington: Island Press.

Stephenson, J., & Moller, H. (2009). Cross-cultural environmental research and management: Challenges and progress. *Journal of the Royal Society of New Zealand, 39*(4), 139-149. doi: 10.1080/03014220909510567

Sterling, S. (2004a). An Analysis of the Development of Sustainability Education Internationally: Evolution, Interpretation and Transformative Potential. In J. Blewitt & C. Cullingford (Eds.), *The Sustainability Curriculum: The Challenge for Higher Education* (pp. 43-62). London: Earthscan.

Sterling, S. (2004b). Higher Education, Sustainabiluity, and the Role of Systemic Learning. In P. B. Corcoran & E. J. W. Arjen (Eds.), *Higher Education and the Challenge of Sustainability: Problematics, Promise and Practice* (pp. 50-70). NY: Kluwer Academic.

Steward, W. C. (nd). The 5 Domains & EcoSTEP: An Introduction Retrieved 3/12/10, from http://www.ecospheres.com/5Domains_EcoStep_introduction.pdf

Storck, I. (2006). The Triple Bottom Line Still Includes People, from http://www.ivanenviroman.com/the-triple-bottom-line-still-includes-people/

Suzuki, H., Dastur, A., Moffatt, S., Yabuki, N., & Maruyama, H. (2010). *Eco2 cities: ecological cities as economic cities*: World Bank.

Svanström, M., Lozano-García, F. J., & Rowe, D. (2008). Learning outcomes for sustainable development in higher education. *International Journal of Sustainability in Higher Education, 9*(3), 339-351.

Talbott, S. (2008). Towards an ecological conversation. In W. Vitek & W. Jackson (Eds.), *The virtues of ignorance: complexity, sustainability, and the limits of knowledge* (pp. 101-108). Lexington: University Press of Kentucky.

Taplin, J. R. D., Bent, D., & Aeron-Thomas, D. (2006). Developing a sustainability accounting framework to inform strategic business decisions: a case study from the chemicals industry. [Article]. *Business Strategy & the Environment (John Wiley & Sons, Inc), 15*, 347-360.

Taylor, D. M. (1994). *Off course: restoring balance between Canadian society and the environment*: International Development Research Centre.

Tett, P., Portilla, E., Gillibrand, P. A., & Inall, M. (2011). Carrying and assimilative capacities: the ACExR-LESV model for sea-loch aquaculture. *Aquaculture Research, 42*, 51-67. doi: 10.1111/j.1365-2109.2010.02729.x

Thomson, J. J., & Parent, W. (1986). *Rights, restitution, and risk: essays, in moral theory*: Harvard University Press.

Tilley, F., & Young, W. (Writers). (2009). Sustainability Entrepreneurs [Article], *Greener Management International*: Greenleaf Publishing.

Tormey, R., Liddy, M., & Hogan, D. (2009). Interdisciplinary Literacy: the ability to critique disciplinary cultures and work effectively across disciplines. In A. Stibbe (Ed.), *The Handbook of Sustainability Literacy: Skills for a Changing World* (pp. 224). Totnes: Green Books.

Tritter, J. Q., & McCallum, A. (2006). The snakes and ladders of user involvement: Moving beyond Arnstein. *Health Policy, 76*(2), 156-168.

Tuan, Y. (1974). *Topophilia: a study of environmental perception, attitudes, and values*: Columbia University Press.

Tufte, E. R. (1983). *The visual display of quantitative information*. Cheshire, Conn.: Graphics Press.

Turner, N. J., Gregory, R., Brooks, C., Failing, L., & Satterfield, T. (2008). From invisibility to transparency: identifying the implications. *Ecology and Society, 13*(2), 7.

United Nations. (1992). *Earth Summit: Agenda 21: The United Nations Programme of Action from Rio "The Rio Declaration on Environment and Development"*. Retrieved from http://www.un.org/esa/dsd/agenda21/index.shtml.

United Nations (1997). *Educating for a Sustainable Future: A Transdisciplinary Vision for Concerted Action*. Paris: UNESCO.

United Nations. (2002). *Plan of Implementation of the World Summit on Sustainable Development*. Johannesburg: Unieted Nations Retrieved from http://www.un.org/esa/sustdev/documents/WSSD_POI_PD/English/WSSD_PlanImpl.pdf.

United Nations (Brundtland, G. (1987). *A/42/427. Our Common Future: Report of the World Commission on Environment and Development, General Assembly Resolution 42/187, 11 December 1987. Retrieved: 5/6/2010*. Retrieved from http://www.un-documents.net/wced-ocf.htm and http://www.worldinbalance.net/intagreements/1987-brundtland.php.

United Nations Environment Programme. (2007). *Global Environmental Outlook 4*.

United Nations. Conference on the Human Environment. (1973). *United Nations Conference on the human environment: report : Stockholm, 5-16 June 1972*.

Vallero, D. A. (2005). *Paradigms Lost: Learning from Environmental Mistakes, Mishaps and Misdeeds*. Amsterdam: Butterworth-Heinemann,.

van Mansvelt, J. D., & van der Lubbe, M. J. (1999). *Checklist for sustainable landscape management: final report of the EU concerted action AIR3-CT93-1210 : the landscape and nature production capacity of organic/sustainable types of agriculture*. Amsterdam: Elsevier.

Vehkamäki, S. (2005). The concept of sustainability in modern times. In A. Jalkanen & P. Nygren (Eds.), *Sustainable use of renewable natural resources - from principles to practice*. Helsinki: University of Helsinki Department of Forestry.

Vitek, B., & Jackson, W. (2008). *The virtues of ignorance: complexity, sustainability, and the limits of knowledge*. Lexington: University Press of Kentucky.

Vugteveen, P. e., Leuven, R. S. E. W., Huijbregts, M. A. J., & Lenders, H. J. R. (2006). Redefinition and Elaboration of River Ecosystem Health: Perspective for River Management. [Article]. *Hydrobiologia, 565*, 289-308.

Wagner, C. (1995). Decision Support for "Messy" Problems. *Information and Management, 28*, 393-403.

Wals, A. E. J., & Jickling, B. (2002). "Sustainability" in higher education: From doublethink and newspeak to critical thinking and meaningful learning. *International Journal of Sustainability in Higher Education, 3*(3), 221-232.

Walters, C. (1986). *Adaptive Management of Renewable Resources*. New York: MacMillan.

Wehi, P. M., Whaanga, H., & Roa, T. (2009). Missing in translation: Maori language and oral tradition in scientific analyses of traditional ecological knowledge (TEK). *Journal of the Royal Society of New Zealand, 39*(4), 201-204. doi: 10.1080/03014220909510580

Welling, B. H. (2009). Ecoporn: on the limits of visualizing the non-human. In S. Dobrin & S. Morey (Eds.), *Ecosee: image, rhetoric, nature* (pp. 53-77). Albany NY: SUNY Press.

White, L. (1967). "The Historical Roots of Our Ecologic Crisis. *Science, 155*(3767), 1203-1212.

Wiens, J. A. (1989). Spatial scaling in ecology. *Functional Ecology, 3*, 385-397.

Wijayadasa, K. H. J. (1997). *Integrating Environmental Considerations into Economic Decision Making Processes in South Asia: Synthesis Paper: Sri Lanka*.

Wilber, K. (2007). *A Brief History of Everything*. Boston, MA: Shambhala.

Willard, B. (2005). *The Next Sustainability Wave: Building Boardroom Buy-in (Conscientious Commerce)*. Gabriola Island, British Columbia, Canada: New Society Publishers.

Wilson, F. A. (1994). Computer support for strategic organisational decision-making. *Journal of Strategic Information Systems, 3*(4), 289-298.

Wirth, T. (1994). *Sustainable development and national security - statement by Timothy E. Wirth before the National Press Club - Transcript*. Paper presented at the US Department of State Dispatch, July 25, 1994

Wood, M. (2000). *Blind memory: visual representations of slavery in England and America, 1780-1865*: Manchester University Press.

WWF/ZSL/GFN, Humphrey, S., Loh, J., & Goldfinger, S. (Eds.). (2008). *Living planet report*. Gland Switzerland: WWF International.

Young, W., & Tilley, F. (2006). Can businesses move beyond efficiency? The shift toward effectiveness and equity in the corporate sustainability debate. *Business Strategy and the Environment, 15*(6), 402-415. doi: 10.1002/bse.510

acknowledgments

This book celebrates the efforts of a great many people who have worked to communicate ideas of sustainability through visual representations. To them the world owes a grateful thank you.

For me I am grateful for the help of an abundance of assistance from many people – from some a simple discussion clarified an idea – others put up with the obsession over months.

So, in no particular order, I acknowledge the contribution of: Richard Morgan; Peter Holland; Kerry Shephard; Forum for the Future; Centre for Alternative Technology; Blekinge Institute of Technology; Natural Edge Project; the Dunedin City Council's Community Resilience Forum – especially Jinty McTavish and Kate Wilson; colleagues at CITRENZ (ex NACCQ); the Sustainability Community at CHI, colleagues from SIGCSE; Eli Blevis; Nathan Shedroff; Andy Williamson; Logan Muller; Hayden Montgomerie; Colin Boswell; Alison Clear; Metiria Turei; David Clark; Clare Curran; Shane Gallagher and Anton Angelo.

I am fortunate to work at the wonderful Otago Polytechnic – where we are committed to every graduate being a sustainable practitioner. These are values well lived. Led by Phil Ker, colleagues from across the institution are passionate about creating a better future – I salute you all, for your passion, and for supporting this book. I am constantly amazed by the greatness of colleagues from across Otago Polytechnic: Nikki Bould, Nicola Mutch, Katie Ellwood (my co-author of 'little book', the design of which prompted the research that lead to this book); Tim Bishop; Ella Lawton; Steve Henry; Barry Law; Anna Hughes; Bridie Lonie; Caro McCaw; Leoni Schmidt; Alistair Regan; Robin Day; Phil Ker, Jenny Aimers; Anni Watkins; Chris Williamson; Khyla Russell. My colleagues in Information Technology deserve special mention – no more books this year I promise - Lesley Smith; Adrienne Dearnley; Ashley Martin; Brian Treanor; Christine Dyer; Dale Parsons; Darrell Love; David Bremer; Hamish Smith; Joy Gasson; Karen Love; Krissi Wood; Mike Goodwin; Patricia Haden; Peter Brook; Rachel Trounson; Ros Westerman; and Thomi Richards.

Diagrams in this book have come to my attention though a variety of methods not least being the legion of folks who have sent links to images (mostly my blog computingforsustainability). This book is not exhaustive – indeed there were twice as many images in the first draft. I am always looking for more – feel free to send ideas through sustainablens.org or email.

I am grateful for the research assistance of Richard West in the early stages. Shane Gallagher and Elizabeth Simmons also helped shaped the book in its early stages. The patient librarians at the Robertson, Central and Science Libraries do a stunning job of finding obscure texts. I am grateful to the authors and publishers who not only granted permission for use of diagrams, but were very supportive of this book.

The book was mustered and polished by NewSplash. I am grateful for the skills and patience of Lynda Henderson, Lucinda McMeeken, Victoria Griffen, Lisa Hodges, Simon Horner. Thankyou to those who contributed to the review process, improving both text and argument.

I would like to thank Graham McGregor for the countless hours of discussion and hot chocolates. His input was invaluable through several restructurings of the book.

And, as always, thank you to my family. Phoebe, Oliver and Henry - you are all awesome.

So, to these people, and countless others – thank you.

Samuel Mann

Sawyers Bay, Dunedin, New Zealand

November 2011

samuel.mann@op.ac.nz

Made in the USA
Lexington, KY
04 March 2014